ST. JOSEPH'S
R.C. CHURCH
67 PUREWELL
CHRISTCHURCH

Sacrifice and Community

D1418723

Illuminations: Theory and Religion

Series editors: Catherine Pickstock, John Milbank, and Graham Ward

Religion has a growing visibility in the world at large. Throughout the humanities there is a mounting realization that religion and culture lie so closely together that religion is an unavoidable and fundamental human reality. Consequently, the examination of religion and theology now stands at the centre of any questioning of our western identity, including the question of whether there is such a thing as "truth."

ILLUMINATIONS aims both to reflect the diverse elements of these developments and, from them, to produce creative new syntheses. It is unique in exploring the new interaction between theology, philosophy, religious studies, political theory and cultural studies. Despite the theoretical convergence of certain trends they often in practice do not come together. The aim of ILLUMINATIONS is to make this happen, and advance contemporary theoretical discussion.

Sacrifice and Community

Jewish Offering and Christian Eucharist

Matthew Levering

Blackwell
Publishing

© 2005 by Matthew Levering

BLACKWELL PUBLISHING
350 Main Street, Malden, MA 02148-5020, USA
9600 Garsington Road, Oxford OX4 2DQ, UK
550 Swanston Street, Carlton, Victoria 3053, Australia

The right of Matthew Levering to be identified as the Author of this Work has been asserted in accordance with the UK Copyright, Designs, and Patents Act 1988.

All rights reserved. No part of this publication may be reproduced, stored in a retrieval system, or transmitted, in any form or by any means, electronic, mechanical, photocopying, recording or otherwise, except as permitted by the UK Copyright, Designs, and Patents Act 1988, without the prior permission of the publisher.

First published 2005 by Blackwell Publishing Ltd

1 2005

Library of Congress Cataloging-in-Publication Data

Levering, Matthew Webb, 1971–
   Sacrifice and community : Jewish offering and Christian Eucharist / Matthew Levering.
      p. cm.
   Includes bibliographical references and index.
   ISBN-13: 978-1-4051-3689-1 (hard cover : alk. paper)
   ISBN-10: 1-4051-3689-8 (hard cover : alk. paper)
   ISBN-13: 978-1-4051-3690-7 (pbk. : alk. paper)
   ISBN-10: 1-4051-3690-1 (pbk. : alk. paper)   1. Lord's Supper—Sacrifice.
2. Isaac (Biblical patriarch)—Sacrifice.   3. Catholic Church—Relations—Judaism.
4. Judaism—Relations—Catholic Church.   I. Title.

   BX2218.L48 2005
   234'.163—dc22
                                                                           2005003347

A catalogue record for this title is available from the British Library.

Set in 10.5/12pt Sabon
by Graphicraft Limited, Hong Kong
Printed and bound in India
by Replika Press Pvt Ltd, Kundli

The publisher's policy is to use permanent paper from mills that operate a sustainable forestry policy, and which has been manufactured from pulp processed using acid-free and elementary chlorine-free practices. Furthermore, the publisher ensures that the text paper and cover board used have met acceptable environmental accreditation standards.

For further information on
Blackwell Publishing, visit our website:
www.blackwellpublishing.com

TO JOY LEVERING

Contents

Acknowledgments

The Dominican theologian Servais Pinckaers has enjoined theologians to penetrate Aquinas's insights by attending more deeply to Aquinas's biblical, patristic, and metaphysical sources. Through this labor, in dialogue with contemporary thought, a distinctive style of contemporary theology, participating in the newness of the gospel from within the Church's tradition of theological reflection, is emerging. This theology has value in illumining the realities of Catholic faith that inspire, in participatory contemplation, our active and radical love. Therefore my first thanks goes to John Milbank and Catherine Pickstock for including this work in their Illuminations series. Gilles Emery, O.P. and Fergus Kerr, O.P. assisted in the book's progress toward publication: I owe an ever-increasing debt to them. Ed Houser and Neil Roy kindly invited me to give lectures that later, in different form, found inclusion in the book. I am grateful too for the encouragement and help during the past years given to me by many others including Lewis Ayres, Stephen Brown, David Burrell, Diane Eriksen, Paul Gondreau, Stanley Hauerwas, Thomas Hibbs, Russell Hittinger, Reinhard Hütter, Daniel Keating, Peter Kwasniewski, Benoît-Dominique de La Soujeole, O.P., Steven Long, Bruce Marshall, Francis Martin, Robert Miner, Charles Morerod, O.P., Francesca Murphy, Roger Nutt, Lauren Pristas, Richard Schenk, O.P., Michael Sherwin, O.P., Gregory Vall, and Thomas Weinandy, O.F.M. Cap. The book could not have been written without the good-spirited assistance in locating and xeroxing secondary sources rendered by Peggy Mary Brooks and Paula Storm. My colleagues Michael Dauphinais, Matthew Lamb, and William Riordan have offered the deep friendship, wisdom, and devotion to Jesus Christ that constitute a true theological community; my appreciation for them runs especially deep. Bernard Blankenhorn, O.P. and Jörgen Vijgen heroically read the entire manuscript more than once during its early and particularly awkward stages. Without their criticisms and keen insights, the book would never have reached a publishable state. Andrew Hofer, O.P. and Guy Mansini, O.S.B. painstakingly critiqued later drafts, and greatly improved the arguments and documentation; Romanus Cessario, O.P., Michael Lang, and John Yocum kindly read and critiqued the penultimate draft. For their efforts, I cannot thank them enough. The love of my parents and in-laws, as well as my brother and sisters-in-law, and our extended family means an enormous amount to me. My grandmother, Irene B. Webb, once again supported me through this project by her love and gifts: may God bless her abundantly, now and forever, for what she has done for my family and me. Reviewing this mountain of graces that God, through these friends and family members, has bestowed upon me, I give great thanks to the Creator. I give special thanks to God for my beloved wife, mother of my children, and dearest friend, Joy. "She is far more precious than jewels. The heart of her husband trusts in her, and he will have no lack of gain. . . . Give her the fruit of her hands, and let her works praise her in the gates" (Prov. 31:10–11, 31).

Introduction

Beyond Eucharist Idealism

This study explores the theology of the Eucharist in light of the necessary union, for Israel and for the Church, of the cultic act of sacrifice and communion in the divine life of wisdom and love. The study is thus grounded by Israel's communion as an elect people marked by their sacrificial desire for union with God. As I hope to show, the Eucharist fulfills, without displacing, Israel's liturgical desire by building up a cruciform people who, in and through their sacramental-sacrificial sharing in the Messiah's saving sacrifice, are united in a communion of charity as the fulfilled Temple.[1]

---

[1] Colman O'Neill, O.P. has pointed out that ecumenical concerns often lead Catholic theologians to begin with communion and downplay sacrifice. He finds, however, that bracketing the aspect of sacrifice often leads to distortions given the significance of sacrifice in Catholic eucharistic theology. See O'Neill, *Sacramental Realism: A General Theory of the Sacraments* (Wilmington, DE: Michael Glazier, 1983): 82. Rowan Williams argues that the aspect of sacrifice must be retained, but in a metaphorical sense: Williams, *Eucharistic Sacrifice: The Roots of a Metaphor* (Bramcote: Grove Books, 1982). Numerous Anglican and Catholic works in the late nineteenth and early twentieth centuries emphasized sacrifice: see, e.g., the German Roman Catholic theologian Nicholas Gihr's massive *The Holy Sacrifice of the Mass: Dogmatically, Liturgically and Ascetically Explained* (London: B. Herder, 1946 [1902, translated from the 6th edition]); the almost equally voluminous study by the Episcopalian Alfred G. Mortimer, *The Eucharistic Sacrifice: An Historical and Theological Investigation of the Sacrificial Conception of the Holy Eucharist in the Christian Church* (London: Longmans, Green, and Co., 1901); as well as more popular books such as J. Brodie Brosnan's *The Sacrifice of the New Law* (New York: Benziger, 1926) and Joseph Kramp, S.J.'s study of the liturgy, *The Liturgical Sacrifice of the New Law*, trans. Leo F. Miller (London: B. Herder, 1926). In his 1877 preface to the first edition of the book, included in the translation cited above, Nicholas Gihr expresses the Eucharist's pedagogical character in configuring us to Christ:

> May God grant His blessing and success to this work – especially in our days, when the Church and her faithful children are necessarily more or less constrained to lead a life of sacrifice. May it awaken and foster in many hearts love for the Eucharistic Sacrifice, as well as a cheerful and courageous spirit to undergo willingly the trials and contradictions that self-immolation demands! (6)

Put another way, the Eucharist is the fulfillment of Israel's cultic, communal liturgy, and, as such, is a sacrificial or cruciform communion. Describing Thomas Aquinas's theology of salvation, Romanus Cessario observes that, in the Eucharist, "the unity established between Christ and his members makes of the whole body a single oblation to the Lord."[2] In this oblation, the sacrifice and meal mutually interpenetrate and define one another, since the communion, as a communion in Christ's Pasch, is cruciform.[3] The perfection of the *imago dei* (deification) accords with the mode of the restoration of the *imago dei*.[4] The character of the Eucharist as communion *in and through sacrifice* thus shapes all aspects of Eucharistic theology, including metaphysical doctrines such as transubstantiation, and establishes the Church as an "ecstatic" people communicating, through Christ's Pasch, in the Trinitarian *ecstasis* of self-giving wisdom and love.

Much of the book engages Aquinas's theology of the Eucharist. Aquinas's sapiential theology provides an entrance through which contemporary theologians can enter into the ecclesial and theological tradition of *sacra doctrina*, the participation of believers by the Holy Spirit in the knowledge and prophetic mission of Christ the Teacher. As Reinhard Hütter has put it, *sacra doctrina* must be "pathic" so that

---

[2] Romanus Cessario, O.P., "Aquinas on Christian Salvation," in *Aquinas on Doctrine: A Critical Introduction*, ed. Thomas Weinandy, Daniel Keating, and John Yocum (New York: T. & T. Clark, 2004): 133.

[3] Louis Bouyer asks, "what, then, according to the primitive view, is properly sacrificial in the Christian *synaxis* (the Christian assembly)? We must answer that, from the ways in which the first Christian authors, beginning with St. Paul, express themselves, everything in the Christian *synaxis* is sacrificial" (Bouyer, *Life and Liturgy* [London: Sheed and Ward, 1956]: 77). Much depends, however, upon whether one includes the meal within the sacrificial offering, or includes the sacrificial offering within the meal. The latter position, toward which Bouyer somewhat tends due to his emphasis on the "ritual *berakoth* of the Jewish meal," may dowlay our liturgical participation in Christ's enacted *justice*, the righteousness of the Cross in and through which true communion is possible. See Bouyer, *Eucharist: Theology and Spirituality of the Eucharistic Prayer*, trans. Charles Underhill Quinn (Notre Dame, IN: University of Notre Dame Press, 1968): 106; cf. Bouyer, *The Christian Mystery: From Pagan Myth to Christian Mysticism*, trans. Illtyd Trethowan (Edinburgh: T. & T. Clark, 1990): 290.

[4] This is the key insight of Romanus Cessario, O.P., *The Godly Image: Christ and Salvation in Catholic Thought from Anselm to Aquinas* (Petersham, MA: St Bede's Publications, 1990). Repeatedly in the *tertia pars* of the *Summa Theologiae*, Aquinas sets forth this twofold movement of "furtherance in good" and "withdrawal from evil" (3, q. 1, a. 2). As Peter Casarella states, "The bread of life who gave himself for the sake of the world nourishes us through the sacrifice that he offers. Through his self-offering, we are made the recipients of an offer of eternal life. His cruciform appearance is not accidental to his offering appearance. The cross of Christ is the very form in which the offer is made to us" (Casarella, "Eucharist: Presence of a Gift," in *Rediscovering the Eucharist: Ecumenical Conversations*, ed. Roch Kereszty, O. Cist. [New York: Paulist Press, 2003]: 199–225, at 214).

it may be "poietic"; fruitful ("poietic") penetration of the revealed mysteries occurs within the "pathic" or receptive tradition of the Church's ongoing contemplation of the Word.[5] The depths of this reception must continually be re-appropriated. As a saint and theologian, Aquinas partakes in this *sacra doctrina* and teaches others how to partake in it.

The first chapter of the book examines Jewish theologies of Abraham's near-sacrifice of Isaac (the aqedah).[6] These Jewish theologies teach us how to interpret communion with God and neighbor through the lens of Israel, as Aquinas does.[7] In light of the connection of the aqedah with the Temple sacrifices, and of both with communion with God, Jewish theologies of the aqedah – taken up by St Paul at the heart of his theology of salvation (Rom. 8:32) – powerfully remind us that the formation of the united people of God (communion) occurs in and through sacrificial worship.

The necessity of interpreting Christian sacrifice and communion through the lens of Israel is likewise affirmed by the patristics scholar Robert Wilken, in commenting upon Justin Martyr's mid-second-century account of the Christian liturgy of the Eucharist:

> The second part of the Christian Eucharist [as described by Justin Martyr] has parallels to the sacrifices in the Temple in Jerusalem in ancient times. From the beginning of Christianity, the death and resurrection of Christ have been understood as a sacrifice. In the Epistle to the Hebrews, an early Christian letter in the New Testament, the author writes: "When Christ appeared as a high priest of the good things that have come

---

[5] See Reinhard Hütter, *Suffering Divine Things: Theology as Church Practice* (Grand Rapids, MI: Eerdmans, 2000).

[6] On the role of Israel in Aquinas's theology of sacrifice, see not only Aquinas's account of the Old Law and of Christ's sacrifice, but also the arguments that inform his account of sacrifice understood as belonging to the moral virtue of religion. When describing how offering sacrifice belongs to the natural law, Aquinas draws upon the story of Isaac, Exodus 22, the Psalms, Leviticus, and Deuteronomy. See *Summa Theologiae* 2-2, q. 85, especially the *sed contras*. Aquinas recognizes that sacrifice is biblically bound up with communion; Christ's fulfillment of Torah is Christ's fulfillment of Temple.

[7] The lens of Israel is crucial for the theology of the Christian Eucharist because, as Catherine Pickstock has written, "all the things pointing towards the Eucharist *retain their pregnant mystery without cancellation*. We are still knights looking for the Grail, just as we are still Israel on pilgrimage" (Pickstock, "Truth and Language," in John Milbank and Catherine Pickstock, *Truth in Aquinas* [London: Routledge, 2001]: 111, emphasis added). Both linear supersessionists *and* those who reject theologies of fulfillment operate from within a Hegelian philosophy of history that does not recognize this sense of a participatory "pregnant mystery without cancellation." On Aquinas's participatory understanding of the time-eternity relationship, see Matthew L. Lamb, "The Eschatology of St. Thomas Aquinas," in *Aquinas on Doctrine: A Critical Introduction*, ed. Thomas Weinandy, Daniel Keating, and John Yocum (New York: T. & T. Clark, 2004): 225–40. Aquinas does not conceive of time in the merely linear fashion of modernity.

. . . he entered once for all into the Holy Place, taking not the blood of goats and calves but his own blood, thus securing an eternal redemption" (Heb. 9:11–12). In the ancient prayers spoken over the bread and wine, the priest said: "We offer to Thee O Lord this fearful and unbloody sacrifice, beseeching Thee that thou deal not with us after our sins nor reward us after our iniquities, but according to thy leniency and thine unspeakable love towards mankind overlook and blot out the handwriting that is against us they suppliants." It is clear from this prayer that Christian worship has deep roots in the sacrificial worship of the ancient Jewish Temple, but in Christian belief there is only one sacrifice, one offering, the offering of Christ's life.[8]

Aidan Nichols similarly provides a summary of St Augustine's understanding, found in Book X of *City of God*, that illumines how Christ's identity as the true Temple (John 2:21) governs the Christian understanding of the Eucharist. Nichols observes, "Augustine brings together the notion that the Church offers herself in the Eucharist with the notion that she offers Christ there . . . As the *De Civitate Dei* continues: 'He [Christ] intended the daily sacrifice of the Church to be the sacramental symbol of this [his own sacrifice]; for the Church, being the body of which he is the Head, learns to offer herself through him.' "[9]

With a particular focus on the sacrificial cult of the Temple, Chapter 2 treats Aquinas's account of expiatory sacrifice – rooted in that of

---

[8] Robert Louis Wilken, "Christian Worship: An Affair of Things as well as Words," in *Christianity in Jewish Terms*, ed. Tikva Frymer-Kensky et al. (Boulder, CO: Westview Press, 2000): 199. He remarks, "In common use, remembering has to do with recalling something that happened in the past but that is no longer actual. But in the Christian liturgy, the term 'remembrance' means re-presenting, re-actualizing, making present what happened in the past" (200). "Remembrance" has similar meanings in Jewish liturgy, as Wilken shows (drawing on the work of Lawrence Hoffman). For discussion of Justin's important use of Isaiah 53, see Daniel P. Bailey, " 'Our Suffering and Crucified Messiah' (*Dial*. 111.2): Justin Martyr's Allusions to Isaiah 53 in His *Dialogue with Trypho* with Special Reference to the New Edition of M. Marcovich," in *The Suffering Servant: Isaiah 53 in Jewish and Christian Sources*, ed. Bernd Janowski and Peter Stuhlmacher, trans. Daniel P. Bailey (Grand Rapids, MI: Eerdmans, 2004 [1996]): 324–417.
[9] Aidan Nichols, O.P., *The Holy Eucharist: From the New Testament to Pope John Paul II* (Dublin: Veritas, 1991): 53; cf. Nichols, "The Holy Oblation: On the Primacy of Eucharistic Sacrifice,"*Downside Review* 122 (2004): 259–72. See also, for the Eastern tradition regarding our communion as attained in and through our eucharistic participation in Christ's sacrifice, Lawrence J. Welch, *Christology and Eucharist in the Early Thought of Cyril of Alexandria* (San Francisco: International Scholars Press, 1994): especially Chapter 4, and Felix Heinzer, "The Suffering Humanity of Christ as the Source of Salvation in Maximus the Confessor," in *Faith in Christ and the Worship of Christ*, ed. Leo Scheffczyk and trans. Graham Harrison (San Francisco: Ignatius Press, 1986): 47–64.

Augustine[10] – as regards both the Cross and the Eucharist. The chapter addresses how the justice accomplished in and through Christ's sacrifice, the fulfillment of the imagery of the aqedah as well as of the Temple sacrifices, is constitutive of communion. Chapters 3 and 4 then discuss the two referents of the Eucharist: the Mystical Body of the Church (the communion of charity) and Christ's "true" body now living and glorified in heaven.[11] Chapter 3 discusses the Eucharist as nourishing the communion of charity – ultimately eschatological – that is the Church. The chapter argues that only in light of a sacrificial and Christological understanding of charity can the specificity of the "communion" attained by Christ and built up by the Eucharist be understood. Chapter 4, in dialogue with contemporary Russian Orthodox theology, examines the doctrine of transubstantiation, and suggests that what is at stake in this doctrine is our radical "presence" or inclusion within Christ's sacrifice. Finally, the last chapter of the book, Chapter 5, explores the liturgy's sacramental representation of Christ's sacrifice as the Church's deifying pedagogy in the sacrificial justice and ascetical contemplation required of those who wish to share in Christ's fulfillment of Israel's law and liturgy. To employ the medieval terminology, Chapters 3, 4, and 5 correspond respectively to the *res sacramenti*, the *res et sacramentum*, and the *sacramentum tantum*.

As William Cavanaugh has observed with regard to the Fathers, whose participatory understanding of the relationship of time to eternity is appropriated by Aquinas:

> In patristic writings on the Eucharist we find . . . a conception of full human participation in the sacrifice of Christ because the historical imagination is superseded by the

---

[10] Augustine's legacy is of course profoundly contested. For Aquinas's indebtedness to Augustine on sacrifice, see *Summa Theologiae* 3, q. 22; 3, q. 48, a. 3; and 2-2, q. 85. At every key point where Aquinas discusses sacrifice, he draws upon Augustine. For a commentary on 3, q. 22 that brings out the influence of Augustine, see Jean-Pierre Torrell, O.P., "Le sacerdoce du Christ dans la *Somme de théologie*," *Revue Thomiste* 99 (1999): 75–100. See also Leo J. Elders, S.V.D., "Les citations de saint Augustin dans la *Somme théologique* de saint Thomas d'Aquin," *Doctor communis* 40 (1987): 115–67.

[11] See 3, q. 60, a. 3, *sed contra*. Wayne Hankey has explored the history of this *sed contra* as emerging from the debate between Lanfranc and Berengar. See his fascinating "Reading Augustine through Dionysius: Aquinas's Correction of One Platonism by Another," forthcoming in Michael Dauphinais, Barry David, and Matthew Levering (eds), *Aquinas the Augustinian*; cf. Pierre-Marie Gy, O.P.'s survey of the Leonine edition's version of 3, qq. 73–83: "Le texte original de la Tertia Pars de la *Somme théologique* de S. Thomas d'Aquin dans l'apparat critique de l'édition Léonine: Le cas de l'eucharistie," *Revue des sciences philosophiques et théologiques* 65 (1981): 608–16. For an introduction to Aquinas's Eucharistic theology in the highly charged context of contemporary liturgical theology, see David Berger, *Thomas Aquinas and the Liturgy*, trans. Christopher Grosz (Ypsilanti, MI: Sapientia Press, 2004).

eschatological imagination. Rather than past and present being linked "horizontally" across historical time, past, present and future are linked "vertically" by participation in the eternal "liturgy" of the Trinity.[12]

This patristic-medieval understanding of time as participation in divine eternity, rather than as a mere linear continuum, requires at once affirming that Christ fulfills Israel (rejecting models that envision one covenant for the Jews, another for the Gentiles) and affirming, against linear-supersessionist models, that God's covenants with Israel have never been revoked.[13] Degrees of cruciform participation in Christ's Paschal mystery, rather than a linear continuum ("progress"), constitute the true measure of historical developments. Given this conception of "full human participation in the sacrifice of Christ," the chapters that follow intend to illumine the Eucharist as an ecclesial (that is, sharing "the richness of the olive tree of Israel" [Rom. 11:17]) reality in which human beings become Christ's Body by participating sacrificially (sacrifice and meal[14]) in Christ's cruciform accomplishment of God-centered

---

[12] Cavanaugh, "Eucharistic Sacrifice and Social Imagination in Early Modern Europe," *Journal of Medieval and Early Modern Studies* 31 (2001): 585–605, at 599. Cavanaugh identifies Irenaeus as an exemplar: "The sense of participation in Christ's sacrifice is strong in Irenaeus, who makes no clear distinctions between our offering and Christ's offering in the Eucharist" (599). Similarly, he notes, "For Augustine, too, there is no question of the eucharistic sacrifice as an external response to God's sacrifice. Sacrifice is that by which we are united to God. Therefore there is no tension between sacrifice and mercy, as there is in Luther" (600).

[13] See my *Christ's Fulfillment of Torah and Temple* (Notre Dame, IN: University of Notre Dame Press, 2002). In his contribution to a symposium on *Dabru Emet*, in *Jews and Christians: People of God*, ed. Carl E. Braaten and Robert W. Jenson (Grand Rapids, MI: Eerdmans, 2003), David Bentley Hart succinctly makes the point: "After all, to say 'completes' is not to say 'supersedes'" (186). See also the superb book edited by Jean-Louis Missika and Dominique Wolton, *Choosing God – Chosen by God: Conversations with Cardinal Jean-Marie Lustiger*, trans. Rebecca Howell Balinski (San Francisco: Ignatius Press, 1991).

[14] See B. Kelly, in "The Eucharist: Sacrifice or Meal?," *Irish Theological Quarterly* 35 (1968): 298–306. Kelly's article is a response to Nicholas Lash, *His Presence in the World: A Study of Eucharistic Worship and Theology* (London: Sheed and Ward, 1968), which argues that the meal *is* the sacrifice. Kelly shows, by contrast, that sacrifice and meal are distinct, although he warns against a "dichotomy" between the two (ibid.: 305). Kelly formulates the meaning of the Eucharist:

To be a christian means ultimately to share in the being of Christ crucified. christian self-realization is Christ realizing Himself in the christian. Hence it is that Baptism, the sacrament whereby we are made Christians, is a putting on of Christ, a being taken up into Christ. Made one with Him in Baptism, and through Him united with our fellows, we are radically capable of a community act in which are realized in us Christ's movement in death towards the Father, and the Father's consequent glorification of Him. Here we have

communion. In the practice of Eucharistic theology and inseparably[15] in our participation in the sacramental rite, we learn that our communion as Christ's Body must be cruciform – and thereby we participate, as repentant sinners who by God's grace desire to be turned radically toward God, in the ongoing conversion and renewal of the Body that is the Church, whose mission is to "proclaim the Lord's death until he comes" (1 Cor. 11:26).[16]

Before proceeding, however, some historical background is necessary regarding the displacement of sacrifice in much contemporary Catholic Eucharistic theology.[17] In mainstream contemporary Catholic approaches

---

> the sacrifice and the sacrament (in the sense of communion) of Calvary: Christ obedient unto death and Christ raised up by the Father. The Eucharist is our way of entry into Calvary under both these aspects. (302)

Kelly notes that the unity of the Church is not found only in the meal; rather the Church is united precisely in and through the Church's sharing in Christ's sacrifice:

> Community is found where many gather to make a common offering . . . The congregation at Holy Mass, children of one Father, offering Christ their victim through the ministry of their priest, are a community, act as a community, and show themselves to be a community . . . We go together, as a people, to God in sacrifice. God comes to us, to all of us together, as a people, in Holy Communion. (306)

Kelly's insights were unfortunately overwhelmed in the rush of his fellow Catholic theologians toward Eucharistic idealism. See also Kelly, "Sacramental Presence: Real Presence," *Irish Theological Quarterly* 37 (1970): 71–9.

[15] Jean-Luc Marion draws out the connection between Eucharistic (ecclesial) theologizing and Eucharistic (ecclesial) practice in *God Without Being*, trans. Thomas A. Carlson (Chicago: University of Chicago Press, 1991): 153–6.

[16] Eucharistic theology thus presupposes the other topics of theology, from the triune God through the Mystical Body of the Redeemer. On this point see John P. Yocum, "Sacraments in Aquinas," in *Aquinas on Doctrine: A Critical Introduction*, ed. Thomas Weinandy, Daniel Keating, and John Yocum (New York: T. & T. Clark, 2004): 159–81, at 159. Denis Farkasfalvy, O. Cist. has argued that the New Testament itself has its provenance in Eucharistic assemblies, thus grounding sacramentally the Church's reflection upon all the mysteries of faith. See Farkasfalvy, "The Eucharistic Provenance of New Testament Texts," in *Rediscovering the Eucharist: Ecumenical Conversations*, ed. Roch A. Kereszty, O. Cist. (New York: Paulist Press, 2003): 27–51, as well as the response in the same volume by Francis Martin (pp. 52–62).

[17] For exploration of whether the early Fathers understood the sacrificial character of the Eucharist in continuity with the later Fathers (and similarly with the great medieval theologians and Trent), see, e.g., Aidan Nichols, O.P., *The Holy Eucharist: From the New Testament to Pope John Paul II* (Dublin: Veritas, 1991); Darwell Stone, *A History of the Doctrine of the Eucharist*, vol. 1 (London: Longmans, Green, and Co., 1909); Willy Rordorf et al., *The Eucharist of the Early Christians*, trans. Matthew J. O'Connell (Collegeville, MN: Liturgical Press, 1978); Robin Darling Young, "The Eucharist as Sacrifice According to Clement of Alexandria," in *Rediscovering the Eucharist*, ed. Roch Kereszty, O. Cist., 63–91 (with responses by Brian Daley, S.J. and Everett Ferguson, the latter arguing the case for discontinuity); and Sebastian Brock, "The Holy Spirit and the

to the Eucharist, believers' sacrificial-sacramental participation in Christ's sacrifice, so central for embodying the "richness" of the "olive tree" of Israel, is effaced.[18] How did this situation come to be? Although we can only sketch some of the major steps by which Catholic theologians came to reject sacrifice as a superseded Jewish mode of worship, such a sketch gives a necessary background to the chapters that follow, since my work is intended as a contribution to contemporary rather than "historical" theology.[19] These steps trace the ascendancy of what I term "Eucharistic idealism," the linear-supersessionist displacement of the Jewish mode of embodied sacrificial communion by spiritualizing accounts of Eucharistic communion with God.[20] Robert J. Daly,

---

Eucharist," in Sebastian Brock, *The Holy Spirit in the Syrian Baptismal Tradition*, 2nd edn (Pune, India: 1998): 175–99. Nichols concludes that while the early Fathers especially were careful to distinguish Christian sacrifice from Jewish and pagan animal sacrifice, the Fathers witness to the continuity of the sacrificial understanding of the Eucharist, linked both with Christ's Passion and with the risen Lord. Robert Daly, S.J. has argued for discontinuity in his *Christian Sacrifice: The Judeo-Christian Background before* Origen (Washington, DC: Catholic University of America Press, 1978); Robert Daly, S.J., *The Origins of the Christian Doctrine of Sacrifice* (Philadelphia, PA: Fortress Press, 1978); the same interpretive emphasis on discontinuity (not only as regards sacrifice) governs Paul F. Bradshaw's *Eucharistic Origins* (Oxford: Oxford University Press, 2004).

[18] The Russian Orthodox theologian, Sergius Bulgakov offers this critique:

> In the later consciousness, first in the Western Church, primarily in Protestantism, the Eucharist is transformed into the sacrament of communion, and its sacrificial significance is even denied. In any case, the significance of the Eucharist is diminished by the fact that it is conceived dually: as sacrifice and as communion, that is, as two (albeit connected) operations, not as one complex act. (This feature of Western theology has been adopted by Eastern theology to a certain degree.) (Bulgakov, *The Bride of the Lamb*, trans. Boris Jakim [Grand Rapids, MI: Eerdmans, 2002]: 286)

[19] This distinction, now omnipresent in theological faculties, between "systematic" and "historical" theology – with its result that training in "systematic" theology paradoxically cuts one off from the theological tradition, which is the purview of "historical" theology – dates from Schleiermacher's development of the theology program at the new University of Berlin.

[20] It will be clear that I disagree with the narrative offered by Liam G. Walsh, O.P. in "The Divine and the Human in St. Thomas's Theology of Sacraments," in *Ordo sapientiae et amoris*, ed. C.-J. Pinto de Oliveira, O.P. (Fribourg: Éditions universitaires, 1993): 321–2. In an otherwise valuable article, Walsh argues that the work of Schillebeeckx and Rahner began as a mere personalist corrective to the neo-scholastic tradition, and should be received as such. He observes that "Catholic theology of the sacraments has been forced to look critically at its dominant scholastic tradition, asking among other things whether it could be developed in a way that would do justice to the human realism of the sacraments that pastoral practice, and the tone of contemporary culture, required" (322). Walsh likewise suggests that Colman O'Neill's work marks something of a break with the Thomistic theology of "sign":

in critiquing post-Tridentine Eucharistic theology, exemplifies the position of contemporary Catholic Eucharistic idealism as regards Israel's sacrificial liturgy:

> That the Christ-event had done away with sacrifice in the history-of-religions sense of the term was not yet clear to theologians. For it was still common for theologians to deal with the Old Testament and the New Testament in a relatively undifferentiated way, i.e. without any historicizing hermeneutic. One took one's definition of sacrifice from the Old Testament and applied it, without differentiating hermeneutic, to the Eucharist, almost as if the paschal event of Christ had not taken place.[21]

For Daly, the Christ-event negates and displaces Israel's understanding of expiatory sacrifice, which must in his view not inform the theology of the Eucharist – thus requiring a radical revision of the doctrinal

---

However, in more recent times this love affair of Thomists with the symbolic has begun to run into trouble. One can find hints of that from the Thomist side already in O'Neill – in a slightly panicky way in his *New Approaches to the Eucharist* where he attempts a theological justification for the concerns of Paul VI regarding the appeal to the symbolic in theories of transignification/transfinalisation, and in a more measured way in his *Sacramental Realism.* (323)

This evaluation misses the transitions that were ongoing in Catholic Eucharistic theology in the 1960s. After attributing to Cajetan's influence the fact that "[m]ost Thomists . . . have interpreted the instrumental efficiency of the sacraments as a kind of physical instrumentality," Walsh remarks, "The personalist sacramental theology of a Schillebeeckx provides a happier solution to the problem of the integration of the symbolic and the causal, because it recognizes that the efficient causality in question is that of persons (divine) on other persons (human)" (336). But the personal character of instrumental causality, which can easily be defended (as Walsh does on 345–6) was never, in my view, the issue truly at stake.

[21] Robert J. Daly, S.J., "Robert Bellarmine and Post-Tridentine Eucharistic Theology," *Theological Studies* 61 (2000): 239–60, at 259. Daly draws upon Edward J. Kilmartin, S.J.'s *The Eucharist in the West: History and Theology* (Collegeville, MN: Liturgical Press, 1998) – a volume which Daly edited – but also seeks to appropriate René Girard's understanding of the scapegoat as evidence for his view. See also Kilmartin, "The Catholic Tradition of Eucharistic Theology: Towards the Third Millennium," *Theological Studies* 55 (1994): 405–57; Daly, "Sacrifice Unveiled or Sacrifice Revisited: Trinitarian and Liturgical Perspectives," *Theological Studies* 64 (2003): 24–42; idem, "Eucharistic Origins: From the New Testament to the Liturgies of the Golden Age," *Theological Studies* 66 (2005): 3–22; as well as the work of Enrico Mazza, David Power, and others. In "Robert Bellarmine and Post-Tridentine Eucharistic Theology," Daly provides a critique of John Paul II's *Dominicae Cenae* (cf. Kilmartin, *The Eucharist in the West*, 196–201), and an overview of the current discussion that reflects the momentum in Catholic theological circles toward centering worship upon the community's production rather than upon the sacramental-sacrificial mediation of Christ's sacrifice.

tradition.[22] Arguing against such views, the Orthodox theologian Theodore Stylianopoulos has observed that

> the centrality of Christ in Christian worship and theology is a matter of a new focus, a new center for life and thought, and not a matter of a radical programmatic rejection of all things Jewish. There is to be sure discontinuity between the New Covenant and the Old but there is also continuity. A radical discontinuity between the two dispensations would lead to dangerous theological ground.[23]

---

[22] For a similar project, see David Power, O.M.I., *The Sacrifice We Offer: The Tridentine Dogma and its Reinterpretation* (New York: Crossroad, 1987), where he qualifies Trent's understanding of propitiary sacrifice. See also his critique of sacrifice in *The Eucharistic Mystery: Revitalizing the Tradition* (New York: Crossroad, 1997 [1992]): 320; as well as his "The Language of Sacramental Memorial: Rupture, Excess and Abundance," in *Sacramental Presence in a Postmodern Context*, ed. Lieven Boeve and Lambert Leijssen (Leuven: Peeters, 2001): 135–60, with a response in the same volume by Werner Jeanrond (161–6), congratulating Power for "freeing our appreciation of sacramental action from narrow ecclesial performance to a creative process" (163). Power identifies John Chrysostom as the key figure in the Church's misunderstanding of sacrifice, a misunderstanding that has lasted, Power argues, from the fourth century to the present day – an extraordinary indictment, calling into question the power of the Holy Spirit, of the Catholic Church and the Eastern Orthodox churches. Like Power and Daly, Thomas Ambrogi, S.J. holds with regard to the Mass as a sacrifice that

> there exists a body of dogmatic statements on the question, principally from the Council of Trent, and these are binding on the faith of the contemporary church. It must be seen, however, that this Tridentine corpus of doctrinal formulations by no means exhausts the total consciousness of the church concerning the sacrificial dimension of the eucharistic celebration. The fathers at Trent had no intention of developing an articulated theology of eucharistic sacrifice. (Ambrogi, "Contemporary Roman Catholic Theology of the Eucharistic Sacrifice," in *Lutherans and Catholics in Dialogue*, vol. 3: *The Eucharist as Sacrifice*, eds. Paul C. Empie and T. Austin Murphy [Minneapolis, MN: Augsburg Publishing, 1968]: 149)

Ambrogi then develops this thought in light of Schillebeeckx's theory of transignification.

[23] Theodore Stylianopoulos, "Holy Eucharist and Priesthood in the New Testament," in Theodore Stylianopoulos, *The Good News of Christ: Essays on the Gospel, Sacraments and Spirit* (Brookline, MA: Holy Cross Orthodox Press, 1991): 80–98, at 83–84. Stylianopoulos is arguing against the Lutheran theologian F. Hahn, *The Worship of the Early Church*, trans. D.E. Green and ed. J. Reumann (Philadelphia, PA: Fortress Press, 1974), but he could equally be responding to the work of many others, Catholic and Protestant, since the 1960s; cf. Raymond E. Brown, S.S., *Priest and Bishop: Biblical Reflections* (New York: Paulist Press, 1970). As Stylianopoulos concludes, "Christian priesthood is rooted in the Eucharist as a sacramental and sacrificial act making present the once-for-all sacrifice of Christ by the power of the Spirit" (94). From the Eucharistic sacrifice flow the ordained priesthood's responsibilities of teaching and governing, corresponding to Christ's threefold office.

The emergence of the widespread critique of sacrifice and its twentieth-century impact upon Catholic Eucharistic theology will here be briefly traced through six major figures: Martin Luther, John Calvin, Friedrich Schleiermacher, Georg W.F. Hegel, Edward Schillebeeckx, and Karl Rahner.[24] A sketch of their perspectives will illumine the growing bifurcation of sacrifice and communion, and will thus indicate the background to our effort to retrieve the resources of Aquinas's theology – and of Jewish liturgical theology – for contemporary Catholic Eucharistic theology. For Aquinas, the Eucharist *radically fulfills* (as a sharing in the once-and-for-all sacrifice enacted by Christ's active *charity*) but *does not negate* the Jewish pattern of communion with God and neighbor in and through expiatory sacrifice.[25]

---

[24] It would be worthwhile to extend this sketch backwards to Abelard, Scotus, and Ockham, among others, but present purposes preclude doing so here.

[25] The division between sacrifice and (communion) meal is defended by the Catholic liturgical theologian, Enrico Mazza, who concludes his historical-critical analysis of passages in Deuteronomy by affirming,

> Since the ritual meal had its origin in the history of Jewish sacrifice, we can say that there is a connection between sacrifice and the liturgy of the Jewish meal. At the same time, however, we must deny that the meal itself had any kind of sacrificial character, since it arose out of the reform in the practice of slaughtering animals, when the distinction between secular slaughtering and sacrificial slaughtering was introduced. (E. Mazza, *The Celebration of the Eucharist: The Origin of the Rite and the Development of Its Interpretation*, trans. Matthew J. O'Connell [Collegeville, MN: Liturgical Press, 1999]: 14)

Having argued that cultic sacrifice was already displaced in Jewish ritual meals, Mazza turns to the ritual meal of the Last Supper and holds that "we must study the customary Jewish ritual meal and decide which of the New Testament data are most compatible with that usage" (24). He then finds a split in New Testament between theology and history. All the Gospels, as well as Paul, are party to a "Passoverization" ibid.: (25) of the Last Supper. Theologically, these authors wish to connect the Last Supper with the Passover sacrifice and Christ's sacrifice on the Cross. But, as Mazza concludes, this position "remains a theological interpretation. The historical fact is that the Last Supper was not a Passover celebration and, consequently, that its liturgy was not that of the Jewish Passover" (25–6). Instead, the Last Supper is a Jewish meal that, as Mazza has already claimed, bears only the faintest historical connection to the cultic sacrifices of the Temple. Mazza's dismissal of the relationship between the Jewish sacrifices and meals ignores the unity of the cult in ancient Israel, and his reconstruction of the New Testament texts to suggest that they have introduced a sacrificial element not present in the event is equally tendentious on historical-critical grounds. Cf. Ben F. Meyer's critique, on historical-critical grounds, of the dismissal of cultic sacrifice found in such books as Gerhard Friedrich's *Die Verkündigung des Todes Jesu im Neuen Testament* (Neukirchen-Vluyn: Neukirchener Verlag, 1982) and Xavier Léon-Dufour's influential *Sharing the Eucharistic Bread: The Witness of the New Testament* (New York: Paulist Press, 1987 [French edition 1982]): Meyer, "The Expiation Motif in the Eucharistic Words: A Key to the History of Jesus?," in *One Loaf, One Cup: Ecumenical Studies of 1 Cor 11 and Other Eucharistic Texts*, ed. Ben F. Meyer (Macon, GA: Macon University Press, 1993): 11–33, at 12–22.

FROM LUTHER TO RAHNER: A SKETCH[26]

Martin Luther argues that the sacrament of the Eucharist is Christ's "testament" or last will.[27] Luther holds that when Jesus says, "this is my blood of the covenant, which is poured out" (Matt. 26:28), Jesus is referring to the primary element of a testament or last will, namely his impending death. Christ's testament promises forgiveness of sins, and God confirms this promise by Christ's death.[28] As a testament, the Eucharist is intended to evoke our faith; it is certainly not a sacrifice. Luther notes, however, that "there is no belief more widely accepted in the church today, or one of greater force, than that the mass is a good work and a sacrifice."[29] He recognizes the unusual importance of his rejection of the Eucharistic sacrifice:

---

[26] John H. McKenna, C.M. has covered much of this same history in sketching his view that the theology of eucharistic presence has guided understanding of eucharistic sacrifice. For McKenna, whose brief survey extends through Louis-Marie Chauvet, the flowering of Eucharistic idealism in Catholic theology is a highly positive development of doctrine. See McKenna, "Eucharistic Presence: An Invitation to Dialogue," *Theological Studies* 60 (1999): 294–317.

[27] Martin Luther, "The Pagan Servitude of the Church," trans. Bertram Lee Woolf, in *Martin Luther: Selections from His Writings*, ed. John Dillenberger (New York: Doubleday, 1962): 273; cf. 274–5, where Luther offers a theology of the covenantal history grounded solely in promise. For further analysis of Luther's eucharistic theology, including his later disputations with Zwingli, see, e.g., M.E. Chapman, "Sacrament and Sacrifice in the Theology of the Mass according to Luther, 1513–1526," *One in Christ* 28 (1992): 248–66; Wolfgang Simon, *Die Messopfertheologie Martin Luthers* (Tübingen: Mohr Siebeck, 2002); Thomas Osborne, "Faith, Philosophy, and the Nominalist Background to Luther's Defense of the Real Presence," *Journal of the History of Ideas* 62 (2002): 63–82; Graham White, *Luther as Nominalist: A Study of the Logical Methods Used in Martin Luther's Disputations in Light of their Medieval Background* (Helsinki: 1994); Herman Sasse, *This Is My Body: Luther's Contention for the Real Presence in the Sacrament of the Altar* (Minneapolis, MN: Fortress, 1959); David Steinmetz, "Scripture and the Lord's Supper in Luther's Theology," in *Luther in Context* (Grand Rapids, MI: Baker Books, 1995): 72–84; Brian A. Gerrish, *Grace and Reason: A Study in the Theology of Luther* (Chicago: University of Chicago Press, 1979 [1962]); Marc Lienhard, *Luther, témoin de Jésus-Christ. Les étapes et les thèmes de la Christologie du Réformateur* (Paris: Cerf, 1973): 197–260; Bernard Lohse, *Martin Luther's Theology: Its Historical and Systematic Development*, trans. and ed. Roy A. Harrisville (Minneapolis, MN: Fortress Press, 1999): 57–9, 127–136, 169–77, 306–13.

[28] On this point, see "The Freedom of a Christian" (1520), written soon after "The Pagan Servitude of the Church."

[29] Luther, "The Pagan Servitude of the Church," 271. As part of his official duties, Cajetan wrote in 1530 a formal letter to Pope Clement VII, entitled "De missae sacrificio et ritu, adversus Lutheranos." Cajetan notes that the Lutherans believe the mass to be a "sacrificium memoriale," instituted by Christ so that the community might remember his sacrificial death, but not a true sacrifice or expiatory offering of Christ's body and blood. See Marie-Vincent Leroy, O.P., "Un traité de Cajetan sur la messe," in *Ordo sapientiae et amoris: Hommage au Professeur Jean-Pierre Torrell OP*, ed. Carlos-Josaphat Pinto de Oliveira, O.P. (Fribourg: Éditions universitaires, 1993): 469–86.

It is a matter which has been confirmed by so many centuries of ancient custom, and has become so ingrained, that to alter or abolish it would require that the great majority of the books which are to-day regarded as authoritative, and almost the whole form of church life, should be changed and done away with. Entirely different rites and ceremonies would have to be introduced, or rather reintroduced. But the Saviour lives, and the word of God must be obeyed with greater care than any nice notions, human or angelic. I will discharge my office by bringing the facts to light, and teaching the truth as I have understood It . . . I mean to labour faithfully as one who must stand before Christ's judgment seat, and in such a way that no one will be able to blame me for his unbelief, or his ignorance of the truth.[30]

---

[30] Ibid., 271. For our purposes in investigating Catholic displacement of Eucharistic sacrifice, Luther's position must be noted for its historical influence. Yet, Catholic-Lutheran dialogue has exposed important points of agreement. See the valuable ecumenical statement "The Eucharist: A Lutheran-Roman Catholic Statement," in *Lutherans and Catholics in Dialogue*, vol. 3: *The Eucharist as Sacrifice*, ed. Paul C. Empie and T. Austin Murphy (Minneapolis, MN: Augsburg Publishing, 1968); as well as the helpful article by the Lutheran theologian Kent S. Knutsen in that volume: "Contemporary Lutheran Theology and the Eucharistic Sacrifice," 167–80. Knutsen draws attention to the works of two Lutheran theologians in particular whose efforts to re-interpret sacrifice positively were influential: Gustaf Aulén's *Eucharist and Sacrifice*, trans. Eric Wahlstrom (Philadelphia, PA: Muhlenberg Press, 1958) and F.C.N. Hicks's *The Fulness of Sacrifice* (London: 1930), which argues that medieval theology overemphasized the place of the death of the victim in sacrificial offering. In contrast, the volume's Catholic contributions on sacrifice are weakened by their reliance upon Rahner and Schillebeeckx (the latter as popularized by the British theologian Charles Davis): see Thomas E. Ambrogi, S.J., "Contemporary Roman Catholic Theology of the Eucharistic Sacrifice," 149–65 and James F. McCue's "Luther and Roman Catholicism on the Mass as Sacrifice," 45–74. McCue, interpreting Trent in light of Rahner, holds that Luther simply "misconstrued the Roman Catholic doctrine of the mass as sacrifice, and that what he was really attacking were certain aspects of popular Catholicism" (73). McCue's proposal was rightly challenged by E. Skibbe, "Roman-Lutheran Dialogue: a question of method," *Una Sancta* 23 (1966): 75–85. Skibbe suggests that only official confession statements should ground ecumenical dialogue. See also the analysis of *Ecclesia de Eucharistia* by George Lindbeck, "Augsburg and the *Ecclesia de Eucharistia*," *Pro Ecclesia* 12 (2003): 405–14 and Frank C. Senn's "The Eucharist and Ecumenical Inter-Communion: Reflections on *Ecclesia de Eucharistia*," *Pro Ecclesia* 13 (2004): 307–22. Senn follows Aulén's view of sacrifice (310), and thereby like Lindbeck distances himself from Eucharistic idealism. For overviews of the Reformers' eucharistic theology, see Francis Clark, S.J.'s *Eucharistic Sacrifice and the Reformation*, 2nd ed. (Oxford: Blackwell, 1967) and Darwell Stone, *A History of the Doctrine of the Holy Eucharist*, vol. 2 (London: Longmans, Green, and Co., 1909). For critical discussion of contemporary efforts to bridge the thought of Luther and Aquinas, especially that of Otto Pesch, see Stephen Pfürtner, "The Paradigms of Thomas Aquinas and Martin Luther," in *Paradigm Change in Theology*, ed. Hans Kung and David Tracy (Edinburgh: T. & T. Clark, 1989): 130–60; cf. Pfürtner, *Luther and Aquinas on Salvation*, trans. Edward Quinn (New York: Sheed and Ward, 1964); Pesch, *Theologie der Rechtfertigung bei Martin Luther und Thomas von Aquin: Versuch eines systematisch-theologischen Dialogs* (Mainz: Matthias-Grünwald-Verlag, 1988 [1967]).

Luther considers this view that "the mass is a sacrifice offered to God" to be so erroneous that "if we do not hold firmly that the mass is the promise, or testament, of Christ, as His words plainly show, we shall lose the whole gospel, and all its comfort."[31] The corrupt Church, in Luther's opinion, replaced the prayers and testament with the sacrifice of the mass; the rightful sacrament or sign of God's gracious gift was replaced with human beings' work.[32]

Calvin's principal concern is the idea that the sacrament of the Eucharist accomplishes expiation and merit. He remarks:

> Satan has attempted to adulterate and envelop the sacred Supper of Christ as with thick darkness, that its purity might not be preserved in the Church. But the head of this horrid abomination was, when he raised a sign by which it was not only obscured and perverted, but altogether obliterated and abolished, vanished away and disappeared from the memory of man – namely, when, with most pestilential error, he blinded almost the whole world into the belief that the Mass was a sacrifice and oblation for obtaining the remission of sins.[33]

Calvin points out that not only do the unlearned possess this belief, but indeed the entire liturgy of the Eucharist, crafted by learned theologians, purposefully inculcates it. On the basis of Hebrews 7, Calvin states that "the right and honour of the priesthood has ceased among mortal men, because Christ, who is immortal, is the one perpetual priest."[34] For Calvin, Christ's sacrifice is not communicated by our sacrificial sharing in it, that is, by further sacrifices. Rather, the reconciling power of Christ's sacrifice comes to us through "the preaching of the gospel and the dispensation

---

[31] Luther, "The Pagan Servitude of the Church," 286. In *Œcuménisme et philosophie: Questions philosophiques pour renouveler le dialogue* (Paris: Parole et Silence, 2004): 51–97, Charles Morerod, O.P. identifies the metaphysics of causality (God "over against" us) as the key factor in Luther's rejection of Catholic sacramental theology.
[32] Ibid., 291. For Luther on the Jews, see Steven T. Katz, *The Holocaust in Historical Context*, vol. 1: *The Holocaust and Mass Death before the Modern Age* (Oxford: Oxford University Press, 1994): 386–94. Katz emphasizes the continuity between Luther and New Testament, patristic, and medieval theological attitudes regarding Jews, but there is discontinuity as well, given Luther's theological polemic against "works."
[33] John Calvin, *Institutes of the Christian Religion*, trans. Henry Beveridge (Grand Rapids, MI: Eerdmans, 1989): Book IV, Ch. 18 (II, p. 607). See also "Calvin's Reply to Sadoleto," in *A Reformation Debate: John Calvin and Jacopo Sadoleto*, ed. John C. Olin (New York: Fordham University Press, 2000), where Calvin writes to Cardinal Sadoleto: "We are indignant that in the room of the sacred Supper has been substituted a sacrifice, by which the death of Christ is emptied of its virtues" (68). For further discussion, see B.A. Gerrish, *Grace and Gratitude: The Eucharistic Theology of John Calvin* (Edinburgh: T. & T. Clark, 1993).
[34] Calvin, *Institutes*, 608.

of the sacred Supper" which we must receive "with true faith."[35] Calvin emphasizes that "as widely as giving differs from receiving, does sacrifice differ from the sacrament of the Supper."[36]

Calvin finds that the Fathers, while not corrupt like their medieval counterparts, "erred somewhat in the mode of action. They imitated the Jewish mode of sacrificing more closely than either Christ had ordained, or the nature of the gospel allowed."[37] Calvin does not condemn the Jewish sacrificial system, but views it as superseded by an entirely different mode of receiving God's blessings. He explains that

> the word of the Lord makes this distinction between the Mosaic sacrifices and our eucharist – that while the former represented to the Jewish people the same efficacy of the death of Christ which is now exhibited to us in the Supper, yet the form of representation was different.[38]

The mistake of the Fathers lay in assuming that the priestly link in Israel between sacrifice and communion would continue, after Christ, in a sacrificial priesthood which would establish the communion of believers upon a sacrificial sharing in Christ's sacrifice. As Calvin concludes regarding the Fathers' position, "they declined too much to the shadows of the law."[39]

---

[35] Ibid.

[36] Ibid. This position influences the Anglican position developed by Cranmer. As Rowan Williams states,

> Several of the Reformers – certainly Luther and Calvin – had no problem about the notions of memorial and thanksgiving sacrifice: Luther could understand the *Sanctus* as a praise, Cranmer however, is more cautious. The third Exhortation and the Preface of the 1552 rite say a certain amount about thanksgiving for the history of salvation, but the rite is rather muted overall; and the idea of a *sacrifice* of thanksgiving is carefully transferred to the post-communion. (Williams, *Eucharistic Sacrifice* [Bramcote: Grove Books, 1982]: 26)

Williams blames the controversy over eucharistic sacrifice on "an exaggerated mediaeval passion-mysticism" that "had pressed the identity of mass and Calvary to its extreme point, so that any 'sacrificing' in the Eucharist *must* be the shedding of Christ's blood for the forgiveness of sins" (26), but it seems to me that the roots lie deeper.

[37] Calvin, *Institutes*, 608.

[38] Ibid., 615.

[39] Ibid. Yet, for Calvin spiritual sacrifice connects the Church with Israel, since sacrifices of praise are extolled in the Old Testament as well as in the New. Calvin holds that "even while the people of God were kept under the external tutelage of the law, the prophets clearly expressed that under these carnal sacrifices there was a reality which is common both to the Jewish people and the Christian Church" (615).

Friedrich Schleiermacher, the founder of Protestant liberalism, radicalizes the Reformers' emphasis on interiority. Inward experience stands at the heart of Schleiermacher's theological project: "In our exposition all doctrines properly so called must be extracted from the Christian religious self-consciousness, i.e. the inward experience of Christian people."[40] Human beings experience a God-consciousness or feeling of absolute dependence, yet this God-consciousness is mixed, to varying degrees, with other elements of consciousness, belonging to the lower powers of the soul, that dilute the God-consciousness. The God-consciousness is the experience of "grace"; the lower states of consciousness are – as we recognize once the God-consciousness has developed in us – the experience of "sin."[41] For Schleiermacher, Christ is the perfect human being because in him the God-consciousness is coterminous with his self-consciousness. Although the God-consciousness is natural to human beings, nonetheless Christ's mediation is necessary to bring about the real activation of the God-consciousness in human beings.[42] The essence of "priesthood," for Schleiermacher, is this sympathetic mediation to all human beings of God-consciousness. All who receive the God-consciousness that Christ mediates become "priests" themselves, and share the God-consciousness with others.

This perspective shapes Schleiermacher's doctrine of the Eucharist. Regarding the Catholic doctrine that the Eucharistic sacrifice offers the sacrifice of Calvary, not a sacrifice other than Christ's, Schleiermacher explains,

> We know nothing of merits or satisfactions as intended here. The evasive suggestion that such sacrifice is not different from but identical with that accomplished on the cross, has

---

[40] Friedrich Schleiermacher, *The Christian Faith*, trans. H.R. MacIntosh and J.S. Stewart, et al. (Edinburgh: T. &. T. Clark, 1989): 265. For discussion of Schleiermacher, see R.R. Niebuhr, *Schleiermacher on Christ and Religion* (New York: 1964); B.A. Gerrish, *Continuing the Reformation: Essays on Modern Religious Thought* (Chicago: University of Chicago Press, 1993): 147–216, 249–73; idem, *A Prince of the Church: Schleiermacher and the Beginnings of Modern Theology* (Philadelphia, PA: Fortress Press, 1984).

[41] Schleiermacher, *The Christian Faith*, 273.

[42] Ibid. Schleiermacher thus states with regard to Christ's "kingship" that

> His kingly power is and remains everywhere and always the same. For those laws and directions do not grow old, but remain valid, with undiminished force, in the Church of Christ; and if for the future He refers His disciples to His spiritual presence, yet even that does not make a distinction between different times. For even His original influence was purely spiritual, and was mediated through His bodily appearance not otherwise than even now His spiritual presence is mediated through the written Word and the picture it contains of His being and influence. (467)

for us no value whatever, for in that case we should have to separate altogether the sacrifice in the death of Christ from the obedience in His life, and His original sacrifice would then be just as arbitrary a transaction and just as magical as the sacrifice of the Mass.[43]

He rejects the idea that the Cross is a "sacrifice" that differs significantly from the "obedience," or supreme God-consciousness, that Christ manifests in his entire life. The conception of "sacrifice" as something other than Christ's sympathetic God-consciousness would make of Christ's death as a "transaction" that changes the position of humankind in relation to God.

In Schleiermacher's view, this idea of a "transaction" can only be "arbitrary" and "magical." He therefore concludes that

while there is no longer any need to describe the Mass as idolatrous, we persist in rejecting unconditionally the whole idea of a sacrifice subsequent to the end of all sacrifices; issuing as it does from a demonstrable misunderstanding, it confuses faith and therefore necessarily encourages superstition, and in particular falsifies the idea of the priesthood of all believers.[44]

Hegel arrives at similar conclusions about the Eucharist, though from a different angle.[45] For Hegel, in propitious climes, the Spirit of a people gradually ripens until it attains "the grade of universality," which destroys the people in their historical manifestation.[46] From this negation, however, emerges "a new principle" which becomes part of the progressive movement – through a series of historical ripenings, negations, and new syntheses – by which the universal Spirit makes itself increasingly manifest, and thereby develops and gradually completes itself, in the history of the world.

Hegel holds that "the formal principle of philosophy in Germany encounters a concrete real World in which Spirit finds inward satisfaction

[43] Ibid., 654.

[44] Ibid., 655. For Schleiermacher's supersessionism, in which like Luther, Calvin, and Hegel he associates the Catholic Church with Judaism, see his *The Christian Faith*, translation of the German 2nd ed. (Edinburgh: T. & T. Clark, 1989): 61, 115.

[45] Georg W.F. Hegel, *The Philosophy of History*, trans. J. Sibree (Buffalo, NY: Prometheus Books, 1991): 78. For further discussion of Hegel that bears upon his understanding of the Eucharist, see, e.g., Cyril O'Regan, *The Heterodox Hegel* (Albany, NY: SUNY Press, 1994): 241–4, 280–1; Jean-Luc Marion, *God Without Being*, trans. Thomas A. Carlson (Chicago: University of Chicago Press, 1991): 169. On Hegel's relationship to Schleiermacher, see Kipton E. Jensen, "The Principle of Protestantism: On Hegel's (Mis)Reading of Schleiermacher's Speeches," *Journal of the American Academy of Religion* 71 (2003): 405–22.

[46] Hegel, *The Philosophy of History*, 78.

and in which conscience is at rest."[47] This result has occurred in Germany thanks to Protestantism, which in rejecting outward works ensured that "it was the Protestant world itself which advanced so far in Thought as to realize the absolute culmination of Self-Consciousness."[48] In Luther, Hegel locates the triumph of idealist principles in Christianity, whose fundamental spiritual core Catholicism had burdened with external Jewish forms. He observes:

> Luther's simple doctrine is that the specific embodiment of Deity – infinite subjectivity, that is true spirituality, Christ – is in no way present and actual in an outward form, but as essentially spiritual is obtained only in being reconciled to God – *in faith and spiritual enjoyment.*[49]

Hegel argues that Luther's "abrogation of externality" required a complete reconfiguration, and purification, of Christian doctrines and institutions, so as to move away from "works" understood as "mere external observances prescribed by authority."[50] Lutheran teachings change Catholic Christianity not in its "substance" or essence, but simply as regards its external forms, "as far as the Catholic Church insists upon that externality."[51]

As a central example of this transition, in which the essence remains but the external form is abrogated, Hegel points to the Eucharist. He identifies Luther's position on the Eucharist as the necessary middle ground between the error of Catholicism, which insists upon the external form, and the error of Calvinism, which seems to obscure the spiritual essence. In this direct eucharistic relationship "in Spirit" between each believer and Christ, the real presence of "Christ" manifests itself as perfect interior communion that translates into an interior union with the universe. In communion, "the individual knows that he is filled with the Divine Spirit," and therefore "all the relations that sprung from that vitiating element of externality . . . are *ipso facto* abrogated."[52] There is here no need for an ordained priesthood because each person stands equally before God, able in interior communion to merge his or her "Subjective Spirit" with "the Spirit of Truth."[53] This unification is the fundamental essence of Christianity. The task of the believer is to appropriate Christ's "work of reconciliation" of individual Spirit with

[47] Ibid., 444.
[48] Ibid., 444–5.
[49] Ibid., 415.
[50] Ibid., 415.
[51] Ibid.
[52] Ibid., 416.
[53] Ibid.

universal Spirit, and come to recognize universal Spirit as the "Spirit of Christ."

In Hegel's view, Luther's new understanding of communion in Christ subverted all authority other than individual reason and conscience, and thereby opened the space for free Spirit, which found its most pure manifestation in Germany. Hegel thus affirms that

> the pure inwardness of the German nation was the proper soil for the emancipation of Spirit; the Romanic Nations, on the contrary, have maintained in the very depth of their soul – in their Spiritual Consciousness – the principle of Disharmony: they are a product of the fusion of Roman and German blood, and still retain the heterogeneity thence resulting.[54]

The Catholic Church remains prominent in the Romanic nations because they continue to cleave to external forms rather than surrender their spirits in union with the universal Spirit. In other words, they are still fleshly rather than spiritual.

Because of their importance for theology, the above four thinkers lay the groundwork for the twentieth-century turn in Catholic Eucharistic theology toward the bifurcation of communion (with God and neighbor) from sacrifice.[55] Schillebeeckx's early study *Christ the Sacrament of the Encounter with God* (1959) almost imperceptibly, through his emphasis on communion as flowing from direct encounter with the risen

---

[54] Ibid., 420–1. For Hegel's displacement of the Jews, see Michael Mack, *German Idealism and the Jew: The Inner Anti-Semitism of Philosophy and German Jewish Responses* (Chicago: University of Chicago Press, 2003). With Hegelian philosophy in mind, Cardinal Lustiger, in *Choosing God – Chosen by God*, warns against "rationalist" and "gnostic" movements in Western thought as "anti-Jewish" precisely as rationalist (69). See also Louis Jacobs, "The Body in Jewish Worship: Three Rituals Examined," in *Religion and the Body*, ed. Sarah Coakley (Cambridge: Cambridge University Press, 1997): 71–89 and two recent studies of modern Jewish philosophy, Jonathan M. Hess, *Germans, Jews and the Claims of Modernity* (New Haven, CT: Yale University Press, 2002) and Martin Kavka, *Jewish Messianism and the History of Philosophy* (Cambridge: Cambridge University Press, 2004).

[55] For related Catholic perspectives on the Eucharist from the same time period as the seminal works of Schillebeeckx and Rahner, see Joseph M. Powers, S.J., *Eucharistic Theology* (New York: Herder and Herder, 1967); Edward Kilmartin, S.J., "The Eucharist in Recent Literature," *Theological Studies* 32 (1971): 233–77; J. A. Appleyard, "How Does a Sacrament 'Cause by Signifying'?" *Science et esprit* 23 (1971): 167–200. Colman O'Neill's criticism of this movement fell generally on deaf or hostile ears: O'Neill, *New Approaches to the Eucharist* (New York: Alba House, 1967). See, for example, the joint review of Powers's and O'Neill's books in *The Thomist* 32 (1968): 129–32, which sharply criticizes O'Neill. See also P.F. Fransen, *Faith and the Sacraments* (London: Blackfriars, 1958).

Christ, marks the beginnings of this turn.⁵⁶ Certainly the language of sacrifice is present throughout his book. For instance, he holds that the biblical account of the Last Supper makes clear that Christ's sacrificial death of "vicarious reconciliation" establishes "community."⁵⁷ He similarly speaks about "the eucharistic People of God" in which "[t]he individual becomes personally united with Christ in his sacrifice of the cross to the extent that, by taking part in the Eucharist and especially in receiving Communion, he enters into the sacrificial community of the Church."⁵⁸

In Schillebeeckx's view, however, the communion with God and neighbor that Jesus establishes flows not from the Cross but rather from the glorified Christ. Schillebeeckx explains that during his earthly ministry, Jesus, like us, experienced a separation from God: not a "local separation" but rather "some kind of 'absence from home' or 'estrangement' from God."⁵⁹ Jesus' humanity, as representative of ours, therefore has to be deified before his humanity can truly become a conduit for communion. Schillebeeckx observes that

> the Spirit has first to overcome the unsaved state of humanity in Jesus, its condition as *sarx*, and has to deify and to renew the whole of humanity through and through, including its very

⁵⁶ Edward Schillebeeckx, O.P., *Christ the Sacrament of the Encounter with God*, trans. Paul Barrett, O.P. et al. from the 3rd edition (New York: Sheed and Ward, 1963); see also his erudite but much less influential doctoral dissertation *De sacrementele heilseconomie* (Antwerp: H. Nelissen, 1952), which has not appeared in English and appeared in French only in 2004: *L'économie sacramentelle du salut* (Fribourg: Academic Press, 2004). The latter book, which amply demonstrates Schillebeeckx's knowledge of the Catholic tradition of sacramental theology, makes clear that his theology possessed the resources to move in a different direction. In contrast, his *The Eucharist*, trans. N.D. Smith (New York: Sheed and Ward, 1968 [1967 Dutch edition]), moves markedly in an idealist direction. An overview of the development of Schillebeeckx's theology through the late 1980s is found in Philip Kennedy, O.P., *Schillebeeckx* (Collegeville, MN: Liturgical Press, 1993). For further engagement with Schillebeeckx's developing thought and its influence, which is now on the wane, see Robert J. Schreiter and Mary Catherine Hilkert, O.P., *The Praxis of Christian Experience: An Introduction to the Theology of Edward Schillebeeckx* (San Francisco: Harper & Row, 1989); A. Haquin, "Vers une théologie fondamentale des sacrements. De E. Schillebeeckx à L.-M. Chauvet," *Anamnesis* 4 (1994): 107–33. See also Schillebeeckx's *Jesus: An Experiment in Christology*, trans. Hubert Hoskins (New York: Seabury, 1979 [1974]) and *Christ: The Experience of Jesus as Lord*, trans. John Bowden (New York: Seabury, 1980 [1977]). Jean-Luc Marion, in *God without Being*, trans. Thomas A. Carlson (Chicago: University of Chicago Press, 1991): 169, sets forth the link between Hegel and (at least the later) Schillebeeckx.
⁵⁷ Ibid., 22. This passage comes from the Dutch 3ʳᵈ edition of 1959, and does not appear in the first two (identical) editions. Jörgen Vijgen generously compared for me the English translation of *Christ the Sacrament of the Encounter with God* with the Dutch editions.
⁵⁸ Ibid., 175.
⁵⁹ Ibid., 26.

bodiliness. Only when this is done can the man Jesus, who is God, give the Spirit of God to us, too, in a sovereign way.[60]

The sacraments present us with "Christ's glorified bodiliness"; they are "an earthly prolongation of Christ's glorified humanity."[61] Schillebeeckx argues that only the glorified Christ can offer us true interpersonal communion: "For the glorious body of Christ gives his soul the outward openness he as man must have if he is really to exercise influence upon us."[62] In his glorified body, removed from the "estrangement" from God that all human beings experience due to our bodiliness (*sarx*), Christ reveals the full spiritual communion he has with God, and thereby influences us by drawing us into this communion. As Schillebeeckx states:

> the Church's sacraments are not things but encounters of men on earth with the glorified man Jesus by way of a visible form. On the plane of history they are the visible and tangible giving of form to the heavenly saving action of Christ. They are this saving action itself in its availability to us; a personal act of the Lord in earthly visibility and open availability.[63]

The saving action of Christ is fundamentally his *heavenly* work. By mediating the encounter with Christ, "Sacramentality thus bridges the gap

---

[60] Ibid., 26–7.
[61] Ibid., 41, 42. A.A. Häussling, in his review of U.M. Lang's *Conversi ad Dominum: Zu Gebetsostung, Stellung des Liturgen am Altar und Kirchenbau* in *Archiv für Liturgiewissenschaft* 42 (2000): 156–7, shows how this position shaped post-conciliar Catholic thought regarding the direction of liturgical prayer. Häussling, invoking the intention of the Council, writes in critique of Lang:

> Against the intention of the Council, the author does not consider the most important argument in favour of the altered direction of the celebrant. The Council wanted to bring home the Paschal Mystery as the central event of salvation history (which is still present!). This means that the Lord, freed from death and exalted, lives in the middle of the Church, that is to say, in the middle of every praying community. Thus there can be no question that, in an age when man has made himself the centre of his own consciousness, when the greatness and the risks of human society shape our experience, the gathering of the faithful around the altar is felt to be more appropriate than the turning towards the east. The latter is often perceived as merely artificial, though "objectively speaking", no less "right".

Communion here is directly with "the Lord, freed from death and exalted." I have taken this valuable quotation of Häussling's review from Lang's *Turning towards the Lord: Orientation in Liturgical Prayer* (San Francisco: Ignatius Press, 2004): 16.
[62] Schillebeeckx, *Christ the Sacrament of the Encounter with God*, 42.
[63] Ibid., 44. The English translation has "the visible and tangible embodiment of," but the Dutch word is "vormgeving," that is, "giving of form" rather than "embodiment."
[64] Ibid. For later development in this direction see Kenan Osborne, O.F.M.'s *Christian*

and solves the disproportion between the Christ of heaven and unglorified humanity."[64] At the center of Schillebeeckx's vision of the sacraments is communion understood as sharing directly in Christ's glorification.

Since for us this communion was made possible *through* the historical sacrifice of the Cross, the heavenly communion always retains a relation to the Cross.[65] Yet the sacraments provide a *direct* participation in the eternal communion of Son and Father, which is signified by the historical Cross. As Schillebeeckx puts it:

> From all this we see that the sacraments, as "mediation" between Christ and ourselves, must be situated not immediately between the historical sacrifice of the Cross and our twentieth-century situation, but rather between the Christ who is living now and our earthly world.[66]

Discounting sacrificial participation in Christ's sacrifice, Schillebeeckx moves directly to glorified communion: "More precisely, what takes place in the sacraments is the immediate encounter in mutual availability between the living *Kyrios* and ourselves."[67]

Karl Rahner's sacramental theology, like the later work of Schillebeeckx, clearly displays the spiritualizing influence of Schleiermacher and Hegel. He decisively moves away from the Jewish mode of communion as arising in and through expiatory sacrifice. Rahner begins with the thesis, "The world is permeated by the grace of God."[68] Every particular experience of sanctifying grace will be

---

Sacraments in a Postmodern World: A Theology for the Third Millennium (New York: Paulist, 1999). The Church's sacraments, according to Osborne, are simply particular instances or events (understood in the occasionalist fashion of nominalist metaphysics) of "sacramentality," described by Osborne as "sacramental *Haecceitas*," and metaphysical discourse about the sacraments exemplifies the "onto-theological" move. See also a further popularization, Joseph Martos, *Doors to the Sacred: A Historical Introduction to Sacraments in the Catholic Church* (Liguori, MO: Liguori Publications, 1991).

[65] Schillebeeckx, *Christ the Sacrament of the Encounter with God*, 61–2.

[66] Ibid., 62.

[67] Ibid. Benoît-dominique de La Soujeole, O.P., by contrast, insists upon the efficacy of Christ's historical acts. See his excellent "La présence dans les saints mystères: Réflexions à propos du *présent* christologique de l'eucharistie," *Revue Thomiste* 104 (2004): 395–419, especially 409f. For a postmodern critique, applied to Schillebeeckx's later work but whose roots are already apparent here, see Lieven Boeve, "The Sacramental Interruption of Rituals of Life," *Heythrop Journal* 44 (2003): 401–17. Boeve warns against correlationist theological method in the contemporary context.

[68] Karl Rahner, S.J., "Considerations on the Active Role of the Person in the Sacramental Event," in his *Theological Investigations*, vol. 14, trans. David Bourke (New York: Seabury, 1976): 161–84, at 166. The original article was written in 1970: "Überlegungen zum personalen Vollzug des sakramentalen Geschehens," in *Geist und Leben* 43 (1970): 282–301. Other works by Rahner with bearing upon sacramental

experienced as an awakening to what has always been present at the heart of our very being.[69] Although the sacraments have at times been understood as if they were God's tools for instrumentally claiming the world, they are in fact God's signs that the world is already permeated by his sanctifying presence.[70] By participation in the Eucharist, therefore, one rediscovers the core both of one's own being and of the world's history: "Under the forms of bread and wine he offers the world in that he knows that it itself is already ceaselessly offering itself up into the inconceivability of God in rejoicing, tears and blood."[71]

Communion means raising our consciousness to the awareness that the very pattern of all historical life is manifested fully in the pattern of Christ's life and stands as the true pattern of our life. Having accepted the presence of this communion as the already definitive character of our being, we are able to embrace its sacrificial pattern fully as our own and allow it consciously to permeate our actions. If the Eucharist is a communion of consciousness that simply ratifies what already is, then does this "make the sacrament superfluous or meaningless"?[72] Rahner

---

theology include: in *Theological Investigations*, vol. 4, trans. Kevin Smyth (Baltimore, MD: Helicon Press, 1966), "The Concept of Mystery in Catholic Theology," 36–73, "Nature and Grace," 165–88, "The Theology of the Symbol," 221–52, "The Word and the Eucharist," 253–86, "The Presence of Christ in the Sacrament of the Lord's Supper," 287–311, "On the Duration of the Presence of Christ after Communion," 312–20; in *Theological Investigations*, vol. 14, "What Is a Sacrament?," 135–48, "Introductory Observations on Thomas Aquinas' Theology of the Sacraments in General," 149–60. *Meditations on the Sacraments* (New York: Seabury, 1977 [1974]); *The Church and the Sacraments* (Edinburgh: 1963); *The Celebration of the Eucharist*, rev. by Angelus Häussling (New York: Herder and Herder, 1968 [1966, based on articles published in the 1950s]). Rahner's debt to Hegel is apparent in *Spirit in the World*, trans. William Dych, S.J. (New York: Continuum, 1994 [1957]). For further discussion see William V. Dych, "Karl Rahner's Theology of the Eucharist," *Philosophy and Theology* 11 (1998): 125–46; Lambert Leijssen, "Rahner's Contribution to the Renewal of Sacramentology," *Philosophy and Theology* 9 (1995): 201–22; Richard Schenk, O.P., *Die Gnade vollendeter Endlichkeit. Zur transzendentaltheologischen Auslegung der thomanischen Anthropologie* (Freiburg: Herder, 1989); John Carmody, "The Realism of Christian Life," in *A World of Grace: An Introduction to the Themes and Foundations of Karl Rahner's Theology*, ed. Leo J. O'Donovan, S.J. (New York: Seabury, 1980): 138–52; Denis J.M. Bradley, "Rahner's *Spirit in the World*: Aquinas or Hegel?" *The Thomist* 41 (1977): 167–99. Carmody identifies Rahner's "Considerations on the Active Role of the Person in the Sacramental Event" as the key text for Rahner's sacramental theology.

[69] Rahner, "Considerations on the Active Role of the Person in the Sacramental Event," 167.

[70] For a defense of Aquinas's account of divine and instrumental causality in the sacraments against the criticisms of Rahner and others, see Liam G. Walsh, "The Divine and the Human in St. Thomas's Theology of Sacraments," in *Ordo sapientiae et amoris*, ed. C.-J. Pinto de Oliveira, O.P. (Fribourg: Éditions universitaires, 1993): 342f.

[71] Rahner, "Considerations on the Active Role of the Person in the Sacramental Event," 172.

[72] Ibid., 175.

answers no, on the grounds that the sacramental sign helps to refocus our consciousness so that we are more deeply present to reality. The sacramental sign reminds us of

> this grace which the recipient of the sacraments already possesses, namely a state of having been drawn into the dynamic process which holds the world together, impelling it toward its goal, the inconceivability of God, uniting all earthly realities and spirits and blending them into a single history of the world as the coming of God through his self-bestowal.[73]

We could continue to trace the development and entrenchment of Catholic Eucharistic idealism through the theologies of the Eucharist and the priesthood of such contemporary figures as Louis-Marie Chauvet, David Power, Kenan Osborne, and many others.[74] Yet the key point should

---

[73] Ibid., 176. Rahner elsewhere describes the sacraments as "the highest stages in the word of grace in the Church in its character as exhibitive and as event" (Rahner, "What Is a Sacrament?," in *Theological Investigations*, vol. 14, trans. David Bourke [New York: Seabury, 1976]: 144). For Rahner's "transcendental Christology," see *Foundations of Christian Faith*, 206–12. For Rahner's account of the Old Testament see his "The Old Testament and Christian Dogmatic Theology," in *Theological Investigations*, vol. 16, trans. David Morland, O.S.B. (New York: Crossroad, 1983): 177–90, at 184–5 and 190, as well as Rahner's dialogue in 1982 with the Jewish New Testament scholar Pinchas Lapide, published in English as Karl Rahner and Pinchas Lapide, *Encountering Jesus – Encountering Judaism: A Dialogue*, trans. Davis Perkins (New York: Crossroad, 1987 [1983]): especially 53–4, 57–9. Stephen B. Chapman has rightly observed:

> For Rahner, the Old Testament's role within the canon is ultimately to provide the modern church with the same kind of salvation-historical background information for the Christ event that it once provided the early church. However, here again, just as in liberal Protestantism, the ability of the OT to speak "vertically" to the contemporary church disappears within the strongly "horizontal" framework of salvation history. (Chapman, "The Old Testament Canon and Its Authority for the Christian Church," *Ex Auditu* 19 [2003]: 125–48, at 133)

See also Bruce Marshall, *Christology in Conflict: The Identity of a Savior in Karl Barth and Karl Rahner* (Oxford: Blackwell, 1987).

[74] For an overview of contemporary trends in sacramental theology, including "Post-Rahnerian," "Liberation Theology," "Postmodern," "Feminist," and "African and Asian" – united by the authors' adherence to what I have termed Eucharistic idealism – see David Power, O.M.I., Regis A. Duffy, O.F.M., and Kevin W. Irwin, "Sacramental Theology: A Review of Literature," *Theological Studies* 55 (1994): 657–705. As David Power notes in his conclusion to the essays, all the approaches surveyed call for significant changes in traditional (pre-Schillebeeckx and Rahner) Catholic understanding of sacraments. Power emphasizes that while these calls for change may seem to indicate a break with Catholic tradition, in fact they mark a profoundly Catholic "faith that Christ and the Spirit are active in the community of disciples in truly human forms" (705).

already be clear: mainstream academic twentieth-century Catholic Eucharistic theology distanced itself from the Jewish (and Catholic) mode of communion in and through sacrifice.[75] William Cavanaugh has connected this displacement of sacrifice with modern ethics from Kant to Derrida, in which "the impartial gift is assumed to be the purer gift,

---

[75] Hans Urs von Balthasar's account of the Eucharist may be read as an exception to this trend, although Steffen Lösel claims that "Balthasar's frequent use even of *sacrificial* terminology itself is not based primarily on the cultic concept. Nowhere does Balthasar develop his concept of sacrifice from the various Hebrew sacrifices in the context of the temple cult or even the sacrifice of the Day of Atonement (cf. Lev. 17). Rather, his notion of sacrifice builds on an existential interpretation of the term. For Balthasar, sacrifice is but an aspect of every loving relationship" (Lösel, "A Plain Account of Christian Salvation? Balthasar on Sacrifice, Solidarity, and Substitution," *Pro Ecclesia* 13 [2004]: 141–171, at 165 fn. 126). Pointing to Mary's sorrowful sharing in her Son's crucifixion (*Theo-Drama*, vol. 4: *The Action*, trans. Graham Harrison [San Francisco: Ignatius Press, 1994], 399f.; see also *Theo-Drama*, vol. 5: *The Last Act*, trans. Graham Harrison [San Francisco: Ignatius Press, 1998 (German edition 1983)], 66–98), von Balthasar argues that the Church eucharistically accompanies Christ in his absolute alienation. The Son's "eucharistic gesture of self-distribution – beyond all the bounds of human finitude" (Hans Urs von Balthasar, *New Elucidations*, trans. Mary Theresilde Skerry [San Francisco: Ignatius Press, 1986 (German edition 1979)], 114) at the Last Supper

> is by no means intended as a merely juridical, moral or satisfactory gesture but beyond that as something real, one could almost say "physical." It is my abandonment by God, which is inherent in my sin, and my dying apart from God and into the darkness of eternal death that he experiences in his "being delivered up"; and he experiences them more deeply and definitely than any mere creature can experience such things. (*New Elucidations*, 116)

The Eucharist enables us to experience the divine "abandonment" that characterizes our sinfulness, but now to experience it as the locus of supreme divine presence. In sharing sacrificially in Christ's alienation, we share in the self-surrender that, by plumbing the depths of our alienation, accomplishes our reconciliation. Grounded upon his theology of the Cross, von Balthasar's theology of the Eucharist thus holds together sacrifice and communion, but does so by positing a "sacrifice" that is radical alienation, and a "communion" based upon Christ's sharing in the hellish state of damnation. Robert Sokolowski adopts von Balthasar's understanding of Christ's Passion in order to ground his account of the Last Supper and the Eucharist (*Eucharistic Presence: A Study in the Theology of Disclosure* [Washington, DC: Catholic University of America Press, 1993], 58–9, 61). For further discussion of von Balthasar's Eucharistic theology, see Peter Casarella, "*Analogia Donationis*: Hans Urs von Balthasar on the Eucharist," *Philosophy & Theology* 11 (1998): 147–77; Aidan Nichols, O.P., "The Holy Oblation: On the Primacy of Eucharistic Sacrifice," *Downside Review* 122 (2004): 259–72, at 269–71; Nicholas J. Healy, III and David L. Schindler, "For the Life of the World: Hans Urs von Balthasar on the Church as Eucharist," in *The Cambridge Companion to Hans Urs von Balthasar*, ed. Edward T. Oakes, S.J. and David Moss (Cambridge: Cambridge University Press, 2004): 51–63. For further discussion of von Balthasar's theology of Cross and Trinity, along with bibliographical references, see my *Scripture and Metaphysics* (Oxford: Blackwell, 2004): 111–43 and Bernhard Blankenhorn, O.P.'s "Balthasar's Method of Divine Naming," *Nova et Vetera* 1 (2003): 245–68.

because it is free of any taint of exchange."[76] Such a "zero-sum" account of sacrifice, Cavanaugh suggests, cannot account for the graced, participatory exchange of gifts made possible in the Eucharist understood as the sacrificial offering of the Mystical Body.[77] For Cavanaugh, "Without a stronger rendition of human participation in the sacrifice of Christ, self-sacrifice is in danger of becoming mere altruism."[78]

John Paul II's encyclical *Ecclesia de Eucharistia* similarly warns against displacement of the sacrificial character of the Eucharist:

> At times one encounters an extremely reductive understanding of the Eucharistic mystery. Stripped of its sacrificial meaning, it is celebrated as if it were simply a fraternal banquet. Furthermore, the necessity of the ministerial priesthood, grounded in apostolic succession, is at times obscured and the sacramental nature of the Eucharist is reduced to its mere effectiveness as a form of proclamation.[79]

Observing that the encyclical employs the words "sacrifice/sacrificial" over 70 times, Richard Schenk has noted that John Paul II's *Ecclesia de Eucharistia* recounts "the ways in which the real presence of Christ involves the Church ever anew in his unique and ultimate sacrifice, the definitive source of all perfected communion."[80] Through sacramentally

---

[76] Cavanaugh, "Eucharistic Sacrifice and the Social Imagination in Early Modern Europe," *Journal of Medieval and Early Modern Studies* 31 (2001): 596. He adds,

> Much of modern moral theory oscillates between utilitarian self-interest and Kantian self-sacrifice. Kant's concept of duty assumes – *pace* Aristotle and Aquinas – that the moral rightness of an act is most secure when it goes directly contrary to the inclinations of the agent, that is, when the act regards only the other and not the self. The choice we have is apparently between altruism and egotism, but neither escapes the logic of self-possession, for pure altruism is parasitical on the misfortunes of others to demonstrate its heroism . . . Self-sacrifice in its modern mode preserves self-possession and precludes mutual participation because there must be an unreturned transfer from one discrete self to another . . . *Agape* thereby appears to exclude *eros*, the desire of the giver to *be with* the recipient. Distance must be preserved. Furthermore, a breach is opened between charity and justice – justice in the classical definition of "giving one his due" – because questions of debt must be excluded from the gift to protect its purity. (596–7)

[77] Ibid., 587, 597–9 (drawing upon John Milbank's "Can a Gift Be Given? Prolegomenon to a Future Trinitarian Metaphysic," *Modern Theology* 11 [1995]: 119–41).

[78] Ibid., 598.

[79] *Ecclesia de Eucharistia*, no. 10.

[80] Richard Schenk, O.P., "The Eucharist and Ecclesial Communion" (a commentary on Chapter 4 of *Ecclesia de Eucharistia*) in *At the Altar of the World: The Pontificate of Pope John Paul II through the Lens of L'Osservatore Romano and the Words of Ecclesia de Eucharistia*, ed. Daniel G. Callahan (Washington, DC: Pope John Paul II Cultural Center, 2003): 83–7, at 85. Schenk comments:

sharing in Christ's sacrifice, the Church herself becomes sacrificial, imbued with radical love.

The Eucharist, as a communion of love in and through Christ's sacrifice, involves learning cruciformity as members of Christ's sacrificial Body.[81] As such, the Eucharist fulfills Israel's mode of sacrificial

---

> The extent of the encyclical's emphasis on the work of Christ in the Eucharist can be gauged by the frequency of the term "sacrifice"/"sacrificial," used over seventy times in the encyclical, not counting synonyms such as "offering," "paschal victim," or "blood poured out." (85)

See also John Paul II's apostolic letter, *Mane Nobiscum Domine*, proclaiming the year of the Eucharist (October 2004–October 2005), nos. 15, 25–6. The Pope comments,

> There is no doubt that the most evident dimension of the Eucharist is that it is a *meal* . . . Yet it must not be forgotten that the Eucharistic meal also has a profoundly and primarily *sacrificial* meaning. In the Eucharist, Christ makes present to us anew *the sacrifice offered once for all on Golgotha*. Present in the Eucharist as the Risen Lord, he nonetheless bears the marks of his passion, of which every Mass is a "memorial." (no. 15)

The primacy of the sacrificial meaning (which is also a great "thanksgiving" as a gift from God) is important because, as John Paul II goes on to say, "the Eucharist is a mode of being, which passes from Jesus into each Christian" (no. 25) and "One who learns to say 'thank you' in the manner of the crucified Christ might end up as a martyr, but never as a persecutor" (no. 26). For further discussion of the primacy of sacrifice in *Ecclesia de Eucharistia*, see Aidan Nichols, O.P.'s insightful "The Holy Oblation: On the Primacy of Eucharistic Sacrifice," *Downside Review* 122 (2004): 259–72.

[81] On "cruciformity" – being configured to Christ's self-giving and redemptive love on the Cross – see Michael J. Gorman's valuable *Cruciformity: Paul's Narrative Spirituality of the Cross* (Grand Rapids, MI: Eerdmans, 2001). See also John D. Laurence, S.J., "The Eucharist as the Imitation of Christ," *Theological Studies* 47 (1986): 286–96. Laurence's article, however, concludes by separating, with regard to the form of the sacrament of the Eucharist, Christ's "external" and "internal" actions, and relegating the former to a position of absolutely no importance – a striking instance of Eucharistic idealism. Laurence writes:

> In determining what is always and everywhere necessary for a true celebration of the Eucharist, those arguments based exclusively on the external actions of Christ at the Last Supper are accordingly unhelpful. For example, that only wheat bread and grape wine can be used, or that only males, because they bear a "natural resemblance" to Christ, can be presiders. If these restrictions are in fact theologically necessary, they can be so only if the Church is otherwise unable to express its fundamental faith in the historical events of Christ's life, death, and resurrection as the unique source of salvation. At the present time, therefore, the only response possible to the question is a continuing docility on the part of the faithful and hierarchy alike to the leadings of Christ through his Spirit in the living faith of the Church. (296)

Laurence's article would benefit from attention to Leo Elders, S.V.D.'s superb "The Inner Life of Jesus in the Theology and Devotion of Saint Thomas Aquinas," in *Faith in Christ and the Worship of Christ*, ed. Leo Scheffczyk and trans. Graham Harrison (San Francisco: Ignatius Press, 1986): 65–79.

worship, in which sacrifice and communion are inextricably integrated. The account of cruciform communion offered in this book, indebted to Aquinas as well as to numerous Jewish and Christian exegetes and theologians, thus belongs to the spiritual and liturgical exercises – the limp of Jacob – by which Israel is moved from creature-centered idolatry to praise of the God who is sheer Act. God sets before Israel the task of fleeing idolatry by embodied wisdom (Torah) and sacrificial communion (Temple), and in Christ the two are one. Union with Jesus Christ in the sacramental-sacrificial liturgy of the Eucharist is both a sharing in Christ's sacrificial fulfillment of Torah and Temple and a contemplative participation in the trinitarian life of the divine Word.[82]

Thus, I hope that the work will contribute to the ongoing effort of believers

> to know the love of Christ which surpasses knowledge, that you may be filled with all the fulness of God. Now to him who by the power at work within us is able to do far more abundantly than all that we ask or think, to him be glory in the church and in Christ Jesus to all generations, for ever and ever. Amen. (Eph. 3:19–21)

---

[82] The present book extends the arguments made in my *Christ's Fulfillment of Torah and Temple* and *Scripture and Metaphysics*. David Bentley Hart has observed that in Greek patristic theology of the Eucharist these two aspects, "sacramental *koinonia*" and "mystical *theoria*," are drawn together in a delicate balance. See Hart's "'Thine Own of Thine Own': Eucharistic Sacrifice in Orthodox Tradition," in *Rediscovering the Eucharist: Ecumenical Conversations*, ed. Roch Kereszty, O. Cist. (New York: Paulist Press, 2003): 155–7.

1

The Desire of Israel

Jon D. Levenson points out that Israel, marked by desire to be in communion with the all-holy God, recognizes that such communion is possible only, after sin, through sacrificial offering.[1] For the rabbinic tradition, Levenson notes, Genesis 22:15–18 makes clear that the people of Israel exist only because of Abraham's willingness to sacrifice the son of the promise. Likewise Genesis 22:2, combined with 2 Chronicles 3:1, indicates for the rabbis both that the place where Abraham went to sacrifice his son was none other than "the mountain on which Solomon built his temple" and that "the aqedah is the origin of the daily lamb offerings (the *temîdîm*) and, less directly but more portentously, of the passover sacrifice as well."[2] Levenson affirms:

> The paschal connection will prove central to the parallel Christian belief that the eucharist is a reenactment of Jesus' final meal before his sacrificial death. Both the Jewish and the Christian systems of sacrifice come to be seen as founded upon a father's willingness to surrender his beloved son and the son's unstinting acceptance of the sacrificial role he has been assigned in the great drama of redemption. Though this is more obviously the case in Christianity, it holds for Judaism more than is generally recognized. The Christian doctrine is incomprehensible apart from the history of Jewish biblical interpretation.[3]

---

[1] I discuss the relation of sacrifice to the state of sin in later chapters.

[2] Jon D. Levenson, *The Death and Resurrection of the Beloved Son: The Transformation of Child Sacrifice in Judaism and Christianity* (New Haven, CT: Yale University Press, 1993): 173–4.

[3] Levenson, *The Death and Resurrection of the Beloved Son*, 174–5. Levenson speaks of "the crucial rabbinic notion that the death of the righteous atones for the sins of others" (195). Kierkegaard has given the most famous Christian reading of the aqedah. While this reading is strongly Lutheran – the aqedah represents the triumph of blind faith – it should be read against the spiritualizing direction of Hegel's Eucharistic idealism,

As theologians such as Louis Bouyer, Joseph Ratzinger, and Rowan Williams have suggested, the aqedah is a crucial locus for Christian reflection on the eucharistic intersection of sacrifice and communion.[4] Williams observes that

> it is clear that the ransoming of Isaac by the provision of a lamb was seen as one of God's decisive acts of honouring his promises – a kind of renewal of the covenant built into creation, expressed in the promise to Abraham, vindicated at the Exodus, consummated in the Messianic age.[5]

Within Jewish theology, the aqedah depicts the reality that radical communion is made possible through radical sacrifice.[6] Likewise for Aquinas, following Augustine's *City of God*, Genesis 22 finds its place as one of what Augustine calls the "many and various signs" of Christ's radical sacrifice, "one being prefigured by many, in the same way as a

---

and is thus closer to Jewish readings than Levenson allows. (See Jerome I. Gellman, *Abraham! Abraham! Kierkegaard and the Hasidim on the Binding of Isaac* [Burlington, VT: Ashgate, 2003]). Marveling at how Abraham's obedience reveals the passion of his faith, Kierkegaard states, "But as for Abraham there was no one who could understand him. And yet think what he attained! He remained true to his love . . . Faith is the highest passion in a man." See his *Fear and Trembling* and *The Sickness unto Death*, trans. Walter Lowrie (Princeton, NJ: Princeton University Press, 1968), 129, 131. Kierkegaard writes earlier in the book, "The ethical expression for what Abraham did is, that he would murder Isaac; the religious expression is, that he would sacrifice Isaac; but precisely in this contradiction consists the dread which can well make a man sleepless, and yet Abraham is not without this dread" (41). See also Robert Hayward, "Appendix: The Aqedah," in M. F. C. Bourdillon and Meyer Fortes, eds. *Sacrifice* (London: Academic Press, 1980): 84–5.

[4] Joseph Ratzinger takes this approach in a meditation entitled " 'The Lamb Redeemed the Sheep': Reflections on the Symbolism of Easter" in *Behold the Pierced One: An Approach to a Spiritual Christology*, trans. Graham Harrison (San Francisco: Ignatius Press, 1986 [German edition 1984]: 111–21. Rowan Williams makes similar remarks in *Eucharistic Sacrifice*, 15. He draws upon an article by Geza Vermes, "Redemption and Genesis xxii," in *Scripture and Tradition in Judaism*, 2nd edn (Leiden: E.J. Brill, 1973). Further surveys of the aqedah and of the growing critical literature can be found in Edward Noort, Eibert J.C. Tigchelaar, and Ed Noort, eds., *The Sacrifice of Isaac: The Aqedah, Genesis 22 and Its Interpretations* (Leiden: Brill, 2001); Robert J. Daly, S.J., "The Soteriological Significance of the Sacrifice of Isaac," *Catholic Biblical Quarterly* 39 (1977): 45–75; C.J.R. Hayward, "The Present State of Research into the Targumic Account of the Sacrifice of Isaac," *Journal of Jewish Studies* 32 (1981): 127–50; and P.R. Davies and Bruce D. Chilton, "The Aqedah: A Revised Tradition History," *Catholic Biblical Quarterly* 40 (1978): 514–46.

[5] Williams, *Eucharistic Sacrifice*, 16. Williams goes on to suggest that the *tamid* offering, associated with remembrance of the aqedah, was not a sin-offering.

[6] Ratzinger's interpretation is similar to that of Avivah Gottlieb Zornberg below: The "laughter" of communion comes about in and through the sacrifice accomplished by God, which we partake in.

single concept of thought is expressed in many words."[7] As Aquinas professes in his eucharistic hymn "Lauda, Zion" (belonging to his sequence of the Mass for the feast of Corpus Christi), "In figuris praesignatur,/ cum Isaac immolatur,/ agnus Paschae deputatur,/ datur manna patribus."[8] Similarly, commenting upon John 1:29 where Jesus is identified as the "lamb of God," Aquinas states that:

> [Christ] is called the Lamb of God, that is, of the Father, because the Father provided man with an oblation to offer that satisfied for sins, which man could not have through himself. So when Isaac asked Abraham, "Where is the victim for the holocaust?2 he answered, "God himself will provide a victim for the holocaust" (Gen. 22:7); "God did not spare his own Son, but delivered him up for all of us" (Rom. 8:32).[9]

---

[7] Aquinas quotes this passage from Augustine in 3, q. 48, a. 3, which discusses whether Christ's Passion accomplished our salvation by way of "sacrifice."

[8] For the authenticity of this hymn and of the office of Corpus Christi, see Jean-Pierre Torrell, O.P., *Saint Thomas Aquinas*, vol. 1: *The Person and His Work*, trans. Robert Royal (Washington, D.C.: Catholic University of America Press, 1996): 129–36; Pierre-Marie Gy, O.P., "L'office du Corpus Christi et s. Thomas d'Aquin. État d'une recherche," *Revue des sciences philosophiques et théologiques* 64 (1980): 491–507; L.J. Bataillon, O.P., "Le sermon inédit de s. Thomas *Homo quidam fecit cenam magnam*. Introduction et édition," *Revue des sciences philosophiques et théologiques* 67 (1983): 353–69. Following Gy, Torrell speaks of the office as "a decisive moment in Thomas's spiritual evolution" (Torrell, 135). The hymn makes clear Aquinas's view that Christ's Eucharist should be understood as the fulfillment of Israel, and cannot be understood outside this context. In the office of Corpus Christi, see Aquinas's beautiful prayers before and after the Eucharist, which express his awareness of his sinfulness and his desire to be in Christ's Mystical Body – an aspect pointed out to me by Andrew Hofer, O.P. On the history and function of the liturgical "office" in the medieval West, see Eric Palazzo, *Le Moyen Âge: Des origines au XIIIe siècle*, Histoire des livres liturgiques (Paris: Beauchesne, 1993): 131–79.

[9] St Thomas Aquinas, *Commentary on the Gospel of Saint John*, Part I, trans. James A. Weisheipl, O.P. and Fabian R. Larcher, O.P. (Albany, NY: Magi Books, 1980): ch. 1, lecture 14, no. 257 (p. 120). Genesis 22 often served in medieval theology to raise questions about divine omnipotence and human freedom, as well as (in Jewish literature) to provide a model of Jewish martyrdom, in response to the pogroms associated with the Crusades. For further analysis of the medieval Jewish and Christian discussion, see from a vast literature Isabelle Mandrella, *Das Isaak-Opfer: Historisch-systematische Untersuchung zu Rationalität und Wandelbarkeit des Naturrechts in der mittelalterlichen Lehre vom natürlichen Gesetz* (Münster: Aschendorff, 2002); Seymour Feldman, "The Binding of Isaac: A Test-Case of Divine Foreknowledge," in *Divine Omniscience and Omnipotence in Medieval Philosophy: Islamic, Jewish and Christian Perspectives*, ed. Tamar Rudavsky (Dordrecht: D. Reidel, 1985): 105–33; Jeremy Cohen, "Philosophical Exegesis in Historical Perspective: The Case of the Binding of Isaac," in *Divine Omniscience and Omnipotence in Medieval Philosophy*, ed. Tamar Rudavsky, 135–42; Norman Kretzmann, "Abraham, Isaac, and Euthyphro: God and the Basis of Morality," in *Hamartia: The Concept of Error in the Western Tradition*, ed. Donald Stump et al. (New York: Edwin Mellen Press, 1983): 27–50.

This insight that after sin, human communion with God and neighbor always is achieved in and through sacrifice lies at the foundation of Israel's and the Church's worship. As Bouyer puts it:

> according to Hebrews, the sacrifice of Christ, which is one with his manifestation to sinful men and the gift of love which is proper to God so that they may share it and live thereby the life of sons, is the sacrifice of the only son which God asked of Abraham, putting him to the test as a parable, because only God, of course, could bring this about and, in so doing, make us capable of it ([Heb.] 11:19).[10]

The present chapter therefore seeks fuller insight into roots of the Aquinas's Christian integration of sacrifice and communion by examining Jewish theology of the aqedah as developed by Jon D. Levenson, Avivah Gottlieb Zornberg, and Michael Wyschogrod.[11] This investigation will enable us to appreciate, when we turn directly to the Eucharist in Aquinas, the precise character and biblical foundations of the integration of expiatory sacrifice and the communion of charity that characterizes all aspects of Aquinas's Eucharistic theology.[12] St Paul's

[10] Louis Bouyer, *The Christian Mystery: From Pagan Myth to Christian Mysticism*, trans. Illtyd Trethowan (Edinburgh: T. & T. Clark, 1990): 289–90. For further discussion of the significance of the aqedah in Hebrews, see Jame Swetnam, *Jesus and Isaac: A Study of the Epistle to the Hebrews in the Light of the Aqedah* (Rome: Pontifical Biblical Institute, 1981).

[11] Immanuel Kant manifests a profound lack of understanding of Genesis 22. See Kant, *The Conflict of the Faculties* (New York: Abaris, 1979): 115. For further insight, arguing that Genesis 22 is about the meaning of sacrifice, see R.W.L. Moberly, *The Bible, Theology, and Faith: A Study of Abraham and Jesus* (Cambridge: Cambridge University Press, 2000): Chapters 3–5, and "Living Dangerously: Genesis 22 and the Quest for Good Biblical Interpretation," in *The Art of Reading Scripture*, ed. Ellen F. Davis and Richard B. Hays (Grand Rapids, MI: Eerdmans, 2003): 181–97. See also Jacob Milgrom, *The Binding of Isaac: The Akedah, a Primary Symbol of Jewish Thought and Art* (Berkeley, CA: University of California Press, 1988). This analysis is extended to Islam by Mishael Maswari Caspi and Sascha Benjamin Cohen, *The Binding (Aqedah) and Its Transformations in Judaism and Islam: The Lambs of God* (Lewiston, NY: Mellen Biblical Press, 1995).

[12] Miri Rubin has warned that beginning in the thirteenth century, in the context of the growth of popular eucharistic piety, "A great intimacy thus developed between the Eucharist and the Jew: the Jew came to be told through his Eucharistic doubts, and the Eucharist through the Jew's rejection" (Rubin, "Whose Eucharist? Eucharistic Identity as Historical Subject," in *Catholicism and Catholicity*, ed. Sarah Beckwith [Oxford: Blackwell, 1999]: 85–96, at 87; cf. Rubin, *Gentile Tales: The Narrative Assault on Late Medieval Jews* [New Haven, CT: Yale University Press, 1999]). See also Joshua Trachtenberg, *The Devil and the Jews: The Medieval Conception of the Jew and Its Relation to Modern Anti-Semitism* (Philadelphia, PA: Jewish Publication Society of America, 1983): chapter 8, "Host and Image Desecration." I hope that the present study contributes to the opposite result.

theological "echo" of the aqedah, quoted by Aquinas in his *Commentary on John* and elsewhere, guides our approach: "He who did not spare his own Son but gave him up for us all, will he not also give us all things in him?" (Rom. 8:32)[13]

1 THE AQEDAH: ABRAHAM'S NEAR-SACRIFICE OF ISAAC (GENESIS 22)

Sacrificing the Beloved Son: *Jon D. Levenson*

In his *The Death and Resurrection of the Beloved Son: The Transformation of Child Sacrifice in Judaism and Christianity*, Levenson devotes significant space to analysis of the aqedah, surveying both historical-critical investigations and the tradition of rabbinic interpretations. He refuses to grant the standard reading, shared by the rabbis and historical-critical scholars, that the aqedah affirms the abolition of child sacrifice (since God provides a ram instead of allowing Abraham to go through with the sacrifice). He points out that "nothing in Gen. 22:1–19 suggests that God's command to immolate Isaac was improper."[14] In his view, the text in Genesis 22 belongs to a period in Israel's history in which child sacrifice, although certainly not the cultic norm, could still be employed in certain serious situations in preference to animal sacrifice.[15]

As evidence, Levenson points to the command in Exodus, "'You shall give Me the first-born among your sons' (Exod. 22:28b)."[16] He then adds that Abraham literally had to obey this command: "Most fathers did not have to carry out this hideous demand. But some did. Abraham knew it was his turn when he heard God in his own voice, ordering the immolation of Isaac."[17] As further explicit examples, he refers to Judges 11 (Jephthah's sacrifice of his daughter) and 2 Kings 3 (the Moabite king Mesha's sacrifice of his firstborn son). He also points to parallels between Genesis 21, in which Abraham sends away Hagar and Ishmael with every reason to believe that this action will probably result in Ishmael's death, and Genesis 22, in which Abraham consents to

---

[13] For exegetical reflection on Romans 8:32, see Luke Timothy Johnson, *Reading Romans* (New York: Crossroad, 1997). Johnson notes that "scholars rightly perceive an echo of Abraham's offering of his son Isaac on the altar" (134). See also the discussion and bibliographical references in Brevard S. Childs, *Biblical Theology of the Old and New Testaments: Theological Reflection on the Christian Bible* (Minneapolis, MN: Fortress Press, 1992): 325–36; Nils A. Dahl, "The Atonement: Adequate Reward for the Akedah?" in *The Crucified Messiah* (Minneapolis, MN: Augsburg, 1974): 146–60.

[14] Levenson, *The Death and Resurrection of the Beloved Son*, 113.

[15] Cf. ibid., 12–13.

[16] Ibid., 17.

[17] Ibid.

sacrifice Isaac. In both cases, Abraham is actively willing to agree to the death of his son.[18]

I do not think that Levenson provides sufficient evidence to sustain his depiction of the aqedah as an affirmation, at the time of its composition, of the continued possibility of divinely approved child sacrifice. He does not, in my view, give adequate weight to the meaning, in the context of the story and of Abraham's place in Israel's history, of God's provision of the ram.[19] Nonetheless, his analysis suffices to give one pause before accepting readings that, by completely spiritualizing the aqedah story, adopt the opposite extreme from Levenson's position. After noting the similarity between von Rad's position and Kierkegaard's, Levenson remarks that "von Rad, like Kierkegaard a Lutheran, replicates the most basic paradigm movement in the theology of his own tradition, the Pauline paradigm that affirms faith in contradistinction to deeds as the supreme and defining element in spiritual authenticity."[20] Levenson seeks to counter this position by holding to the concrete sacrifice, as *commanded* by God, as irreducibly significant. The aqedah's significance is not solely that Abraham evidences the spiritual quality of trust or faith. Rather, Abraham's *actions* – in this case actively obeying God's command to sacrifice Isaac and bringing Isaac to the very point of sacrificial immolation – carry meritorious weight in the eyes of God. Summarizing von Rad's position, Levenson writes, "In and of itself, Abraham's obedience accomplishes nothing. It serves only as a demonstration of his superlative faith, and it is this demonstration of faith that constitutes his passing the great test."[21]

Levenson finds such readings to be reductive in their refusal to grant the importance of Abraham's *action*, his active willingness to sacrifice his son. When, under the name of objective historical-critical work, Christian anti-"works" lenses govern the interpretation of the aqedah, Abraham's active surrender/sacrifice, which is more than passive trust

---

[18] Ibid., 104–5.

[19] In contrast to St Augustine, *City of God*, trans. Henry Bettenson (New York: Penguin, 1972): Book XVI, ch. 32 (pp. 694–5).

[20] Levenson, 125. See David Steinmetz's "Abraham and the Reformation," in Steinmetz, *Luther in Context* (Grand Rapids, MI: Baker, 1995): 32–46. Steinmetz writes that for Luther, "Abraham's faith is not so much an act (e.g., believing that Sarah will become pregnant in spite of her advanced years) as a disposition (e.g., believing that whatever God promises, however startling, he is able to perform)" (41). The tradition in which Luther operates has its roots in the theology of Peter Abelard, who dismisses the value of deeds in both his account of salvation (see his commentary on Romans 3:19–26) and his ethics, in the short work *Know Yourself*. Bernard was entirely correct to see in Abelard's moves a serious threat to Christian doctrine and ethics, as understood in the Catholic tradition.

[21] Levenson, 125–6. Augustine holds together an appreciation of Abraham's faith (influenced by Hebrews 11:17–19) with a recognition of the full value of obedient *sacrifice*.

or faith, is obscured. Worse, such surrender/sacrifice loses its value in the eyes of God, and is replaced solely by the spiritualized attitude of trust. Levenson remarks:

> Abraham's willingness to heed the frightful command may or may not demonstrate faith in the promise that is invested in Isaac, but it surely and abundantly demonstrates his putting obedience to God ahead of every possible competitor. And if this is so, then if Abraham had failed to heed, he would have exhibited not so much a lack of faith in the promise as a love for Isaac that surpassed even his fear of God. He would, in other words, have elected Isaac his own son over Isaac the beloved son in the larger providential drama, the son whose very existence, from the moment of the angelic annunciation of his impending birth, has run counter to the naturalness of familial life. The aqedah, in short, tests whether Abraham is prepared to surrender his son to the God who gave him.[22]

What God tests in Abraham goes beyond merely a test of Abraham's attitude of trust. The issue rather is whether Abraham will sacrifice every created thing, *even the beloved son of the promise*, to God at God's command.[23] Not mere trust, but active willingness to sacrifice the most prized creaturely reality is at stake. Sacrifice embodies and enacts radical willingness to give up everything creaturely for the sake of the Creator; sacrifice is the true enactment, and therefore the true test, of right worship of God. Levenson focuses our attention upon the radically transcendent God who demands sacrifice, and who therefore does not fit into our attempts to domesticate him: "What is tested in Gen 22:1–19 is not Abraham's knowledge, as knowledge is generally understood today, but his devotion to God, the God who now demands the ultimate sacrifice."

Levenson's point is that God, because he is the true God, *can* demand such ultimate sacrifice. He faults Kierkegaard for attempting to domesticate sacrifice to God. Summarizing Kierkegaard's view, he writes:

> Here again the profound Pauline–Lutheran wellsprings of Kierkegaard's interpretation assert themselves again. It is not just that Abraham acts according to an inward faith that offers exemption from legal norms; the basis of that faith may even be an expectation of bodily resurrection: if he is slain, Isaac will be recalled to life. The influence of the New Testament could not be more obvious.[24]

---

[22] Ibid., 126; cf. 142.
[23] Ibid., 128.
[24] Ibid., 131.

As Levenson emphasizes, the aqedah is not actually about Abraham's subjectivity. Rather, it is about the embodied action of sacrifice – and God demands and approves the most radical sacrifice conceivable. Levenson sees in Kierkegaard's and von Rad's readings of Abraham, in short, an implicit, unjustifiable critique of Jewish understandings of sacrifice. More importantly, such readings miss the point that Abraham's active willingness to sacrifice even the beloved son, rather than desiring the beloved son over and against God, counteracts the sin of Adam and Eve in the Garden.[25] Radical sacrifice – and not merely faith – embodies the very opposite of the selfish cleaving to creatures manifested by Adam and Eve in their Fall. Thus, Levenson can conclude that the aqedah displays "the profound and sublime meaning in the cultic norm that the beloved son belongs to God: 'You shall give Me the first-born among your sons' (Exod. 22:28b)."[26]

Levenson's emphasis on the centrality of the action of sacrifice for Israel's relationship with God both superbly undermines accounts of the aqedah that focus merely on Abraham's subjectivity, and suggests that sacrifice, as the reversal of the state of sin, must remain constitutive of any Jewish or Christian understanding of personal communion with God. Yet, as I have already suggested, in pressing his case against the spiritualizers Levenson sometimes goes too far in insisting that the aqedah commends child sacrifice. Stating clearly that God's command to sacrifice Isaac is a "horrendous command"[27] and a "hideous demand,"[28] Levenson nonetheless asks,

> Were the practice of child sacrifice always so alien to YHWH, so "worthy of severest condemnation," would there have survived a text in which it is this act and no other that constitutes YHWH's greatest test of his servant Abraham?[29]

In other words, although the command is horrendous and hideous, nonetheless it was not, in Levenson's view, always "alien to YHWH." This is to suggest that aspects of God's nature, at least as depicted in the Old Testament, find expression in the horrendous and hideous. The aqedah itself, however, never approves of child sacrifice. Rather, the story, as Levenson otherwise sees so well, is about the requirement of detaching oneself radically, by sacrifice, from every created good in order to love God above all things, rather than cleaving idolatrously

---

[25] Ibid., 140.
[26] Ibid., 142.
[27] Ibid., 140.
[28] Ibid., 17.
[29] Ibid., 12.

(as do Adam and Eve) to a created good – no matter whether the most beautiful.[30]

Sacrifice and Feasting: *Avivah Gottlieb Zornberg*

Drawing primarily upon the rabbinic tradition of interpretation as well as upon contemporary psychology, Avivah Gottlieb Zornberg interprets Genesis 22 by focusing (as the rabbinic tradition does) upon Abraham's interior life and spiritual development.[31] She thus sees the events of Genesis 22 as completing the story of Abraham by means of a divine judgment of Abraham's life. She points out, "As a burnt offering, Isaac will – technically – be consumed totally; emotionally, existentially, this will leave Abraham with nothing to show for his life."[32] In the *Bereshit Rabbah*, she notes, the rabbinic midrash argues that Abraham should have made animal sacrifice to God during the feast that celebrated Isaac's birth (cf. Gen. 21:8). Abraham's festive communion with his friends appears to lack the foundational element of sacrificial offering to God. Abraham's feasting or "communion" thereby threatens to become mere solipsism, and Sarah's "laughter" and sharing of laughter with her friends (Gen. 21:6) may well ring hollow. Laughter, for Zornberg, "is

---

[30] Levenson also discusses 4 Maccabees (probably early first century AD), which develops a theology of redemptive martyrdom on the basis of the aqedah, understood as involving Isaac's *free choice* to be bound to the altar of sacrifice. 4 Maccabees 17:20–2 differs from Romans 3:25 because

> [t]o *all* Jews who die the consecrated death it [4 Macc] applies the language of propitiation or expiation that Paul was to apply to Jesus alone. Isaac, in 4 Maccabees, both is and is not thus a spiritual forebear of Jesus as reinterpreted by Paul and kindred Christians. Isaac is a forebear of Jesus in that, as a martyr, he helps bring reconciliation and redemption. He is not a forebear of Jesus, however, in that his death is not *uniquely and exclusively* redemptive: it is one scriptural example, albeit an especially poignant one, of the sort of death that the author asks of Jews facing the horrific choice of martyrdom or violation of the Torah" (189)

Levenson contrasts 4 Maccabees with Romans also in the fact that the norms of the Torah, for which Jews accept martyrdom in 4 Maccabees, are according to Paul "set aside by the new aeon inaugurated by the death and reported resurrection of Jesus" (189; cf. Levenson's further discussion on 215–17). Flavius Josephus, in *Jewish Antiquities*, also interprets the aqedah cultically, emphasizing the free will (self-sacrifice) of Isaac, as do the rabbis of the second and third centuries AD, who in addition sometimes depict Abraham as shedding the blood of Isaac. Levenson speaks of "the crucial rabbinic notion that the death of the righteous atones for the sins of others" (195).

[31] Avivah Gottlieb Zornberg, *The Beginning of Desire: Reflections on Genesis* (New York: Doubleday, 1995), 97–122. I will focus upon her use of rabbinic exegesis to draw together communion and sacrifice by paying attention to the generally overlooked links between the celebration of Genesis 21 and the sacrifice of Genesis 22.

[32] Ibid., 97.

an image representing the end of days, the overcoming of separateness and closure."[33] Yet, Sarah's laughter with her friends and Abraham's feasting, lacking the aspect of sacrificial thanksgiving to God, may seem to be "self-indulgence" rather than true communion.[34]

During the period after Isaac's birth and before God's command to sacrifice Isaac, Abraham lives in the territory of the Philistines. He makes a covenant with Abimelech the Philistine, and "planted a tamarisk tree in Beersheba, and called there on the name of the Lord, the Everlasting God" (Gen. 21:33). This tamarisk tree signifies, in the rabbinic tradition, Abraham's hospitality. Zornberg quotes the Talmud:

> R. Yehudah said that this *eshel* [tamarisk] was an orchard, while R. Nehemiah said it was a hotel . . . Abraham caused God's name to ring out in the mouth of every traveler. How was that? After they had eaten and drunk, they would stand up to give him a blessing. He would tell them, "Was it my food you ate? Was it not God's food you ate?" So they thanked and gave praise and blessing to the One Who spoke and the world came into being.[35]

Guided by the *Bereshit Rabbah*, Zornberg extends this midrash to signify a place where travelers receive any delectable food that they desire, a place where people "eat of the substance of God," food that belongs to God.[36] In this midrashic view, Abraham's tamarisk tree, coming as it does after Isaac's birth and the feasting that had taken place then, indicates Abraham's status as a dispenser of communion not only with

---

[33] Ibid., 100.
[34] Ibid., 98.
[35] Ibid., 102.
[36] Ibid., 104. On the significance of food and feasting, see also Catherine Pickstock, "Truth and Language," in John Milbank and Catherine Pickstock, *Truth in Aquinas* (New York: Routledge, 2001). Pickstock's work has been appropriated by Nathan Mitchell to advance his view that

> open companionship at table (a meal practice that emphasized radical egalitarianism, inclusivity and abundance) was replaced by a focus on the presence of Jesus himself. *The bread-breaker became the bread broken.* Concern for cultic moments and cultic elements replaced concern for "feeding the five thousand," for multiplying loaves and fishes on behalf of the hungry. Gradually the community meal itself (as a time of joyful assembly, feasting, care of the needy and instruction) assumed less importance, and a cultic eucharistic meal (with emphasis on the bread and cup as Christ's body and blood) grew ever more significant. (Mitchell, *Real Presence: The Work of the Eucharist*, 2nd edn [Chicago: Liturgy Training Publications, 2001]: 57–8)

Pickstock's work is far from this perspective.

neighbor but also with God. Zornberg notes that the twelfth-century scholar Rashi, commenting on *Ketubot* 8b, "explains 'Abraham's covenant' as referring to the verse we are discussing: 'We learn from his *eshel*, his "orchard-hotel," that Abraham dealt in loving kindness.' "[37]

The meaning of Abraham's life, then, is the personal communion of love. Yet, this meaning is true only if the communion, the feasting and laughter, flows from communion with God. Zornberg articulates Abraham's position as envisioned by the rabbinic midrash: "I live in the world of feasting and laughter, which imposes no overt constraints; but, really, my life *means* total *korban* (sacrifice), total closeness to God, even if this has never been literally translated into sacrifice."[38] The sacrificial stance characterizes the person whose communion with others flows from a radical communion with God, in which the self is entirely given over (sacrificially) to union with God. She quotes the nineteenth-century Hasidic rabbi Mordecai Yosef Leiner, who writes that God commands Abraham to sacrifice Isaac so that Abraham, near the end of his life,

> should begin to evaluate himself and to evaluate all the preceding trials. On this trial depended all the others, and he might have lost all of them, God forbid . . . But when he saw that it lay in his power to deliver everything to God, then he understood that in everything that he had undergone till now he had done the will of God.[39]

Precisely because Abraham is able to obey God's command to sacrifice everything that he has (that is, his son Isaac), Abraham manifests that the laughter and feasting of the previous chapter (Gen. 21) are not mere self-indulgent communion but rather constitute the true and lasting personal communion that flows from offering everything sacrificially to God.[40]

---

[37] Ibid., 105.

[38] Ibid., 114. For a Christian articulation of "korban," see David Bentley Hart, " 'Thine Own of Thine Own': Eucharistic Sacrifice in Orthodox Tradition," in *Rediscovering the Eucharist: Ecumenical Conversations*, ed. Roch Kereszty, O. Cist. (New York: Paulist Press, 2003): 142–69, at 143.

[39] Ibid., 115.

[40] On such laughter, Ratzinger remarks:

> Jesus is Isaac, who, risen from the dead, comes down from the mountain with the laughter of joy in his face. All the words of the Risen One manifest this joy – this laughter of redemption: if you see what I see and have seen, if you catch a glimpse of the whole picture, you will laugh! (cf. John 16:20). In the Baroque period the liturgy used to include the risus paschalis, the Easter laughter. The Easter homily had to contain a story which made people laugh, so that the church resounded with a joyful laughter. (*Behold the Pierced One*, 119)

Following Rabbi Akiva (and Kierkegaard), Zornberg notes that this attitude of sacrificial obedience is so complete that Abraham does not even reply when God commands him to sacrifice the son of whom God, only a chapter earlier, had promised that "through Isaac shall your descendants be named" (Gen. 21:12). Rabbi Nahman of Bratzlav, who died in the early nineteenth century, interprets this silence as a kind of dark night of the soul, through which spiritual sacrifice emerges the most profound communion with God. This dark-night experience, or mystical prayer, fits with Abraham's journeying toward the place of sacrifice. Zornberg points out that the Talmud holds that journeying toward a more distant synagogue, when one could have prayed at a closer synagogue, is meritorious. She draws upon the sixteenth-century rabbi Judah Loew ben Bezalel and other rabbis to argue that traveling expresses "yearning in action," and therefore expresses the desire for God that belongs to inexhaustible communion with him.[41] She thereby presents Abraham as consumed by spiritual yearning or desire for God, an attitude that is fundamentally sacrificial.

Sacrifice expresses the "deepest intentionality" of Abraham's feasting (communion); Abraham's willingness to sacrifice everything (Isaac) confirms the personal communion with God manifested in the earlier feasting.[42] Zornberg argues, "In the end, the 'prodigious paradox' [Kierkegaard] of the Akedah focuses on the question of *korban* (sacrifice). Satan insinuates [in the Talmud] that Abraham's feasting is essentially babble; closeness to God is not Abraham's underlying passion."[43] Abraham's actions, however, reveal the opposite. Abraham grasps that true interpersonal communion, true feasting, laughter, and hospitality, must flow from profound sacrifice of everything to God the giver of all true communion. Abraham's feasting is "of God's substance" because it flows from his sacrificial offering, manifested in his willingness to participate obediently in the covenantal sacrifice commanded by God. In short, "the sheer force of Abraham's desire" for union/communion with God is manifested perfectly in his sacrificial act.[44] God's Presence to Abraham in interpersonal communion becomes apparent in the sacrifice of the ram.[45] God himself provides the sacrifice that grounds and ratifies the communion.

Sacrifice and Community: *Michael Wyschogrod*

For the Jewish philosophical theologian Michael Wyschogrod, sacrifice's central role in the communion of Israel with God mandates theologically

[41] Zornberg, 119.
[42] Ibid., 120.
[43] Ibid., 119.
[44] Ibid., 120
[45] Ibid., 121.

the eventual rebuilding of Israel's Temple.[46] Communion with Israel's God, Wyschogrod notes, requires of Israel her whole life, all that she is. He affirms, "The Jewish people must be and is prepared to be sacrificed for the sanctification of God's name."[47] Does this mean that Wyschogrod holds that the Jewish people must come to desire their own destruction? While the answer is no, he comes perilously close to this position. For Wyschogrod, the Jewish people, precisely in knowing themselves as wondrously loved, can only expect that they, as a people, will be God's presence in the world: "If there is no need for a sacrament in Judaism, it is because the people of Israel in whose flesh the presence of God makes itself felt in the world becomes the sacrament."[48] Israel's rabbis accepted the destruction of the Temple, on this view, because they knew that the sacrificial liturgy was not ended, but rather would continue literally in Israel's flesh.

As with Levenson's insistence that YHWH commends child sacrifice, this account gives one pause. Wyschogrod, like Levenson, compels us to take seriously the notion of radical, and not merely spiritualized, sacrifice. Yet his position also raises some troubling questions. Wyschogrod goes so far as to explain the Jews' history of suffering by arguing that when the Temple and its sacrifices were present, Israel's death was not required, but that the destruction of the Temple (and loss of the sacrificial worship) meant that Israel itself, as a people, would be the sacrificial offering. He states:

> It is almost as if the world of the Jerusalem Temple, with its animal sacrifices, were an unreal suspension of the sacrifice of Israel. In the Temple, the people are forgiven and protected. There, the death that everywhere else hovers over them is diverted to animals, so that while the animals die, the people is strengthened by its proximity to God. But everywhere else, this diversion is not permitted. Everywhere else, and particularly when there is no Temple, the people is the sacrifice, as Jewish history has shown so many times.[49]

---

[46] See Michael Wyschogrod, *The Body of Faith: God in the People Israel* (Northvale, NJ: Jason Aronson, 1996). Wyschogrod argues for the eventual rebuilding of the Temple and renewal of its sacrificial liturgy (245–7). For a similar view on the necessity of rebuilding the Temple, and an explanation and defense of its animal sacrifices, see Joshua Berman, *The Temple: Its Symbolism and Meaning Then and Now* (Northvale, NJ: Jason Aronson, 1995). As a follower of Christ, and also as an observer of the explosive religious politics of the Middle East, I would consider the rebuilding of the Temple to be a gravely mistaken enterprise, even while I recognize the necessary integration of communion and sacrifice. A taste of the perils involved is given by David B. Burrell, C.S.C.'s contribution to a symposium on *Dabru Emet* in *Jews and Christians: People of God*, ed. Carl E. Braaten and Robert W. Jenson (Grand Rapids, MI: Eerdmans, 2003): 190–2.
[47] Wyschogrod, *The Body of Faith*, 24.
[48] Ibid., 25.
[49] Ibid., 24–5.

Why would true communion with God in the world be manifested by the Jewish people as embodied sacrifice? For Wyschogrod, to conceive of a communion with God outside such sacrifice is to fall into rationalism. He writes:

> Above all, sacrifice is not idea but an act. Prayer and repentance are ideas. They are contemplative actions, of the heart rather than the body. For this reason, rationalists of all times have been delighted by the termination of the sacrifices. For them, the "service of the heart" is self-evidently more appropriate for communication between rational man and their rational God than the bloodbaths of a Temple-slaughterhouse.[50]

In contrast to rationalism, Wyschogrod argues that Israel's communion with God is incarnational.[51] The sacrificial system confronts the reality of death. In the act of sacrifice, human beings stand before God as bodily creatures who will themselves one day soon be devoid of life, as the sacrificial victim is now. No "communion" with God that leaves out the human reality of death can be a true communion, because death is integral to what it now means to be a human being. In sacrifice, death is sanctified by God's presence; the whole human being is drawn into divine communion, a communion that encompasses death. As Wyschogrod states:

> Sacrificial Judaism brings the truth of human existence into the Temple. It does not leave it outside its portals. It does not reserve sacred ground only for silent worship. Instead, the bruiting, bleeding, dying animal is brought and shown to God.[52]

Wyschogrod calls us to recognize that Israel manifests the true status of human beings. We are bound to death. We must give ourselves up, literally, to the judgment of God. God alone, by his sheer gift, can give meaning to the onrushing dying of human beings. In sacrificial posture, human beings recognize themselves not as autonomous subjects, but as dying "objects" who become subjects (in truth) only in God. Wyschogrod reminds us,

---

[50] Ibid., 18.
[51] Steven D. Kepnes makes a similar point with regard to Moses Mendelssohn's favorable view, following Maimonides, of the ceremonial laws in "Moses Mendelssohn's Philosophy of Jewish Liturgy: A Post-Liberal Assessment," *Modern Theology* 20 (2004): 185–212. Kepnes argues that "Moses Mendelssohn glimpsed, in liturgy, a form of mediation between the universal and the particular which postliberal Jews at the turn of the twenty-first century have been searching for" (197).
[52] Wyschogrod, *The Body of Faith*, 19.

In the Temple, therefore, it is man who stands before God, not man as he would like to be or as he hopes he will be, but as he truly is now, in the realization that he is the object that is his body and that his blood will soon flow from his body as well.[53]

A "communion" with God that left out this aspect of sacrifice would be built upon false premises: we cannot uphold our "communion," since we are dying. Rather, we rely completely (sacrificially) upon God to ground real "communion." It follows that the communion, from our side, is only real if sacrificial. Sacrificial worship affirms that communal sacrifice is the only posture in which we can, as creatures, truly enter into communion with God. Wyschogrod states,

> Enlightened religion recoils with horror from the thought of sacrifice, preferring a spotless house of worship filled with organ music and exquisitely polite behavior. The price paid for such decorum is that the worshiper must leave the most problematic part of his self outside the temple, to reclaim it when the service is over and to live with it unencumbered by sanctification.[54]

Non-sacrificial communion involves neither the human being's true (completely dependent) self, nor God's presence transforming and embracing the full human being.

As Wyschogrod points out with some dismay, then, "it took the Reform Judaism of the nineteenth century to cleanse the prayer book of its supplications for the return of sacrifices."[55] Once we understand the

---

[53] Ibid.

[54] Ibid.

[55] Ibid., 20. Wyschogrod argues in this vein that

> if the Jewish return to the land is to be taken seriously, then the cultic dimension of Judaism, which is so closely tied to the land of Israel, must gradually reappear in Jewish consciousness. The cultic in Judaism revolves around the Temple worship. Temple worship, in turn, revolves around the sacrifices that were brought in the Temple in Jerusalem and so carefully pre-scribed in the Pentateuch, particularly in the book of Leviticus. At present, the sacrifices are but a memory for most Jews, for many Jews an embar-rassing memory. Is this an aspect of Judaism that is permanently dead or is a future for it possible? It is a question that cannot be ignored . . . To the modern mind, of course, repentance is a far more rational basis for God to forgive human sin than sacrifice. The net result is that sacrifice has faded from Jewish consciousness, for secular and liberal Jews in practice and in theory, and for Orthodox Jews in practice but not in theory. Orthodox Jews recite the prayers for the restoration of sacrifices, yet one wonders how real

role of sacrifice in mediating real "communion" to a world of dying human beings, we can understand how Israel, in Wyschogrod's eyes, continues to play this sacrificial role for the world by her communal sacrifices in the diaspora, if not in the Temple. Like Zornberg, Wyschogrod turns to the story of Abraham's near-sacrifice of Isaac in Genesis 22 in order to hone this vision of a sacrificial people who thereby embody God's presence or divine communion in the world. He notes,

> The original sacrifice to which all subsequent sacrifice points is the sacrifice of man before God. More specifically, it is the sacrifice of Isaac, who is Abraham's promised son of his old age, the son through whom his seed will become a great nation.[56]

The "sacrifice of man before God" means that God's love (communion with God) requires of human beings that they be willing "to accept death at the hands of God."[57]

If we are to receive and reciprocate God's love, then we cannot rebel at death. We must, by accepting death, cede autonomy and accept God's loving rule and our complete dependence upon him. Wyschogrod states:

> Both Abraham and Isaac are obedient, one to the command of God and the other to that of his earthly father. Just as Abraham obeys God, so does Isaac obey his father. And both

---

such a prospect is even for Orthodox Jews. And yet the sanctity of Jerusalem, of the Temple Mount and of the Western Wall, is a palpable fact . . . In concrete terms, the rebuilding of the Temple will, in time, become thinkable. This does not mean that the project will commence tomorrow. One of the necessary conditions for the resumption of sacrifice is the reappearance of prophecy in Israel. Only by means of prophecy will certain determinations be possible that are not possible at present. While most Jews have family traditions as to whether they are or are not members of the priestly class, these traditions are not fully reliable and only by prophecy will it be possible to make definitive determinations, a necessity if sacrifices are to be restored. But while the rebuilding of the Temple and the reestablishment of sacrifice is not an immediate prospect, it must become a thinkable idea. It is a thinkable idea because it is commanded in the word of God. It is inextricably interwoven with everything else in the Torah that Jews hold so dear. And it acts as a necessary corrective to the secularization of Judaism, which consists in its ethicization. There is a large portion of Judaism that does not deal with the moral law but with the pleasing of God as he commanded. And it is curious that the most striking manifestation of holiness is not connected with the ethical but with the cultic. It is this cultic holiness that will reappear in Jerusalem. (245–7)

[56] Ibid., 20.
[57] Ibid.

trust him whom they obey. The obedience is not based on terror but on love. It is as if both knew that they are loved by him who demands and that therefore nothing bad can come of it.[58]

In Wyschogrod's view, Abraham thus enacts Israel's experience of (divine) fatherhood and obedient sonship. Abraham plays the role of the divine father who, in his wise and loving plan, wills the penalty of death. Abraham also embodies obedient Israel by, renouncing autonomous subjectivity, offering his whole self sacrificially to his (divine) father. This role of obedient son is played, as well, by Isaac in relation to his father Abraham. Wyschogrod emphasizes that in Israel, the parent–child relationship took the place of the obsession "with the problem of death" and the "elaborate assurances of immortality" that characterized "Egyptian religion and Near Eastern religion in general."[59] God's promise that Abraham's descendants would be a blessing enables Abraham (and Jews) to be far more concerned with the interests of his descendants than in his own interests, including immortality. Wyschogrod therefore points out, "It is for this reason that Abraham's sacrifice of Isaac must be understood above all as self-sacrifice or, more accurately, sacrifice of what is even more precious than the self."[60]

In Abraham's loving, obedient willingness literally to sacrifice his son Isaac, then, Wyschogrod finds a paradox of self-confidence and self-laceration. To be in communion with God offers, on the one hand, a profound assurance and security, and on the other hand a "terrible danger"[61] because communion with the infinite proceeds upon the basis of self-surrender, rejecting any claim to autonomous self-possession. Wyschogrod finds self-sacrifice at the heart of the divine communion that Israel, by her election, embodies: "The love that Israel receives from God cries out for a return, for the giving by Israel to God of its substance, as God gives of his. And this giving is self-sacrifice, in some form."[62] Communion with God is not only life-giving; it is also life-taking, since our lives are owed to God, as expressed by Israel's sacrificial laws.

---

[58] Ibid., 21.
[59] Ibid., 22.
[60] Ibid.
[61] Wyschogrod succumbs somewhat to the modern tendency to envision God "over against" the creature. For the late-medieval understanding of God as over against us, an understanding that influenced Luther and Enlightenment philosophy, see Michael Allen Gillespie, *Nihilism before Nietzsche* (Chicago: University of Chicago Press, 1995); Charles Morerod, O.P., *Œcuménisme et philosophie: Questions philosophiques pour renouveler le dialogue* (Paris: Parole et Silence, 2004): Part II, pp. 55–148; Matthew L. Lamb, "The Resurrection and Christian Identity as *Conversatio Dei*," *Concilium* 249 (1993): 111–23.
[62] Wyschogrod, *The Body of Faith*, 23.

Authentic communion with God will include this life-surrendering aspect, because in surrendering ourselves to God we receive his life-giving power, rather than our insubstantial claims to autonomy, as the basis of our lives. In the "terrible danger" of sacrifice, dying to ourselves, we live in communion with God.

To sum up: Wyschogrod's description of Israel as a "sacrificial people" goes perhaps too far in seeking to explain the Jewish people's experience of suffering, rather than allowing it to remain unexplained and, outside of God's mysterious providence, unexplainable except in terms of the sins of those who have oppressed and murdered Jews. Yet, Wyschogrod's presentation of the relationship of sacrifice to our encountering our own dying, with its demolition of the "autonomous self," powerfully exposes how, outside of radical (embodied) sacrifice, *communion fails.*

2 CONCLUSION

In what way should Christians share in Jewish understanding of sacrifice? Does this intrinsic link between sacrifice and personal/communal communion with God hold for Christianity, as it does for Israel? Levenson remarks regarding the Catholic understanding of the Eucharist:

> in some Christian communions, most conspicuously the Roman Catholic, the eucharist is seen not only as a commemoration of the Last Supper ("Do this in remembrance of me," 1 Cor. 11:24), but as a ceremony of prayer and feasting that is also and most importantly *sacrifice*, an effective reenactment of Jesus' atoning death. In their different ways, both the *Shemoneh Esreh* and the mass have roots in the sacrificial ordinances of the Torah and a substantial debt to post-biblical Jewish exegesis on the story of the binding of Isaac. The indisputable differences between the two great liturgical practices should not be allowed to obscure their profound commonalities.[63]

---

[63] Levenson, *The Death and Resurrection of the Beloved Son*, 186. In the final two chapters of the book, Levenson offers an account of the Christian transposition of the aqedah, but this account is weakened by his reading of Paul without the lens of Paul's fulfillment-theology. Deeming the New Testament, especially Paul, to be naively supersessionist, Levenson holds that for the dominant strands of the New Testament, in a way parallel to certain Rabbinic texts on the Ishmaelites and Edomites, "[t]he break is total: contrary to what the biblical archetype might have suggested, the Jews and the Church are not even related, and the discord between them is, by both accounts, something very different from a squabble within the family" (232). More positively, Levenson concludes his book:

Christians find in the Eucharist a fulfillment of Israel's desire, not a supersessionist displacement, so long as sacrifice (the Messiah's sacrificial offering and the people's sharing in it) remains at the center of the Church's communion with God and each other.[64] Moreover, communion in the sacrifice of the Eucharist, like communion in Israel's sacrifices, is not the final "end." The Eucharist propels all humankind toward a deeper fulfillment, involving the full inclusion of Israel, in which the sacrament will no longer be necessary, since the heavenly Jerusalem's "temple is the Lord God the Almighty and the Lamb"

> That relationship [between Judaism and Christianity], usually characterized as one of parent and child, is better seen as the rivalry of two siblings for their father's unique blessing. Judaism and Christianity are both, in substantial measure, midrashic systems whose scriptural base is the Hebrew Bible and whose origins lie in the interpretive procedures internal to their common Scripture and in the rich legacy of the Judaism of the late Second Temple period. The competition of these two rival midrashic systems for their common biblical legacy reenacts the sibling rivalry at the core of ancient Israel's account of its own tortured origins. In light of the universalistic dimensions of that legacy (e.g., Gen. 9:1–17), it is not surprising that both Judaism and Christianity have proven able to affirm the spiritual dignity of those who stand outside their own communities. But the two traditions lose definition and fade when that universalistic affirmation overwhelms the ancient, protean, and strangely resilient story of the death and resurrection of the beloved son. (232)

[64] This does not suggest, of course, that Jewish thinkers would consider the Eucharist, even as retaining the sacrificial mode of worship, to be a fitting fulfillment. But for parallels between the Eucharist and the Passover seder, specifically regarding the relationship of the Passover *matsah* to the sacrificial *pesach*, see Lawrence A. Hoffman, "A Symbol of Salvation in the Passover Seder," in Paul F. Bradshaw and Lawrence A. Hoffman, eds., *Passover and Easter: The Symbolic Structuring of Sacred Seasons* (Notre Dame, IN: University of Notre Dame Press, 1999): 109–31. Hoffman writes:

> That the salvational symbolism of *matsah* was widely assumed at an early date is indicated by almost unanimous agreement of post-Talmudic authorities on the subject. Though they do not always speak explicitly of deliverance, they generally do refer to a common tradition identifying *matsah* as a replacement for the *pesach*, or Passover offering. (110)

He goes on to note that "*matsah* was used as a salvational symbol. It was held aloft as the seder began, precisely at that point where the lamb had been brought; and around it participants were constituted as a legal company, just as would have been required for a paschal lamb" (123). In the same volume, Frank C. Senn sets forth the connections and differences between the Jewish Passover seder and the Christian Easter Pasch, and cautions against Christians celebrating the Jewish seder: "Until congregations have learned to observe and celebrate well their own paschal feast, they have no business trying to celebrate someone else's" (Senn, "Should Christians Celebrate the Passover?," 183–205, at 202).

(Rev. 21:22).[65] Both Jewish and Christian sacrifice envision an unspeakably richer consummation, in which the sacrificial liturgy will pass into perfect communion.[66] This element of spiritual desire for perfect communion with God characterizes both Israel's sacrifices and the sacrament–sacrifice of the Eucharist.

The Eucharist, when its sacrificial dimension is not obscured, forms a people in this mode of cruciform communion. Thus, while acknowledging the imperfection of medieval social arrangements, William Cavanaugh notes, "In the eucharistic sacrifice, nevertheless, the people were ritually incorporated into the slain Body of Christ, sacrificed for their redemption, and became 'blody bretheren, for God boughte us alle.'"[67] Our communion flows from our incorporation into Christ's sacrifice. The sacrifices of Israel, as fulfilled in Christ's sacrifice and participated in the Eucharist, remind us that God, in both creation and redemption, calls us forth as members of his historical Body, a community whose characteristic mark, despite its failures, is the *imitatio Christi*, self-sacrificing love.

---

[65] On the full inclusion of Israel at the heart of Christian eschatology, see the *Catechism of the Catholic Church*, no. 674. For further discussion of the Temple in Christian theology, see Gregory K. Beale, *The Temple in the Church's Mission: A Biblical Theology of the Dwelling Place of God* (Downers Grove, IL: InterVarsity Press, 2004).

[66] Cf. Catherine Pickstock, "Truth and Language," in John Milbank and Catherine Pickstock, *Truth in Aquinas* (New York: Routledge, 2001). Noting the connection between development of Eucharistic theology and the emergence of the Grail narratives, Pickstock remarks:

> The allegory of the Grail helped to ensure that the seemingly most commonly available thing in every church in every town and village was made the object of a difficult quest and high adventure, a quest indeed so difficult that it was almost impossible to attain, as if it were scarcely possible even to locate and receive the Eucharist. Nonetheless, the ultimate vision accorded Galahad ensures that the postmodern festishization of pure postponement is also here avoided. (109)

[67] William T. Cavanaugh, "Eucharistic Sacrifice and the Social Imagination in Early Modern Europe," *Journal of Medieval and Early Modern Studies* 31 (2001): 592; the quotation in the text is from *Piers Plowman*. Cf. Sarah Beckwith, *Christ's Body: Identity, Culture, and Society in Late Medieval Writings* (London: Routledge, 1993); Eamon Duffy, *The Stripping of the Altars* (New Haven, CT: Yale University Press, 1992); Rachel Fulton, *From Judgment to Passion: Devotion to Christ and the Virgin Mary, 800–1200* (New York: Columbia University Press, 2002); Ernst Kantorowicz, *The King's Two Bodies* (Princeton, NJ: Princeton University Press, 1957). Cavanaugh is sensitive to the fear of "Christendom" expressed by, e.g., David Aers, "Altars of Power: Reflections on Eamon Duffy's *The Stripping of the Altars*," *Literature and History* 3 (1994): 90–115. See also Cavanaugh's instructive comments in "Eucharistic Sacrifice and the Social Imagination," p. 593, on Kyle Pasewark's "The Body in Ecstasy: Love, Difference, and the Social Organism in Luther's Theory of the Lord's Supper," *Journal of Religion* 77 (1997): 511–40.

For Aquinas, Isaac is a paradigmatic instance of such sacrificial communion, even though Isaac himself does not, unlike Abraham and Jacob, offer sacrifice in the Genesis narratives: "Isaac was a type of Christ, being himself offered in sacrifice; and so there was no need that he should be represented as offering sacrifice."[68] Even so, does Aquinas's account of the sacrament of the Eucharist live up to the insights, drawn from the story of Abraham's near-sacrifice of the beloved son, of Levenson, Zornberg, and Wyschogrod? The answer hinges upon Aquinas's understanding of the sacrificial and expiatory character of the Cross and the Eucharist, as well as upon how well he integrates this understanding of sacrificial expiation into his understanding of the communion of charity – the fulfilled Temple, the Church – that is the fruit of the Eucharist. In taking up these topics in the two chapters that follow, I will build upon the insights attained through the Jewish theologies of the aqedah. I will therefore first explore biblical sacrifice and the sacrifices of the Temple that Christ fulfills. On the basis of this biblical portraiture, I will address the theme of expiatory sacrifice in the theology of St Thomas Aquinas. Only in light of such biblical grounding can Aquinas's theology of the Eucharist be understood.[69]

---

[68] 2-2, q. 85, a. 1, ad 2.

[69] As Leo Elders, S.V.D. states in an article that treats Christ's Cross and the Eucharist:

> It is to be observed at the outset that the Christology of St Thomas is not subordinated to any philosophical views or categories of thought; it is subject only to the Word of God. What supports his theological structure are the biblical quotations in the *sed contra* arguments and in the *corpus* of the individual articles. A careful and reflective reading of the relevant texts makes it clear that the Christology of St Thomas is truly the fruit of meditation in the area of biblical theology, inspired by prayer and devotion. At the same time, it is by no means an uncritical theology but a *quasi explicatio* of the Church's doctrine of faith; it was based on the whole of the tradition available to him and it took into account penetrating counterarguments. (65)

2

The Eucharist and Expiatory Sacrifice

It should already be clear that descriptive terms taken from human conceptions of justice, such as sacrifice, expiation, and ransom, have a constitutive place in the Old and New Testament. As Walter Brueggemann has pointed out, "Israel is never far away from legal language."[1] This "legal language," as the medieval debate between Abelard and Bernard reminds us, requires of the Christian theologian an exploration of the startling claim that God the Father wills that human reconciliation be achieved by the bloody sacrifice of his incarnate Son and our Eucharistic participation in that sacrifice.[2] By way of undertaking such an exploration, I will first inquire more broadly into the relationship of sacrifice and communion in the Old and New Testaments, as an extension of our reflection upon the aqedah. Second, I will focus in particular upon the meaning of the Temple sacrificial offerings in light

---

[1] Walter Brueggemann, *Isaiah 40–66* (Louisville, KY: Westminster John Knox Press, 1998): 147. Brueggemann is here treating Isaiah 53, but his statement applies to the entire scriptures of Israel. See also Jon D. Levenson, *Theology of the Program of Restoration of Ezekiel 40–48* (Missoula, Montana: Scholars Press, 1976): 129ff.; Frank H. Gorman, Jr., *The Ideology of Ritual: Space, Time and Status in the Priestly Theology* (Sheffield: Sheffield Academic Press, 1990). As Gorman notes,

> there has been a general bias in Old Testament scholarship, particularly among its Protestant practitioners, against Priestly ritual. Wellhausen gave voice to this perspective and, in many ways, established the direction that study of Priestly ritual texts would take. From this perspective, the Priestly ritual texts represent a view of religion and worship that by its very nature takes away the life of true religion and worship. (8)

[2] For the medieval discussion, see the brief sketch in my *Christ's Fulfillment of Torah and Temple* (Notre Dame, IN: University of Notre Dame Press, 2002): 3–8. The debate between Abelard and Bernard, rooted in their differing views of Anselm's and the Fathers' approaches to the Cross and resulting in the condemnation of Abelard's views, can be found in Abelard's commentary on Romans 3:19–26 and Bernard's *Letter 190*. See also G. H. Williams, "The Sacramental Presuppositions of Anselm's *Cur Deus Homo*," *Church History* 26 (1957): 245–74.

of contemporary exegetical debates. On this basis, I will explore Aquinas's account of the fulfillment of Israel's sacrificial liturgy in Christ's Cross and the Eucharist, a fulfillment that governs the entire shape of Eucharistic theology.[3]

1 SACRIFICIAL LITURGY AND COMMUNION IN THE BIBLE: A SKETCH

To see the Old Testament's various cultic and sacrificial events and images, including the aqedah which we have already discussed at length, as "fulfilled" in Christ requires the eyes of faith. Thus, any broad sketch seeking to trace the continuity between sacrifice in Israel and Christ's expiatory sacrifice will necessarily be contested exegetically at almost every step, because of the discontinuity that is also present. In offering such a broad sketch, I hope to make clear that the sacrificial dimension – centered upon the obedient giving up of life understood as enabling relationship with God[4] – is at the center of Israel's and the Church's understanding of communion.

According to the Torah, Israel received her divine liturgy in the law given to Moses. Indeed, liturgy governs the Exodus event, since Moses and Aaron request from Pharaoh permission to travel "a three days journey into the wilderness" so as to "sacrifice to the Lord our God, lest he fall upon us with pestilence or with the sword" (Exod. 5:3). God wills that the people of Israel offer liturgical sacrifice to him; Pharaoh commands them to keep working. The people of Israel thus cannot do the work of God – liturgy – because they are enslaved to the work of Pharaoh. On the night before the Exodus, Moses commands the people of Israel to prepare for the Lord's Passover. Those marked by the blood will be spared; all the other first-born, not included in the (sacrificial) covenantal

---

[3] Greek and Latin theological modes are not at odds here. The fourteenth-century Byzantine theologian Nicholas Cabasilas, familiar with Latin theology, adopts an account of satisfaction, and of Eucharistic participation in Christ's Cross, that largely mirrors Aquinas's: see Nicholas Cabasilas, *The Life in Christ*, trans. Carmino J. deCatanzaro (Crestwood, NY: St Vladimir's Press, 1998): Book IV, pp. 117–22. Richard Schenk, O.P. notes that the Council of Trent "referred to Nicolas' erudition on the patristic sources for the theology of the sacrificial nature of the Eucharist" (Schenk, "The Eucharist and Ecclesial Communion," in *At the Altar of the World*, ed. Daniel G. Callahan [Washington, DC: Pope John Paul II Center, 2003]: 84). See also the Orthodox theologian David Bentley Hart's section on Anselm in *The Beauty of the Infinite: The Aesthetics of Christian Truth* (Grand Rapids, MI: Eerdmans, 2003): 360–73.

[4] The question of whether the meaning of "sacrifice" for the ancient Israelites is found in the death or in the blood lies outside the scope of our investigation. For our purposes, it suffices to note that if the blood of Christ sanctifies, purifies, or expiates, then it is the death of Christ, his free giving up of his life, that does these things. I have benefited from discussions with Guy Mansini, O.S.B. and John Yocum regarding this point.

relationship of divine mercy, will be doomed to destruction for their sins (Exod. 12:21–4).

Similarly, at Mount Sinai, where they are to receive the Torah and learn how to worship, Moses marks the people with sacrificial blood. After Moses has written "all the words of the Lord," he builds an altar, whose construction mirrored the twelve tribes of Israel, for the Lord at the base of Mount Sinai. The people of Israel offer sacrifice to the Lord. Moses then throws the sacrificial blood upon the altar and upon the people as a sign of their newfound obedience, rooted in sacrifice, to God's word (Exod. 24:6–8). Accompanied by seventy elders along with Aaron and Aaron's two oldest sons, Moses then ascends Mount Sinai and enjoys a meal – partaking in the sacrifice – in God's presence: "they saw the God of Israel . . . they beheld God, and ate and drank" (Exod. 24:10–11). After this meal, Moses alone ascends farther up the mountain, where after six days waiting in the "cloud" (the Holy Spirit) Moses enters into the "seventh day," indicative of the new creation, and receives the Law and the commandments about the construction of the tabernacle for the Lord.[5]

Similar sacrificial renewals of God's merciful covenant with Israel are offered by Joshua, David, Solomon, and Josiah. Isaiah speaks prophetically of an ultimate sacrifice:

> Behold, my servant shall prosper, and he shall be exalted and lifted up, and shall be very high. As many were astonished at him – his appearance was so marred, beyond human semblance, and his form beyond that of the sons of men – so shall he startle many nations; kings shall shut their mouths because of him; for that which has not been told them they shall see, and that which they have not heard they shall understand. Who has believed what we have heard? And to whom has the arm of the Lord been revealed? For he grew up before him like a young plant, and like a root out of dry ground; he had no form or comeliness that we should look at him, and no beauty that we should desire him. He was despised and rejected by men; a man of sorrows, and acquainted with grief; and as one from whom men hide their faces he was despised, and we esteemed him not. Surely he has borne our griefs and carried

---

[5] Brevard Childs observes that Hebrews 9:18–21 redefines Exodus 24 in terms of expiation. While this may be true, I would also argue that expiatory elements are not completely absent even from Exodus 24. In and through the sacrificial blood (which responds to the context of sin witnessed to in the earlier chapters of Exodus), the people, through the mediation of Moses and the elders, are made capable of communion with God. See Childs, *The Book of Exodus: A Critical, Theological Commentary* (Louisville, KY: The Westminster Press, 1974): 511.

our sorrows; yet we esteemed him stricken, smitten by God, and afflicted. But he was wounded for our transgressions, he was bruised for our iniquities; upon him was the chastisement that made us whole, and with his stripes we are healed. All we like sheep have gone astray; we have turned every one to his own way; and the Lord has laid on him the iniquity of us all. (Isa. 52:13–53:6)

Isaiah goes on depict the servant as an innocent "offering for sin" who shall "make many to be accounted righteous; and he shall bear their iniquities" by being "numbered with the transgressors" (Isa. 53:10–12).[6]

The mystery of the salvific suffering of an innocent man is also found in various forms in, among other places, Job, Jeremiah, and the Book of Wisdom.[7] The Book of Wisdom describes materialist hedonists, with

---

[6] The meaning of Isaiah 53:10, and especially the notion of an "offering for sin" or a "guilt offering," are contested by exegetes. For an argument that both Jesus and his followers employed Isaiah 53 to interpret his death as a messianic sacrifice, see Peter Stuhlmacher, "Isaiah 53 in the Gospels and Acts," in *The Suffering Servant: Isaiah 53 in Jewish and Christian Sources*, ed. Bernd Janowski and Peter Stuhlmacher, trans. Daniel P. Bailey (Grand Rapids, MI: Eerdmans, 2004 [1996]): 147–62. In the same volume, Otfried Hofius argues that the New Testament letters reinterpret Isaiah 53 by drawing upon an inclusive notion of "place-taking" rather than a merely substitutionary notion: "Jesus Christ, in his person and in his work, is not merely and not primarily explained by Isaiah 53: Isaiah 53 is rather explained *by him*" (Hofius, "The Fourth Servant Song in the New Testament Letters," in *The Suffering Servant: Isaiah 53 in Jewish and Christian Sources*, 163–88, at 188). Similarly, against earlier readings that de-emphasize the cultic aspects of Isaiah 40–55, Christopher Seitz has noted that although the servant's identity is obscure, the servant's mission of atonement is clear. By means of the servant, Zion will be vindicated and restored. See Seitz, "Isaiah and Lamentations: The Suffering and Afflicted Zion," in his *Word without End: The Old Testament as Abiding Theological Witness* (Grand Rapids, MI: Eerdmans, 1998): 130–49, at 148. See also, from the vast literature on the topic, Donald P. Bailey, "The Suffering Servant: Recent Tübingen Scholarship on Isaiah 53" and "Concepts of *Stellvertretung* in the Interpretation of Isaiah 53," in *Jesus and the Suffering Servant: Isaiah 53 and Christian Origins*, ed. W. Bellinger and W. Farmer (Harrisburg, PA: Trinity Press International, 1998): 223–50 and 251–9, as well as Brevard Childs's fascinating historical study *The Struggle to Understand Isaiah as Christian Scripture* (Grand Rapids, MI: Eerdmans, 2004). For Jewish midrashic readings of Isaiah 53 as prophesying a suffering messiah, see Michael Fishbane, *The Exegetical Imagination: On Jewish Thought and Theology* (Cambridge, MA: Harvard University Press, 1998): Chapter 5, "Midrashic Theologies of Messianic Suffering," pp. 73–85.

[7] Such suffering analogously expands the conception of "sacrifice," by moving beyond the communion or expiation accomplished through the blood of an animal. Adopting a strict sense of "sacrifice" (leaving, for example, the aqedah out of consideration), Albert Vanhoye, S.J. writes,

From the point of view of Old Testament cult, the death of Jesus in no way appeared as a priestly offering; it was in fact the very opposite of a sacrifice. Indeed, sacrifice did not consist in the putting to death of a living person,

no hope of life after death and thus no ultimate goal beyond earthly pleasure (however defined) and no rule of life other than might makes right (Wisd. 2:11), as saying:

> "Let us lie in wait for the righteous man, because he is inconvenient to us and opposes our actions; he reproaches us for sins against the law, and accuses us of sins against our training. He professes to have knowledge of God, and calls himself a child of the Lord. He became to us a reproof of our thoughts; the very sight of him is a burden to us, because his manner of life is unlike that of others, and his ways are strange. We are considered by him as something base, and he avoids our ways as unclean; he calls the last end of the righteous happy, and boasts that God is his father. Let us see if his words are true, and let us test what will happen at the end of his life; for if the righteous man is God's son, he will help him, and will deliver him from the hand of his adversaries. Let us test him with insult and torture, that we may find out how gentle he is, and make trial of his forbearance. Let us condemn him to a shameful death, for, according to what he says, he will be protected." Thus they reasoned, but they were led astray, for their wickedness blinded them, and they did not know the secret purposes of God, nor hope for the wages of holiness, nor discern the prize for blameless souls. (Wisd. 2:12–22)

---

still less in his sufferings, but in rites of offering performed by the priest in the holy place. The Jewish Law carefully distinguished between slaughter and ritual sacrifice (Deut. 12:13–16). Now Jesus' death had taken place had taken place outside the Holy City. It had not been accompanied by liturgical rites. It was viewed as a legal penalty, the execution of a man condemned to death. (Vanhoye, *Old Testament Priests and the New Priest According to the New Testament*, trans. J. Bernard Orchard, O.S.B. [Petersham, MA: St Bede's Publications, 1986]: 50)

Vanhoye goes on to point out, "The Old Testament never says that a victim offered in sacrifice 'has died for our sins'" (51). Nonetheless, he argues that Jesus' understanding of himself as the new Temple and the accounts of the Last Supper provide at least implicit grounds for interpreting Jesus' death as sacrificial. While agreeing with Vanhoye that the discontinuity between Jesus' death and the various manifestations of Old Testament sacrificial language means that Jesus' sacrificial death cannot be simply "read off" from the Old Testament – in other words, Jesus' priesthood is radically new – I think that Vanhoye's lack of attention to the aqedah leads him to underestimate the inner depths of Old Testament sacrificial language. See also Hermann Spieckermann's examination of Jeremiah and Ezekiel in "The Conception and Prehistory of the Idea of Vicarious Suffering in the Old Testament," in *The Suffering Servant: Isaiah 53 in Jewish and Christian Sources*, ed. Bernd Janowski and Peter Stuhlmacher, 1–15.

St Paul thus reminds his fledgling churches that "Christ died for our sins in accordance with the scriptures" (1 Cor. 15:3) and returns often to the theme that "one has died for all" (2 Cor. 5:14).[8] Echoing Isaiah 53 (and Isa. 59 and 63) and proclaiming the fulfillment of the covenantal sacrifices of Israel, he teaches in his summary of the gospel in Romans 3:

> But now the righteousness of God has been manifested apart from law, although the law and the prophets bear witness to it, the righteousness of God through faith in Jesus Christ for all who believe. For there is no distinction; since all have sinned and fall short of the glory of God, they are justified by his grace as a gift, through the redemption which is in Christ Jesus, whom God put forward as an expiation by his blood, to be received by faith (Rom. 3:21–5).[9]

Christ's sacrificial death is an "expiation" (Rom. 3:25) and we are "justified by his blood" (Rom. 5:9). In order to appropriate this justification interiorly, St Paul makes clear, we must, by the power of the Holy Spirit and through the sacramental mediation of the Church, be "baptized into his death" (Rom. 6:3): "For if we have been united with him in a death like his, we shall certainly be united with him in a resurrection like his" (Rom. 6:5). The key is to be joined, in a participatory fashion, to his sacrifice. We must suffer "with him" in order to share in the reconciliation that he has accomplished:

> When we cry, "Abba! Father!" it is the Spirit himself bearing witness with our spirit that we are children of God, and if children, then heirs, heirs of God and fellow heirs with Christ, provided that we suffer with him in order that we may also be glorified with him. (Rom. 8:15–17)[10]

---

[8] For an explication of Christ's death as a true (not metaphorical) sacrifice according to the New Testament, see S.W. Sykes, "Sacrifice in the New Testament and Christian Theology," in *Sacrifice*, ed. M.F.C. Bourdillon and Meyer Fortes (London: Academic Press, 1980): 61–83. See also Jean-Hervé Nicolas, O.P., "Le Christ est mort pour nos péchés selon les Écritures," *Revue Thomiste* 96 (1996): 209–34.

[9] For a thorough discussion of Isaianic influences on Romans, see J. Ross Wagner, *Heralds of the Good News: Isaiah and Paul in Concert in the Letter to the Romans* (Leiden: Brill, 2002). Wagner discusses the Suffering Servant text most importantly on p. 335. On Isaiah 53 and Jesus' intention, expressed in his eucharistic words, to offer his death "as covenant sacrifice and expiatory offering" (33), see Ben F. Meyer, "The Expiation Motif in the Eucharistic Words: A Key to the History of Jesus?," in *One Loaf, One Cup: Ecumenical Studies of 1 Cor 11 and Other Eucharistic Texts*, ed. Ben F. Meyer (Macon, GA: Macon University Press, 1993): 11–33.

[10] Luke Timothy Johnson likewise emphasizes that for Paul the Christian life is "*sharing the suffering* of the messiah" (Johnson, *Reading Romans* [New York: Crossroad, 1997]: 126). See also John R. Meyer:

As the gospels emphasize, Christ's whole life is ordered to his sacrificial death.[11] The Gospel of Mark affirms that Christ came "to give his life as a ransom for many" (10:45). At the heart of Simeon's prophecy in the Gospel of Luke, similarly, is sacrificial suffering. He tells Mary, "Behold, this child is set for the fall and rising of many in Israel, and for a sign that is spoken against (and a sword will pierce through your own soul also), and thoughts out of many hearts may be revealed" (Luke 2:34–5).[12] In the Gospel of Matthew, Jesus warns his disciples, "He who

---

Sharing in Christ's Death and the Holy Spirit," *Irish Theological Quarterly* 66 (2001): 125–40. Meyer writes, "The Christian must therefore become identified with Christ, re-experiencing his suffering for the spiritual benefit of self as well as others. God the Father sees sin within the reality of the sacrificial death of Jesus, viewing all sinners through the prism of sacrificial love . . . So while we could rightly say that the generative centre of Paul's thought is the resurrection, it is more precise to assert that the *locus vivendi* of that eschatological promise is fellowship in the suffering of Christ. The Christian *ekklesia Theou* takes up the Hebrew *qâhâl YHWH* (cf. Num. 16:20, 20:4), becoming the final perfection of the covenant in which everyone is now a temple of sacrifice. (140)

In contrast, Elochukwu E. Uzukwu, C.S.Sp. grasps in Paul only the element of spiritual sacrifice: "The gods have no need for the blood of sacrifice. Paul brings this spiritualization to its peak: life lived for God or the whole self dedicated to God is perfect sacrifice or worship" (Uzukwu, *Worship as Body Language: Introduction to Christian Worship: An African Orientation* [Collegeville, MN: Liturgical Press, 1997]: 175).

[11] N.T. Wright makes this point in *Jesus and the Victory of God* (Minneapolis, MN: Fortress Press, 1996): e.g. 565, 594. In *The New Testament and the People of God* (Minneapolis, MN: Fortress Press, 1992): 273f., Wright shows that the Temple's sacrificial system, with its associated purity laws, operated to remind Israelites of the redemptive (community-formative) sacrifices of the past, especially the Passover, and to highlight the promise of a new restoration of the community through a definitive act of God that would bring to fulfillment the history of sacrifice in Israel. Further, the people's status as members of the covenant community was framed by the sacrificial system. In sacrificing to YHWH, Jews not only worshiped their God, but also participated in the events (Abraham's near-sacrifice of Isaac, the Passover sacrifice) by which God, through sacrifice, had formed and covenantally set apart his people. For a far more negative portrayal of sacrifice in ancient Israel, and a brief polemical foray into the Eucharistic sacrifice, see Joseph Blenkinsopp, "Sacrifice and Social Maintenance in Ancient Israel," in *Treasures Old and New: Essays in the Theology of the Pentateuch* (Grand Rapids, MI: Eerdmans, 2004): 53–66. Blenkinsopp's critique of Jewish sacrifice is indicative of why proponents of Eucharistic idealism think supersessionism – though not anti-Judaism – is ultimately necessary.

[12] Colman O'Neill, O.P. evocatively compares the congregation's role in the liturgy of the Eucharist to that of the Virgin Mary at the foot of the Cross, sharing in the sufferings of her Son. See O'Neill, *Meeting Christ in the Sacraments*, rev. ed. by Romanus Cessario, O.P. (New York: Alba House, 1991): 231. Similar indication of Mary's role in Eucharistic theology as expressive of the Church's insertion into Christ's sacrifice is found more recently in Aidan Nichols, O.P., "The Holy Oblation: On the Primacy of Eucharistic Sacrifice," *Downside Review* 122 (2004): 259–72, at 269–72.

finds his life will lose it, and he who loses his life for my sake will find it" (Matt. 10:39).[13]

It is at the Last Supper, in sharing with his disciples the Eucharist of his body and blood, that Jesus makes most clear how our sharing in his sacrifice is to come about. Matthew reports:

> Now as they were eating, Jesus took bread, and blessed, and broke it, and gave it to his disciples and said, "Take, eat; this is my body." And he took a cup, and when he had given thanks he gave it to them, saying, "Drink of it, all of you; for this is my blood of the covenant, which is poured out for many for the forgiveness of sins." (Matt. 26:26–8; cf. Mark 14:24)

Luke describes the event in similar language:

> And he took bread and when he had given thanks he broke it and gave it to them, saying, "This is my body which is given for you. Do this in remembrance of me." And likewise the cup after supper, saying, "This cup which is poured out for you is the new covenant in my blood." (Luke 22:19–20)[14]

Jesus, in the Gospel of John, reveals how his exaltation – being "lifted up" – corresponds with the profound vicarious suffering endured by the Servant in Isaiah. Christ says, "Now is my soul troubled. And what shall I say? 'Father, save me from this hour?' No, for this purpose I have come to this hour. Father, glorify thy name" (John 12:27–8). The glory

---

[13] In "On the Suffering of God's Chosen: Christian Views in Jewish Terms," contained in *Christianity in Jewish Terms*, ed. Tikva Frymer-Kensky et al. (Boulder, CO: Westview Press, 2000): 203–20, Leora Batnitzky raises the concern that the Christian understanding tends to valorize suffering. In a response entitled "Suspicions of Suffering" contained in the same volume, the Jewish philosopher Robert Gibbs rightly distinguishes between a "representative view of suffering" and "the subordinating and totalizing views." Gibbs points out that both Isaiah 53 and Christian theology contain a representative view of suffering, in which one suffers for many.

[14] Luke is often seen as the evangelist least interested in sacrifice, but see the observation of Bernard Cooke, S.J., "Synoptic Presentation of the Eucharist as Covenant Sacrifice," *Theological Studies* 21 (1960): 1–44, at 3–4: "By beginning his Gospel narrative with a scene of Temple sacrifice, Luke places his history of Christ's life in a Temple framework that continues right up to the final verse of his Gospel, where he tells us that the disciples returned from the Ascension to praise God in the Temple. The significant prominence of the OT priest, Zachary, at the beginning of the Gospel; the priestly meaning Zachary attaches to the promises of salvation and to their realization; the fact that John, the 'greatest of the prophets,' comes from a priestly family – all this quite clearly sets a sacerdotal tone for Luke's Gospel." Cf. Gregory K. Beale's valuable discussion of the book of Acts in *The Temple in the Church's Mission: A Biblical Theology of the Dwelling Place of God* (Downers Grove, IL: InterVarsity Press, 2004): 201–44.

or exaltation of the Trinitarian name will be the Cross and Resurrection: "Now is the judgment of this world, now shall the ruler of this world be cast out; and I, when I am lifted up from the earth, will draw all men to myself" (John 12:31–2).[15] The language of the Cross and the Eucharist cannot be separated from cultic sacrifice: Christ's body given for us, his blood spilled for the forgiveness of our sins.[16]

When Jesus has been "lifted up," he will "draw all men" to himself. It is in sharing in the Eucharist that believers come to apprehend, and truly share in, Christ's sacrificial Cross. Luke relates,

> When he [the risen Lord] was at table with them, he took the bread and blessed it, and broke it, and gave it to them. And their eyes were opened and they recognized him; and he vanished out of their sight. They said to each other, "Did not our hearts burn within us while he talked to us on the road, while he opened to us the scriptures?" (Luke 24:30–2).[17]

John is even more explicit. He relates Jesus' words to the stunned crowd,

> Truly, truly, I say to you, unless you eat the flesh of the Son of man and drink his blood, you have no life in you; he who eats my flesh and drinks my blood has eternal life, and I will raise him up at the last day. For my flesh is food indeed, and my blood is drink indeed. He who eats my flesh and drinks my blood abides in me, and I in him. (John 6:53–6).[18]

---

[15] The explicit reference to Isaiah 53 occurs in verse 38. For further discussion regarding John's concern with why God's fulfillment, in Christ, of Isaiah 53 was not recognized by many Jews, see Francis J. Moloney, *The Gospel of John* (Collegeville, MN: Liturgical Press, 1998): 346–69.

[16] The Protestant biblical theologian Peter Stuhlmacher argues regarding the Last Supper that Jesus, uniting communion and sacrifice, sought to share "eschatological table fellowship" with his disciples by sharing with them his "vicarious death" in the Eucharist. See Stuhlmacher, "The New Testament Witness Concerning the Lord's Supper," in his *Jesus of Nazareth – Christ of Faith*, trans. Siegfried S. Schatzmann (Peabody, MA: Hendrickson, 1993): 68–9.

[17] See the cultic passages cited by Rowan Williams, *Eucharistic Sacrifice: The Roots of a Metaphor* (Bramcote: Grove Books, 1982): 13. Williams describes the Church on earth as "a fundamentally sacrificial phenomenon" (15).

[18] For historical-critical discussion of John 6, see, e.g., the essays in R. Alan Culpepper, ed., *Critical Readings of John 6* (Leiden: Brill, 1997), particularly those of Maarten J.J. Menken, "John 6:51c–58: Eucharist or Christology?," 183–204 and Marianne Meye Thompson, "Thinking about God: Wisdom and Theology in John 6," 221–42; also William S. Kurz, S.J., "Bread of Life in John 6: Intertextuality and the Unity of Scripture" and "Feeding the 5000 in John 6 and the Eucharist: Spiritual Senses and Actualization," in Luke Timothy Johnson and William S. Kurz, S.J., *The Future of Catholic Biblical Scholarship: A Constructive Conversation* (Grand Rapids, MI: Eerdmans, 2002):

Paul is similarly explicit:

> The cup of blessing which we bless, is it not a participation
> in the blood of Christ? The bread which we break, is it not
> a participation in the body of Christ? Because there is one bread,
> we who are many are one body, for we all partake of the one
> bread. Consider the practice of Israel; are not those who eat
> the sacrifices partners in the altar? (1 Cor. 10:16–18)[19]

Thus, neither Israel nor the Church can get away from what
Brueggemann calls "legal language," the language of expiatory sacrifice.

But this truth actually intensifies the problem for the theology of the
Eucharist. How are we to understand "the practice of Israel" (1 Cor.
10:18) in light of the radical newness that Christ's death and resurrection brings? As the letter to the Hebrews says,

---

203–36. See also Michel Corbin, "Le pain de la vie. La lecture de Jean VI par S. Thomas
d'Aquin," *Recherches de Science Religieuse* 65 (1977): 107–38; my "The Pontifical
Biblical Commission and Aquinas' Exegesis," *Pro Ecclesia* 13 (2004): 25–38; and Michael
Dauphinais's comparison of Raymond Brown's interpretation of John 6 with that of
Aquinas, "'And they shall all be taught by God': Wisdom and the Eucharist in John 6,"
in *Reading John with St. Thomas Aquinas*, ed. Michael Dauphinais and Matthew
Levering (Washington, DC: Catholic University of America Press, 2005): 312–17.

[19] For further discussion, see Jerome Kodell, O.S.B., *The Eucharist in the New
Testament* (Collegeville, MN: Liturgical Press, 1988). Kodell suggests that the *koinonia*
described in 1 Corinthians 10 has the strong sense of insertion of the believer into Christ's
sacrificial mode of existence. Kodell goes on to review the twentieth-century historical-
critical discussion over whether Jesus' meal is sacrificial. He makes note of, and rejects,
the thesis of Hans Lietzmann in 1926 that there were originally two forms of the
Eucharist, a Jerusalem one that focused on communion, and a Pauline/Marcan one "characterized by Hellenistic sacrificial concepts" (Kodell, 25). This misleading thesis reappears
today in the work of Nathan Mitchell. Paul F. Bradshaw deconstructs the texts even further, arguing that "the historical setting of the sayings or any close link with the death
of Christ was not regarded as of importance in early traditions of eucharistic thought"
(Bradshaw, *Eucharistic Origins* [Oxford: Oxford University Press, 2004]: 14–15). He sees
the Synoptic and Pauline eucharistic texts as "catechetical" rather than "liturgical," a
distinction that he applies to the fragmentary texts from the early Fathers as well in light
of his reconstructions of early liturgies. This distinction begs the question, among others,
of what content the "catechesis" sought to convey. Cf. Bernard Cooke, S.J.'s pre-conciliar
(in contrast to his later work) defense of Eucharistic sacrifice, "Synoptic Presentation of
the Eucharist as Covenant Sacrifice," *Theological Studies* 21 (1960): 1–44 responding
to Gustaf Aulén's *Eucharist and Sacrifice*, trans. Eric Wahlstrom (Philadelphia, PA:
Muhlenberg Press, 1958). Cooke argues that "Jesus as depicted by the Synoptics recapi-
tulates and fulfils, in their various stages of evolution, the priesthood, the Temple, and
the sacrifices of Israel" (2) and that Jesus is

> the fulfilment of the OT Temple and its priesthood. He is not only the per-
> fect ontological mediator; He also effected the perfect and unique redemp-
> tive sacrifice. His priesthood is at the very heart of the new covenant, for it
> is exercised in the Supper and the Passion when He instituted this new
> covenant. (43–4)

> But when Christ appeared as a high priest of the good things that have come, then through the greater and more perfect tent (not made with hands, that is, not of this creation) he entered once for all into the Holy Place, taking not the blood of goats and calves but his own blood, thus securing an eternal redemption. For if the sprinkling of defiled persons with the blood of goats and bulls and with the ashes of a heifer sanctifies for the purification of the flesh, how much more shall the blood of Christ, who through the eternal Spirit offered himself without blemish to God, purify your conscience from dead works to serve the living God. (Heb. 9:11–14)

If "the blood of Christ" accomplishes the purification of our souls, is "sacrifice" from thenceforth displaced? Does "sacrifice" belong to how we are united to Christ's sacrifice, or does faith alone suffice? Certainly Christ's sacrifice reconciles and unites to God, and so the purpose of sacrifice is fulfilled forever in his sacrifice: "But when Christ had offered for all time a single sacrifice for sins, he sat down at the right hand of God, then to wait until his enemies should be made a stool for his feet. For by a single offering he has perfected for all time those who are sanctified" (Heb. 10:12–14).[20] Of what purpose would be a sacrificial Eucharist?

It might seem that new liturgy, grounded in Christ's perfect sacrifice, should be rooted not in sacrifice (since no further sacrifice is needed) but in faith. Hebrews goes on to say,

> But you have come to Mount Zion and to the city of the living God, the heavenly Jerusalem, and to innumerable angels in festal gathering, and to the assembly of the first-born who are enrolled in heaven and to a judge who is God of all, and to the spirits of just men made perfect, and to Jesus, the mediator of a new covenant, and to the sprinkled blood that speaks more graciously than the blood of Abel. (Heb. 12:22–4)[21]

---

[20] Albert Vanhoye, S.J. argues that this passage reflects a liturgical, eucharistic context. See Vanhoye, *Old Testament Priests and the New Priest*, 228–9.

[21] Paul Ellingworth identifies Hebrews 12:24 as the rhetorical climax of the whole epistle. See Ellingworth, *The Epistle to the Hebrews* (Grand Rapids, MI: Eerdmans, 1993): 681. See also Gilles Berceville, O.P., "Le sacerdoce du Christ dans le *Commentaire de l'épître aux Hébreux* de saint Thomas d'Aquin," *Revue Thomiste* 99 (1999): 143–58; Mario Caprioli, O.C.D., "Il sacerdozio di Cristo nella *Somma Theologica* e nel Commento *Super Epistolam ad Hebraeos*," in *Storia del tomismo* (Vatican City: Libreria Editrice Vaticana, 1992): 96–105.

How does, in the words of the exegete Paul Ellingworth, "the once-for-all sacrifice of Jesus" have "continuing significance for the worship of God's people in the heavenly Jerusalem"?[22] What kind of liturgy do Christians enact? Is Hebrews, with its striking liturgical and cultic language, describing the displacement in Christ of "the practice of Israel," or the fulfillment of the sacrificial practice of Israel in and through our liturgical (sacrificial) practice of participation in the saving sacrifice of Christ? It will be helpful to inquire further into the meaning of the sacrificial liturgy of Israel's Temple, in light of Christ's saving work.

2 INTERPRETING THE PRACTICE OF ISRAEL

In the *Summa Theologiae*, Aquinas argues that the ceremonial precepts of Israel's law had both literal and figurative meaning – literal as suitable offerings to the one Creator God, and figurative as foreshadowing Christ and the Church.[23] With regard to the animal sacrifices of Israel, Aquinas explains:

> The animals which were offered in sacrifice were slain, because it is by being killed that they become useful to man, forasmuch as God gave them to man for food. Wherefore also they were burnt with fire: because it is by being cooked that they are made fit for human consumption. – Moreover the slaying of the animals signified the destruction of sins: and also that man deserved death on account of his sins. – Again the slaying of these animals signified the slaying of Christ.[24]

Aquinas understands the first two reasons (food for consumption and the signification of the destruction of sins) to be literal, whereas the third is figurative. Yet, contemporary exegetes have challenged such a depiction of expiatory sacrifice in Israel.

Thus, after noting the medieval controversy between Maimonides and Ramban on the efficacy of the animal sacrifices, the Jewish exegete Jacob Milgrom observes:

> Researchers in primitive and comparative religions distinguish four possible purposes behind the institution of sacrifice: (1) to provide food for the god (cf. Eichrodt 1961: 1.141–4); (2) to assimilate the life force of the sacrificial animal (James 1933);

---

[22] Ellingworth, 682–3.
[23] 1-2, q. 102, a. 2.
[24] 1-2, q. 102, a. 3, ad 5.

(3) to effect union with the deity (Smith 1927); and (4) to induce the aid of the deity by means of a gift.[25]

Milgrom rules out the first three as not present in ancient Israel, and finds the fourth, which includes expiation "to ward off or forgive sin or impurity,"[26] to be the heart of Israelite sacrifice. In Milgrom's view, sacrificial expiation in Israel is focused upon the purification not of individuals but rather of the Temple sanctuary.[27]

Baruch Levine argues that ancient Israel did not understand sacrificial expiation to *cause* anything. He states with regard to ritual offerings for sin and purification:

> As a result of the performance of certain rites, God grants expiation or atonement. In such instances, expiation, forgiveness, etc. are not the direct *physical effects* of the rites performed.

---

[25] Jacob Milgrom, *Leviticus 1–16: A New Translation with Introduction and Commentary* (New York: Doubleday, 1991): 440. For Maimonides's view, see Moses Maimonides, *The Guide for the Perplexed*, trans. from the original Arabic by M. Friedländer, 2nd edn (New York: Dover, 1956): chapters 32 and 46. For comparative study of sacrifice, see, e.g., M.F.C. Bourdillon and Meyer Fortes, eds., *Sacrifice* (London: Academic Press, 1980). See also Jacob Milgrom, *Studies in Cultic Theology and Terminology* (Leiden: E.J. Brill, 1983). Milgrom rejects the translation "sin offering," and instead prefers "purification offering" (*Studies in Cultic Theology and Terminology*, 67). For an extended discussion of this important point, see Milgrom, *Leviticus 1–16*, 253ff. Milgrom states as regards the "purification offering": "Whom or what does it purge? Herein lies the first surprise: it is not the offerer of the sacrifice" (*Leviticus 1–16*, 254). Instead, it purifies the Temple sanctuary. Such purification is needed because of Israel's understanding, according to Milgrom, of sin:

> Impurity was feared [by all Near Eastern cults] because it was considered demonic. It was an unending threat to the gods themselves and especially to their temples, as exemplified by the images of protector gods set before temple entrances . . . and, above all, by the elaborate cathartic and apotropaic rites to rid buildings of demons and prevent their return . . . Thus for both Israel and her neighbors impurity was a physical substance, an aerial miasma that possessed magnetic attraction for the realm of the sacred. As will be shown below, Israel thoroughly overhauled this concept of impurity in adapting it to its monotheistic system, but the notion of its dynamic and malefic power, especially in regard to the sancta, was not completely expunged from P. (*Leviticus 1–16*, 256–7)

While largely agreeing with Milgrom, Patrick D. Miller points out that the "purification" offering is said to purify the individual by forgiving his or her sins, in addition to purifying the sanctuary. See Miller, *The Religion of Ancient Israel* (Louisville, KY: Westminster John Knox Press, 2000): 114–15. This difference between Milgrom's and Miller's views is crucial.

[26] Milgrom, *Leviticus 1–16*, 441.

[27] Cf. for a brief summary Jacob Milgrom, *Leviticus: A Book of Ritual and Ethics* (Minneapolis, MN: Fortress Press, 2004): 14–16.

Such acts are prerequisite, but not causational. It is God who grants the desired result!"[28]

For Levine, furthermore, sacrificial expiation belongs within a mythological framework not fully consonant with monotheism. Arguing against covenantal readings of sacrificial atonement, in which the offering of the animal's blood rebinds the covenantal relationship, Levine finds that

> expiation addressed itself to the presence of impurity, the actualized form of evil forces operative in the human environment. This was the function of expiation as a phenomenon. It was not so much that Yahweh had to be appeased for the offenses committed. To the extent that this was the case, such mollification took the form of sacrifice, itself. The accompanying expiation through blood, as distinct from the sacrificial gift, itself, became necessary because Yahweh demanded that the forces of impurity, unleashed by the offenses committed, be kept away from his immediate environment. There is a reason for Yahweh's wrath. It was not mere displeasure at being disobeyed. His wrath was a reaction based on a vital concern, as it were, for his own protection. The sacrificial blood is offered to the demonic forces who accept it in lieu of God's "life", so to speak, and depart, just as they accept it in lieu of human life in other cultic contexts.[29]

Levine thus speaks of Israel's understanding of expiatory sacrifices as "bearing an essentially magical character."[30]

Neither Milgrom nor Levine interprets sacrifice in the context of the particular justice intrinsic to the creature–Creator relationship (cf. Gen. 1–1), a lacuna that weakens their understanding of biblical sacrifice. Even so, Milgrom's understanding of the sacrificial purification of the Temple sanctuary illumines Christ's claim to be, in his sacrificial death, the new (holy) Temple.[31] Levine's view that Israel's expiatory sacrifices operate

---

[28] Baruch A. Levine, *In the Presence of the Lord: A Study of Cult and Some Cultic Terms in Ancient Israel* (Leiden: E.J. Brill, 1974): 65–6.

[29] Ibid., 77–8.

[30] Ibid., 77. For further discussion of "magic," see Gary A. Anderson, *Studies and Offerings in Ancient Israel: Studies in Their Social and Political Importance* (Atlanta, GA: Scholars Press, 1987): 5–25. For a response to Milgrom and Levine regarding Leviticus 17:11 that argues that "[t]he life of the people is 'ransomed' by the life of the animal when its blood is properly manipulated" (189), see Frank H. Gorman, Jr., *The Ideology of Ritual: Space, Time, and Status in the Priestly Theology* (Sheffield: Sheffield Academic Press, 1990): 181–9.

[31] Cf. Milgrom's analysis of the Day of Atonement in his "Israel's Sanctuary: The Priestly *Picture of Dorian Gray*," in *Studies in Cultic Theology and Terminology*

within an "essentially magical" frame, in contrast, misunderstands juridical language. Interpreting Leviticus 1:9, the medieval rabbinic commentator Nachmanides offers a more perceptive explanation of the juridical aspect of Israel's sacrificial system as aimed at awakening the offerer to the truth of his or her own position before God. Nachmanides writes:

> All these acts are performed in order that when they are done, a person should realize that he has sinned against God with his body and his soul, and that "his" blood should really be spilled and "his" body burned, were it not for the loving-kindness of the Creator, Who took from him a substitute and a ransom, namely this offering, so that its blood should be in place of his blood, its life in place of his life.[32]

This position does not require a substitutionary account of expiation (once one distinguishes between "substitution" and "satisfaction"), but it does require an awareness of the juridical dimension of the creature–Creator relationship.

In light of Nachmanides's insights, the contemporary Jewish theologian Joshua Berman discusses the four kinds of Temple sacrifices described in the Torah: *korban chatat*, *korban asham*, *korban olah*, and *korban shelamim*. Each presents a different aspect of Israel's sacrificial communion with God. *Chatat* – "sin/purification offering" – involves purification, whether ritual purification or purification from sinful transgression. The two cannot be opposed since both involve the danger of slipping out of liturgical communion with God. *Asham*, or "guilt offering," constitutes a restitution or indemnity. Even civil offenses require *asham* because of the community's relationship to God; whatever harms the community, is done against God. *Olah*, or "burnt offering," indicates the person's completely dispossessive gift of self to God, the aqedah being an example of *olah*. Finally *shelamim*, or "free-will offering," depicts the festive aspect, grounded in thanksgiving, of the communion with God. The full context of sacrifice, in other words,

---

(Leiden: E.J. Brill, 1983): 75–84. On Christ as the fulfillment of the Temple, see Ben Meyer, "The Temple at the Navel of the Earth," in *Christus Faber: The Master-Builder and the House of God* (Allison Park, PA: Pickwick Publications, 1992): especially 250–1, 259–66. I am grateful to Guy Mansini, O.S.B., who is developing an article on this topic, for this insight and the citations. As Mansini has also pointed out to me, Levine's position, with the exception of the language of myth, has affinities with the patristic theories of redemption from the devil (the demonic forces that require their "due") that Anselm, followed by Aquinas, critiqued.

[32] Joshua Berman, *The Temple: Its Symbolism and Meaning Then and Now* (Northvale, NJ: Jason Aronson, 1995): 119; the quotation is from Nachmanides, *Commentary on the Torah*, Leviticus 1:9, trans. Charles B. Chavel (New York: Shilo Publishing House, 1974).

envisions expiation, purification, restitution, complete self-gift, and thankful communion. In and through this regular and multi-faceted sacrificial liturgy, the communion of God's people with God is liturgically attained in a mode that takes sin seriously and that has, at its core, dispossessive thanksgiving to the Creator.[33]

For Israel, Berman notes, sacrifice generally involves a meal (*zevach*). This is due neither to lingering anthropomorphisms in Israel's conception of God, nor to the self-satisfied focus on the human community that Jean-Luc Marion has identified as central to the anti-sacrificial approach of what I have termed Eucharistic idealism. Instead, "When the Torah speaks of [God's] sensual responses to the *korbanot* . . . it highlights the extent to which the *zevach* is a shared experience; man, literally, and God, figuratively, partake of the same feast."[34] Sacrifice is completed in feasting; far from being simply renunciatory, sacrifice is profoundly fulfilling. These festive meals, often involving bread and wine dedicated to the Temple service, indicate the reality of divine communion. Yet the feast would have no meaning outside the context of the sacrificially governed relationship, because the feast is the realization or crowning or the sacrificial movement. Cut off from the context of sacrifice, from the sacrificial spectrum that moves from expiation to thanksgiving, the feast would, as Avivah Gottlieb Zornberg makes clear, indicate selfish cleaving to the world, a solipsistic and sinful satisfaction grounded upon human pride. Thus this feasting occurs properly within the liturgical context of the "service of God in the Temple."[35]

Berman goes on to point out that when interior service of God is lacking, the bodily offering of animal sacrifices and the liturgical feasts go against their divinely ordained meaning. Since our bodily and spiritual acts constitute a unified whole, the sacrificial liturgy should form a sacrificial people. On this basis he interprets Jeremiah's critique of the Temple sacrifices: "Jeremiah's message is that it is a mockery to bring an *olah* when Israel's actions belie the true meaning of this symbol of self-sacrifice to God."[36] It follows as well that the expiatory meaning of the sacrificial rituals are not opposed to the celebratory covenantal feasting. An emphasis on the community and communal meals (even when these are interpreted as God-centered) cannot do without expiation. This is so because sin damages communion, and so the sins of the individual

---

[33] Ibid., 120–6. Gary A. Anderson, in an essay entitled "The Praise of God as a Cultic Event," points out that "just as 'life' was experienced in the cult as being before the very presence of God in the (heavenly) temple, so 'death' was experienced in the cult as being cut off from that presence outside the temple." See Anderson, "The Praise of God as a Cultic Event," in Gary A. Anderson and Saul M. Olyan, eds., *Priesthood and Cult in Ancient Israel* (Sheffield: Sheffield Academic Press, 1991): 15–33, at 28.

[34] Berman, *The Temple*, 130.

[35] Ibid., 138.

[36] Ibid., 144.

weaken not only the individual, but also the community's relationship with God. Berman states, "Infractions not only diminish the spiritual stature of the transgressor, they strain the covenantal bond."[37] It makes sense, therefore, that the Temple, as the covenantal center of Israel, should also be the locus of expiation. Just as the outward sacrifices cannot do without interior sacrifice, so also communion cannot perdure without expiation. For Berman, the Temple is the center of communication between God and human beings precisely because it is also the place where sin is sacrificially expiated.

As Berman depicts it, in short, sacrifice and communion are united in the Temple. In and through the sacrificial communion mediated by the Temple, Israel participates in God's reconciling action. This position finds no resonance in Reform Judaism, significantly influenced by idealist modes: as Ruth Langer remarks approvingly, "The modern liberal branches of Judaism rejected mourning for the Temple as a determinative basis for Jewish practice and thought."[38] Christian Eucharistic idealism, likewise, rejects the sacrificial mode of the Temple liturgy.[39] Nonetheless, with the Eastern Orthodox theologian David Bentley Hart we can recognize that for Israel

> [b]efore all else, though, sacrifice is a *qurban*, a drawing nigh, an approach in love to the God who graciously approaches

---

[37] Ibid., 142.

[38] Ruth Langer, "Liturgy and Sensory Experience," in *Christianity in Jewish Terms*, ed. Tikva Frymer-Kensky et al. (Boulder, CO: Westview Press, 2000): 189–95, at 191. For insight into rabbinic approaches to the loss of the sacrificial cult of the Temple, see Michael Fishbane, *The Exegetical Imagination: On Jewish Thought and Theology*, chapter 8, "Substitutes for Sacrifice in Judaism." In light of the probability that the Mishnah sought to prepare for the restoration of the Temple liturgy, Fishbane remarks:

> The centrality of sacrifice in ancient Judaism explains the acts of ascetic renunciation adopted by early and later "mourners of Zion," as well as the rabbinic effort to institute concrete acts in "remembrance (of the destruction of the Temple in) Jerusalem" (*zekher li-yerushalayim*). (125)

Fishbane pays special attention to the "mystics of the Zoharic corpus," active in the thirteenth and fourteenth centuries, who

> conceive of the ancient sacrifice ritual (subject of extensive commentaries) in terms of maintaining, purifying, and rebalancing the supernal divine spheres – thrown into disrepair, pollution, and imbalance by human sin. Sacrifice also allows the human being to realign himself, through the offerings, their officiants, and their consumption in fire, to the great chain of divine Being. (132)

The Zoharic mystics spiritualize sacrifice without displacing it.

[39] For exegetical work that cuts against this grain, see Margaret Barker, *The Great High Priest: The Temple Roots of Christian Liturgy* (New York: T. & T. Clark, 2003).

his people in love. If there are currents of stress in the history of Israel's cult, they do not run between the idea of sacrifice as such and a prophetic rejection of sacrifice, but between different ways of understanding the motion of sacrifice that Israel is, the gift it makes of itself – of its body – to the God who gives it its being and its name. For Christian thought this gift is perfectly made in the life and body of Jesus, with unique finality, but in such a way that all that Israel is, is borne up to the Father, and with it the world.[40]

As Joseph Ratzinger puts it, "As the chosen people, Israel has the mission to be the place of true adoration and thus to be at once priesthood and temple for the whole world."[41] Christ's sacrificial death, his Pasch, thus draws together and illumines the various sacrificial deeds and images found within Israel – in which the cult of the Temple, with its festivals (above all Passover), plays a central role.

And yet in fulfilling Israel's sacrifices, Christ radically transforms them, going beyond the limitations of animal sacrifices by his free self-offering in perfect charity.[42] Christian participation in the Temple is participation in Jesus Christ; believers are therefore Christ's "body" (Rom. 12:4–5; 1 Cor. 11:29; 1 Cor. 12:12–27; Eph. 1:23; Eph. 4–5; Col. 1–3). As Christ's Body, believers pay the penalty of death, owed for sin, *in* Christ. In his Paschal fulfillment of Israel's Torah, Christ himself is thus the true Temple (John 2:19–21; Mark 14:58), the locus of true purification and communion. As St Paul says:

There is therefore now no condemnation for those who are in Christ Jesus. For the law of the Spirit of life in Christ Jesus has set me free from the law of sin and death. For God has done what the law, weakened by the flesh, could not do: sending his own Son in the likeness of sinful flesh and for sin, he condemned sin in the flesh, in order that the just requirement of the law might be fulfilled in us, who walk not according to the flesh but according to the Spirit. (Rom. 8:1–4)

Given the simultaneous continuity and discontinuity between Christ and Israel, the particular character of Christ's self-offering (and the Eucharist) as a "sacrifice" – in other words, the saving efficacy of God

---

[40] David Bentley Hart, *The Beauty of the Infinite*, 350.
[41] Joseph Cardinal Ratzinger, *Called to Communion: Understanding the Church Today*, trans. Adrian Walker (San Francisco: Ignatius Press, 1996): 125.
[42] Roch Kereszty emphasizes this element of transformation: see Kereszty, "The Eucharist of the Church and the Offering of Christ," in *Rediscovering the Eucharist: Ecumenical Conversations*, ed. Roch Kereszty, O. Cist. (New York: Paulist Press, 2003): 240–60, at 243.

active in Christ's Cross – remains difficult to articulate. How does Christ's sacrificial death satisfy for our sins, and how do we, as Christ's mystical Body, participate in the sacrifice offered by Jesus, the fulfilled and radically transformed Temple?[43]

3 AQUINAS ON CHRIST'S EXPIATORY CROSS

John Milbank has warned against "extrinsicism" in accounts of the atonement, by which he means the danger that the doctrine of salvation is seen simply as another "ahistorical hypostasisation of Jesus's person."[44] Milbank's solution is to focus on the Kingdom that Jesus inaugurates. Without denying the significance of the Kingdom or New Creation, Aquinas presupposes that Christ's Cross must be first viewed in light of the metaphysics of creation, whose significance such thinkers as Josef Pieper, David Burrell, and Robert Sokolowski have pointed out.[45] The

---

[43] In "The Eucharist as Sacrifice," in *Rediscovering the Eucharist: Ecumenical Conversations*, ed. Roch Kereszty, O. Cist., 175–87, Avery Dulles, S.J. summarizes Christ's satisfactory sacrifice, the Eucharist as Christ's sacrifice, and the Eucharist as the Church's sacrifice. Quoting Scripture and ecclesial documents almost exclusively, Dulles advances a position that accords with Aquinas's as outlined in this chapter. See also Dulles, "The Death of Jesus as Sacrifice," *Josephinum Journal of Theology* 3 (1996): 4–17.

[44] John Milbank, "The Name of Jesus: Incarnation, Atonement, Ecclesiology," 314f., 329.

[45] The same move is made by Athanasius in *On the Incarnation*. For the significance of the metaphysics of creation for Aquinas's whole theology, see Josef Pieper, "The Negative Element in the Philosophy of St. Thomas Aquinas," in his *The Silence of St. Thomas*, trans. John Murray and Daniel O'Connor (South Bend, IN: St Augustine's Press, 1999). For Burrell's important work on this topic, see, e.g., David B. Burrell, C.S.C., "Creation, Will and Knowledge in Aquinas and Duns Scotus," in H. Stachowiak, ed., *Pragmatik* (Hamburg: 1985): 246–57; David B. Burrell, C.S.C., "Creation, Metaphysics, and Ethics," *Faith and Philosophy* 18 (2001): 204–21; David B. Burrell, C.S.C., "Incarnation and Creation: The Hidden Dimension," *Modern Theology* 12 (1996): 211–20; David B. Burrell, C.S.C., "Creation and 'Actualism': The Dialectical Dimension of Philosophical Theology," *Medieval Philosophy and Theology* 4 (1994): 25–41; David B. Burrell, C.S.C., "Creation in St. Thomas Aquinas's *SuperEvangelium S. Joannis Lectura*," forthcoming in Michael Dauphinais and Matthew Levering, eds., *Reading John with St. Thomas Aquinas* (Washington, DC: Catholic University of America Press); David B. Burrell, C.S.C., "Act of Creation with its Theological Consequences," in Thomas Weinandy, Daniel Keating, and John Yocum, eds., *Aquinas on Doctrine* (New York: T. & T. Clark, 2004): 27–44. For Sokolowski, see his *The God of Faith and Reason: Foundations of Christian Theology* (Washington, DC: Catholic University of America Press, 1982); R. Sokolowski, *Eucharistic Presence*, especially 34–54, 107–17, 152–4, 159–72. In the latter book, commenting upon Paul and Barnabas's visit to Lystra where they are mistaken for gods (Acts 14), Sokolowski remarks, "Nothing can be said about Redemption until we know what kind of God it is who redeems us" (41). Only the transcendent Creator God, Sokolowski shows, could be the God of the Eucharist. Joseph Wawrykow adds his voice to this chorus: "Burrell has re-focused our attention on what I think is the most important insight informing Thomas's theology, that God is the Creator of all that is" (Wawrykow, *God's Grace and Human Action* [Notre Dame, IN: University of Notre Dame Press, 1995]: 186, fn. 84).

cogency of Aquinas's account of the Cross as expiatory of sin depends upon apprehending creation as an intelligible "order" characterized, as a participation in the divine wisdom, by a pattern of "justice."[46] Admittedly, as Rik Van Nieuwenhove has observed:

> When one examines the Catholic theological scene of the last fifty years or so, one is bound to be struck by the fact that the most important Catholic theologians (such as Schillebeeckx, Rahner and Küng) fail, or refuse, to attribute salvific significance to the crucifixion itself.[47]

Even for Colman O'Neill, who certainly recognized the salvific significance of the Cross, one of Aquinas's central achievements lay in removing the concept of satisfaction "from the context of penal justice."[48] If the language of juridical expiation has solely ascetical rather than juridical significance, however, one might ask whether such language, given its tendency to distort our understanding of the unchanging God of love, could be dispensed with and replaced by language that emphasizes God's presence as love and our need to encounter (through purification to be sure) that presence. As we will see, however, Aquinas insists that justice belongs at the heart of the Christian account of salvation, precisely because of the significance of justice as a framework descriptive of the creature–Creator relationship in creation.[49]

---

[46] The recent work of Milbank has focused upon this aspect of participation: see John Milbank and Catherine Pickstock, *Truth in Aquinas* (London: Routledge, 2001). See also C.-J. Pinto de Oliveira, O.P., "Ordo rationis, ordo amoris: La notion d'ordre au centre de l'univers éthique de S. Thomas," in *Ordo sapientiae et amoris*, ed. C.-J. Pinto de Oliveira, O.P. (Fribourg: Éditions universitaires, 1993): 285–302.

[47] Rik Van Nieuwenhove, "St Anselm and St Thomas Aquinas on 'Satisfaction': or how Catholic and Protestant understandings of the Cross differ," *Angelicum* 80 (2003): 159–76, at 159. See also the articles of Emmanuel Perrier, O.P., "L'enjeu christologique de la satisfaction (I)" and "L'enjeu christologique de la satisfaction (II)," *Revue Thomiste* 103 (2003): 105–36 and 203–47, which provide both a survey of contemporary criticisms of the doctrine of "satisfaction" and the biblical, patristic, and dogmatic foundations of the doctrine; as well as Kevin McMahon's helpful brief presentation of Anselm's position in "The Cross and the Pearl: Anselm's Patristic Doctrine of the Atonement," in *Saint Anselm: His Origins and Influence*, ed. John R. Fortin (Lewiston, NY: Edwin Mellen Press, 2001): 56–69.

[48] Colman O'Neill, O.P., *Sacramental Realism: A General Theory of the Sacraments* (Chicago: Midwest Theological Forum, 1998 [1983]): 34.

[49] For discussion of this juridical relationship, which is taken up into Aquinas's account of divine and human charity, see Joseph P. Wawrykow, *God's Grace and Human Action: "Merit" in the Theology of Thomas Aquinas* (Notre Dame, IN: University of Notre Dame Press, 1995): 149f. As regards merit, which depends upon the "justice" established by the gift of grace, Wawrykow concludes:

Guided by the biblical narrative, Aquinas affirms that the first state of the human creature was one of perfect rectitude; otherwise, human beings would not have been created "good," but instead would have been sinful by nature rather than by choice. On this basis, Aquinas asks what constitutes human "rectitude."[50] He reasons that rectitude must consist primarily in the right ordering, or subjection, of human reason and will to God's "eternal law" or plan for the government of things – a right ordering that will necessarily be "political" or social.[51] Since human beings are not simply rational creatures, but also possess sense powers, more than simply the well-ordered soul is required for perfect human rectitude. In order for a condition of true rectitude to exist, Aquinas recognizes, our lower appetites (the sense appetites and apprehensive powers) must be subject to our higher, rational powers. Aquinas cannot imagine that full rectitude of the soul would be possible in a person who is experiencing riot and rebellion on the part of the senses and the body: if the soul is to be just, the senses and the body must share in its justice by being subject to the rational order that the soul makes possible. Body and soul are a unified dynamism: as created participation in the divine Wisdom, the human body is created to express the self-giving rational dynamism of the human soul, as John Paul II has shown in his *Theology of the Body*.[52]

Properly speaking, justice regards the action of one person to another. With Aristotle, Aquinas defines the virtue of justice as "a habit whereby a man renders to each one his due by a constant and

---

Thomas's teaching about merit in the *Summa* is clearly "juridical": He explains merit to be a quality of an act by which one deserves, in justice, a reward from God. Yet Thomas's "juridicism" is highly nuanced, and he is careful to focus our attention on the context in which justice can govern divine–human relations. Most important, he argues that this justice only holds sway when there exists a special community between God and the human person, and this community is itself created by the gift of God. The "communal" basis of justice is disclosed by Thomas's description of grace in terms of sonship. By grace, God freely elevates people to God's own level, treating them as "sons" to whom what belongs to the Father can also belong. As the term "sonship" suggests, the community which lies behind merit is itself Christ-centered. It is through the action of the Son of God that others are enabled to be adopted as God's children. (203–4)

[50] *Summa Theologiae*, 1, q. 95, a. 1.
[51] See 1-2, q. 19, a. 4, where Aquinas shows that the goodness of the human will is measured by its conformity to the eternal law. Aquinas recognizes that the first subjection, that of the soul to God (which causes the other two subjections), is a gift of God, indeed "a supernatural endowment of grace." It must be so, he argues, because otherwise it would not completely disappear after sin, which perverts our natural gifts but does not destroy them.
[52] See John Paul II, *The Theology of the Body: Human Love in the Divine Plan* (Boston: Pauline Books and Media, 1997); cf. Paul Gondreau, *The Passions of Christ's Soul in the Theology of Thomas Aquinas* (Münster: Aschendorff, 2002).

perpetual will."[53] Metaphorically, one may distinguish within the same person various principles of action, and speak of an interior "justice" insofar as these principles are rightly ordered.[54] Regarding justice properly speaking, Aquinas notes that justice towards others can either be "commutative" or "distributive."[55] Commutative justice concerns the interactions of two persons, while distributive justice has to do with the distribution of the goods of the community. Reflection upon commutative justice leads Aquinas to qualify the virtue of justice even further. In some cases, such as in our relations to God or to our parents, it is impossible to repay the equivalent, although this would be required by strict commutative justice.

Citing Psalm 10:8, "The Lord is just, and hath loved justice,"[56] Aquinas asks what it means for God to be "just." Commutative justice, he points out, cannot belong to God, since God infinitely transcends creatures, and does not owe them anything. On the other hand, distributive justice can apply to God, since the order of the universe, which is contained within the eternal law, may be said to represent God's just distribution of goods to each creature according to its degree of being.[57] Aquinas emphasizes that God's justice is not arbitrary: "Since good as perceived by intellect is the object of the will, it is impossible for God to will anything but what His wisdom approves."[58] The justice that characterizes the order of the universe is the expression of God's wise eternal law, which spans the whole of human history and expresses history's ordering to the ultimate end of creation, namely union with God in what Augustine calls the "City of God." In this sense, creaturely justice is ultimately an eschatological (and "political") reality.

At this point, however, Aquinas raises another important dilemma.[59] God's distributive justice is grounded, on his side, in his wisdom; but

---

[53] 2-2, q. 58, a. 1. For discussion of the range of Aquinas's sources, see Wayne J. Hankey, "Political, Psychic, Intellectual, Daimonic, Hierarchical, Cosmic, and Divine: Justice in Aquinas, Al-Fârâbî, Dionysius, and Porphyry," *Dionysius* 21 (2003): 197–218.
[54] 2-2, q. 58, a. 2.
[55] 2-2, q. 61, a. 1.
[56] 1, q. 21, a. 1, *sed contra*. On the structural importance of the biblical *sed contras* in the *Summa Theologiae*, see Leo J. Elders, S.V.D., "Structure et fonction de l'argument 'sed contra' dans la *Somme théologique* de Saint Thomas," *Divus Thomas* 80 (1977): 245–60. See also related articles by Elders, emphasizing the importance of Scripture for Aquinas's theology: "Aquinas on Holy Scripture as the Medium of Divine Revelation," in *La doctrine de la révélation divine de saint Thomas d'Aquin*, ed. Leo J. Elders (Vatican City: Libreria Editrice Vaticana, 1990): 132–52; "La relation entre l'ancienne et la nouvelle Alliance, selon saint Thomas d'Aquin," *Revue Thomiste* 100 (2000): 580–602; "St. Thomas and the Bible," in *Aquinas's Sources: The Notre Dame Symposium*, ed. Timothy L. Smith (South Bend, IN: St Augustine's Press, forthcoming).
[57] See for the neo-Platonic influence, Wayne Hankey, "Political, Psychic, Intellectual, Daimonic, Hierarchical, Cosmic, and Divine," 214–15.
[58] 1, q. 21, a. 1, ad 2.
[59] Ibid., ad 3.

distributive justice also regards what is "due" on the side of the one who receives. How can anything be "due," or owed by God, to a creature? Or does the idea of distributive justice lock God into an extrinsic juridical schema to which God must conform himself? Aquinas replies that by giving what is "due" to creatures, God is in fact primarily giving what is due to himself, although secondarily he is also giving what is due to creatures.[60] This is so because God, in a sense, owes to himself (as an expression of his goodness) that what he, in his wisdom, freely deems fitting for creatures, should be fulfilled in creatures. Furthermore, God's justice towards creatures is itself an act of mercy, since God distributes goods to creatures freely, out of love.[61] Justice is thus never something extrinsic to the relationship of God and creatures. Justice describes in a theologically specific way a central aspect of God's "presence" to his people, ordered toward an eschatological fulfillment. Juridical categories are the very means by which the creature's intrinsic relationship to the gifting God is most truly expressed.[62]

Thus far, however, we have described justice without reference to its punitive element. Justice becomes a problem when it appears that the relationship between God and human beings, because of sin, will be marked by punishment. Aquinas discusses sin with regard to good and evil in human acts. He has already argued that evil is privation in being, not a substance in its own right.[63] A human action is evil insofar as it lacks something "due to its fulness of being."[64] Evil acts, therefore, are those actions that turn away from or weaken one's ordering to the perfective end of union with God. By sinning, the person comes to lack something of the true being that God intends for him to possess.[65]

---

[60] See Wawrykow, *God's Grace and Human Action*, 160–2.

[61] 1, q. 21, a. 4.

[62] Cf. Serge-Thomas Bonino, O.P., "Le sacerdoce comme institution naturelle selon saint Thomas d'Aquin," *Revue Thomiste* 99 (1999): 33–57. In my view, this insight that juridical categories express the relationships of *free persons* answers concerns raised by Peter Casarella regarding the "underdeveloped anthropology of sacrifice" that, in the view of Casarella, limits the Anselmian approach (Casarella recognizes that Aquinas emphasizes the "greatness of God's love"). See Casarella, "A Response to Cardinal Avery Dulles on 'The Eucharist as Sacrifice,'" in *Rediscovering the Eucharist: Ecumenical Conversations*, ed. Roch Kereszty, O. Cist., 188–92, at 189.

[63] 1, q. 48, a. 1. John Crosby rejects privation-theories of evil (Crosby, "Is All Evil Really Only Privation?," *Proceedings of the American Catholic Philosophical Association* 75 [2001]: 197–209, at 208). In chapter 5 of Book VII of the *Confessions*, Augustine raises the same phenomenological questions that plague Crosby, and comes to the recognition that these questions can only be answered once one has moved metaphysically away from idolatry. If anything exists that is not Pure Act or created act (finite participation in Pure Act), that is to say that is not metaphysically good, then something would exist "over against" God, and God would be metaphysically limited – an entity among entities.

[64] 1-2, q. 18, a. 1.

[65] See 1-2, q. 71, a. 2.

The phenomenological concept of "alienation" may thus serve to describe this state of sin, insofar as "alienation" suggests lacking something proper to one's being.[66] In this sense, alienation is the sinner's lack of right order towards God. But alienation is not a merely passive state, which the sinner "endures." On the contrary, the alienated person is necessarily implicated in his or her alienation. Thus the debt of punishment is not an extrinsic juridical penalty.[67] Rather, the concept of a "debt of punishment" expresses the fact that if we sin, the order of justice (grounded in the eternal law or divine wisdom) by which God has connected us to himself does not simply disappear. Aquinas puts it succinctly: "whatever rises up against an order, is put down by that order or by

---

[66] For the historical development of the concept of "alienation," which in the medieval period signified positive ecstatic self-transcendence (*alienatio mentis*), see Nathan Rotenstreich, "On the Ecstatic Sources of the Concept of 'Alienation,'" *Review of Metaphysics* 16 (1961): 550–5; cf. Rotenstreich, *Alienation: The Concept and Its Reception* (Leiden: E.J. Brill, 1989). This work was brought to my attention by Peter A. Kwasniewski, "Aquinas on Eucharistic Ecstasy: From Self-Alienation to Gift of Self," forthcoming in *The Liturgical Subject: Subject, Subjectivity, and the Human Person in Contemporary Liturgical Discussion and Critique*, ed. James Leachman, O.S.B. (Notre Dame, IN: University of Notre Dame Press). Kwasniewski summarizes Rotenstreich's argument:

> Nathan Rotenstreich traces out the evolution of the meaning of the term *alienatio* (1) from its origin in courts of law, where it describes the formal act of transference by which something is removed from one man's ownership and given into the hands of another, (2) to its Platonic, Augustinian, and medieval meaning of what happens in *excessus mentis* or *extasis* when God seizes possession of one's soul and becomes principal actor in her, (3) to its function in Hegel's dialectical system, where union of subject and object is achieved through mutual diremption, (4) to the psychological critique given by Feuerbach and Marx, for whom *alienatio* takes on the derogatory meaning of man's abandonment of his rightful liberty and autonomy in favor of subjection to an illusory Other, be it human or divine; and thus Marx, in a distorted return to the term's origins, speaks of man's being converted into property alienated from its rightful owner, the self. In this way, what was for the medievals the active summit of *theosis* becomes for Marx the primary objection against theism.

Kwasniewski notes the fascination of many modern and postmodern thinkers, including Kierkegaard, Nietzsche, Heidegger, Marcel, Ricoeur, Gadamer, and Levinas, with *ecstasis* and alterity (drawing upon the work of Merold Westphal), and also explores the consequences of this shift for the liturgy, now understood in mainstream academic theology as human production rather than deifying *ecstasis*. Cf. Peter A. Kwasniewski, "Solitude, Communion, and Ecstasy," *Communio* 26 (1999): 388–92, as well as Joseph Ratzinger's comments, noted by Kwasniewski, on self-giving and *ablatio* in Ratzinger's *Called to Communion: Understanding the Church Today*, trans. Adrian Walker (San Francisco: Ignatius Press, 1996): 95, 142, 155.

[67] Aquinas treats the debt of punishment in 1-2, q. 87. For further analysis of the "evil of fault" according to Aquinas, as contrasted with the "evil of punishment," see Romanus Cessario, O.P., *The Godly Image* (Petersham, MA: St Bede's Publications, 1990).

the principle thereof."[68] This order of justice is threefold. First, there is an order in the person that consists in the governing power of the rational faculties, and on this level sin draws forth the punishment of being condemned by one's own conscience, the interior judge. Second, there is the order of human communities, by which justice is preserved in the interactions between human persons. Third, there is the order of Providence, by which God governs all things. Aquinas holds that a sufficiently grave sin incurs an eternal punishment: having destroyed the right order by which we were connected to God (that is, our order to the "ultimate end"), we cannot of ourselves restore this right order.[69] As St Paul says, "Wretched man that I am! Who will deliver me from this body of death?" (Rom. 7:24).

Justice and juridical categories are rightly understood in the Bible within the context of God's profoundly merciful covenantal love.[70] This context provides the background for Aquinas's treatment, through the concept of expiatory "satisfaction," of how human beings can be restored to justice in relation to God. He holds that God could restore the order of justice, if he so willed, simply by a divine decree of forgiveness.[71] However, in his mercy, God willed to restore the order of justice by means of the action of a human being.[72]

By sinning, human beings took away from God what, according to the justice intrinsic to the creature–Creator relationship, they owed him. For the relationship of justice to be restored, human beings would have to return what original sin lost.[73] Yet no mere human being could make such a return, since what was lost was *charity*, and no person in a state of sin possesses the virtue of charity. Second, the human being who sought

---

[68] 1-2, q. 87, a. 1.

[69] 1-2, q. 87, a. 3. This account of due punishment does not make impossible *innocent* suffering. People who oppress others cannot fall back on the doctrine of universal guilt, since oppressive actions against other persons can never be justified on the grounds that they deserved them – precisely because such actions are injustices, they are not deserved. As Guy Mansini, O.S.B. has stated in correspondence with me: Even though it is just for us, because of original sin, to be liable to unjust suffering at the hands of others, the inflictors of unjust suffering are acting unjustly. See Robert Gibbs, "Suspicions of Suffering," 226.

[70] This point is rightly emphasized by Wawrykow, *God's Grace and Human Action*, 163–4. This is also the point of Bernard's response to Abelard's effort (in his commentary on Romans 3:19–26) to bypass the expiatory character of Christ's Cross: see Bernard, *Letter 190*.

[71] 3, q. 46, a. 2, ad 3. Romanus Cessario has shown that here Aquinas moves beyond both his own early account and that of Anselm. Previously, Aquinas, like Anselm, had been concerned that it would be unbecoming for God to forgive sin without satisfaction, on the grounds that sin requires – in justice – due punishment. See Cessario, "Aquinas on Christian Salvation," in *Aquinas on Doctrine*, 122.

[72] 3, q. 46, a. 3.

[73] 1-2, q. 87, a. 6.

to restore the order of justice would need to be able to act on behalf of *all* human beings, which no mere human being could do. Third, in light of St Paul's statement that "by sin death entered the world" (Rom. 5:12), Aquinas notes that the just penalty of the interior disorder caused by original sin is pain and suffering, culminating in death.[74] As creatures all human beings owe a "debt" to God of bodily life. Rebellion against God does not do away with this debt; rather it requires it to be paid in the form of corruption and death, experienced as a punishment. Aquinas notes that under certain conditions, an innocent human being may undergo such "satisfactory" punishment on behalf of others to whom he (or she) is "one in will by the union of love."[75] Yet a mere human being could not satisfy for all sinners in this way, since a mere human being could not love every sinner individually.[76] Thus, in order to restore the powers of the soul to justice, a human being would need *freely* (that is, in perfect charity) to undergo suffering and death on behalf of all sinners – a perfect act of priestly mediation – so that "the disorder," which originated in the rejection of the order of justice (when the first human being chose a finite good over the infinite Good), "might be remedied [interiorly] by the contrary of that which caused it," in other words by the free offering of the debt/penalty as it embodies God's order of justice.[77]

Granting Christ's perfect charity and his ability to act on behalf of all others, it might nonetheless seem that the third point – the payment of the debt/penalty – is explained by Aquinas in a manner that lacks existential understanding of the penalty of sin. Eleonore Stump has suggested in this vein that Aquinas provides no explanation of how "Christ somehow actually bears all human sin; that is, in some way all the sins ever committed in human history are transferred to Christ's soul in his

---

[74] Cf. 1, q. 97, a. 1; 3, q. 14, aa. 1–3.

[75] 1-2, q. 87, a. 7. Rik Van Nieuwenhove differentiates punishment and satisfaction on two grounds: satisfaction's free character and the fact that satisfaction can involve enduring, out of love, the punishment merited by another person ("St Anselm and St Thomas Aquinas on 'Satisfaction'").

[76] Like the character of Ivan in Dostoevsky's *The Brothers Karamazov*, Aquinas recognizes that abstract love for "all humanity" is truly not love at all. Regarding Ivan Karamazov's rejection of God on the grounds that God has permitted evil, see Robert V. Wharton's "Evil in an Earthly Paradise: Ivan Karamazov's 'Dialectic' against God and Zossima's 'Euclidean' Response," *The Thomist* 41 (1977): 567–84.

[77] 1-2, q. 87, a. 6, ad 3. On Christ's priesthood on the Cross (in connection with his kingly and prophetic offices), see my *Christ's Fulfillment of Torah and Temple* (Notre Dame, IN: University of Notre Dame Press, 2002): 51–79. See also Jean-Pierre Torrell, O.P., "Le sacerdoce du Christ dans la *Somme de théologie*," *Revue Thomiste* 99 (1999): 75–100; Gérard Remy, "Sacerdoce et médiation chez saint Thomas," *Revue Thomiste* 99 (1999): 101–18; Benoît-Dominique de La Soujeole, O.P., "Les *tria munera Christi*: Contribution de saint Thomas à la recherche contemporaine," *Revue Thomiste* 99 (1999): 59–74.

suffering on the Cross."[78] For Stump and others, the main penalty of sin is the anguished *despair* that sinners, separated from God, experience.[79] This interior anguish, caused by the free rejection of God, is nothing less than hellish. It would seem that in order for Christ to bear our sins and expiate them interiorly, he would need to undergo fully this anguish, this "dark night." Indeed, both Matthew and Mark report that on the Cross "Jesus cried with a loud voice, 'Eloi, Eloi, lama sabachthani?' which means 'My God, my God, why hast thou forsaken me?'" (Mark 15:34). Jesus here quotes the first line of Psalm 22, in which we also read:

> I am poured out like water, and all my bones are out of joint; my heart is like wax, it is melted within my breast; my strength is dried up like a potsherd, and my tongue cleaves to my jaws; thou dost lay me in the dust of death. Yea, dogs are round about me; a company of evildoers encircle me; they have pierced my hands and feet – I can count all my bones – they stare and gloat over me; they divide my garments among them, and for my raiment they cast lots. (Ps. 22:14–18)

Mark had earlier reported: "they crucified him, and divided his garments among them, casting lots for them, to decide what each should take" (Mark 15:24). Jesus' cry of dereliction, with its reference to his physical dissolution, the nails in his feet and hands, and the division of his garments, reflects the terrible reality of his crucifixion, even if the conclusion of the psalm, which proclaims God's radical victory, reflects his resurrection.[80]

---

[78] Eleonore Stump, "Atonement According to Aquinas," in *Philosophy and the Christian Faith*, ed. Thomas V. Morris (Notre Dame, IN: University of Notre Dame Press, 1988): 61–91, at 84.

[79] This is Robert Sokolowski's point in *Eucharistic Presence: A Study in the Theology of Disclosure* (Washington, DC: Catholic University of America Press, 1993): 58.

[80] Psalm 22 ends, "Yea, to him shall all the proud of the earth bow down; before him shall bow all who go down to the dust, and he who cannot keep himself alive. Posterity shall serve him; men shall tell of the Lord to the coming generation, and proclaim his deliverance to a people yet unborn, that he has wrought it" (Ps. 22:29–31). Cf. Heb. 2:12, which cites Ps. 22:22 in the context of Christ's salvific suffering. The full passage is,

> But we see Jesus, who for a little while was made lower than the angels, crowned with glory and honor because of the suffering of death, so that by the grace of God he might taste death for every one. For it was fitting that he, for whom and by whom all things exist, in bringing many sons to glory, should make the pioneer of their salvation perfect through suffering. For he who sanctifies and those who are sanctified have all one origin. That is why he is not ashamed to call them brethren, saying, "I will proclaim thy name to my brethren, in the midst of the congregation I will praise thee" [Ps. 22:22]" (Heb. 2:9–12).

Cf. Sigmund Mowinckel's comments on the psalms and the "Messiah" in his *The Psalms in Israel's Worship*, trans. D.R. Ap-Thomas (Grand Rapids, MI: Eerdmans, 2004 [1962]): 49.

Does Aquinas underestimate the "cry of dereliction," so emphasized by Hans Urs von Balthasar and others?[81] Does Aquinas, as Stump suggests, "eviscerate the [biblical] text"?[82] Aquinas agrees that the primary penalty of sin is interior anguish, and yet he argues that the innocent man, not the sinner, experiences the fullness of this anguish. The sinner's anguish, in this life, is dulled by the reality that sin obscures our apprehension of the good. Our vices do indeed cause an ache in the soul, and even grave sorrow; and yet the same vices that separate us from God cause us no longer to apprehend him, and to love him, as we otherwise would. If we only knew the great Wisdom and Love that we were rejecting, we would experience much greater sorrow.[83] Citing Augustine, Aquinas speaks of a penitential "holy love" in which one "is saddened over his own or others' sins." Christ's interior suffering is this kind of penitential holy love, and is "the greatest in this present life."[84] Aquinas

---

[81] For discussion, see Thomas G. Weinandy, O.F.M. Cap., *Does God Suffer?* (Notre Dame, IN: University of Notre Dame Press, 2000): 17–18, as well as David Coffey, *Deus Trinitas: The Doctrine of the Triune God* (Oxford: Oxford University Press, 1999): 105–50.

[82] Stump, "Atonement According to Aquinas," 84.

[83] Guy Mansini, O.S.B. rightly observes that

> it is sometimes the very presence of our happiness in the possession of some good that increases our sorrowfulness over some evil . . . Thus, is it really so strange to hold that our Lord's identification with the experience of our alienation from God as sinners, which is partially, at least, what it means to say he loves us while we are still enemies of God (Rom. 5:8), and which it is the concern of many moderns to impute to him, should co-exist with his beatifying immediate knowledge of God? It is rather because of the abiding love of Christ for his Father, a love the human perfection of which is radically a function of his immediate knowledge of the Father, that all the more he can be sorrowful unto death at the sin because of which he dies, at sinners for whom he dies, and at the consequences of sin, even the most interior, that he bears in identifying himself in love with sinners. (Mansini, "Understanding St. Thomas on Christ's Immediate Knowledge of God," *The Thomist* 59 [1995]: 91–124, at 120).

Some theologians have argued that Aquinas's position on Christ's "vision" is both Nestorian (separating the humanity and divinity of Christ by seeing the former as a separate "subject" over against the Son of God) and Monophysite (conflating the two natures so that the divinity necessarily floods the humanity). This view, however, is rooted in misunderstanding of what the "vision" is, and also entails an *a priori* and unnecessary limiting of the human capacities of Christ. What is at stake is the revealed truth of the incarnate Son's non-conceptual, radically intimate knowledge as man of his Father and of each and every human being for whom Christ dies. Various alternatives to the "vision," from a profusion of infused conceptual knowledge to a "human hypostatic knowledge" that is still not "vision," have been proposed. None of these alternatives approaches the intimacy and scope requisite for Christ's intimate knowledge as man of his Father – a knowledge that given its unimaginable greatness simply cannot be mere conceptual knowledge – and of us.

[84] 3, q. 46, a. 6, ad 2.

notes that Christ accepted this greatest sadness in order "to satisfy for the sins of all men."[85] Christ's penitential sorrow or holy love for sinners on the Cross is not weakened, as our sorrow for sin always is, by forgetfulness (allowing ourselves to think about other consoling things), emotional breakdown, or simple lack of apprehension of the profound ugliness of sin in light of the infinite beauty of God's love. Christ cannot and does not hide in these normal ways from the fullness of sin's horror, as we can and do.

Rather, Christ on the Cross intimately (in his human knowing) knows God, and therefore knows exactly what we sinners are rejecting and devaluing.[86] By so knowing, Christ knows the depths of our loss in a way that no person, lacking such knowledge, could ever know it. Aquinas explains that Christ's sadness has an unapproachable intensity because of the *focus* of his sorrow for our sins (a focus conjoined to his focus on God's goodness, in light of which – and only in light of which – our sins take on their true horror):

> the magnitude of Christ's suffering can be estimated from the singleness of His pain and sadness. In other sufferers the interior sadness is mitigated, and even the exterior suffering, from some consideration of reason, by some derivation or redundance from the higher powers into the lower; but it was not so with the suffering Christ, because *He permitted each one of His powers to exercise its proper function*, as Damascene says (*De Fide Orthod.* iii).[87]

In his intense interior suffering, he does not permit consoling thoughts to distract him from his anguish; nor is his anguish in any way eased,

---

[85] Ibid. In so doing, Christ is the mediator between human beings and God: "Although it belongs to Christ as God to take away sin authoritatively, yet it belongs to Him, as man, to satisfy for the sin of the human race. And in this sense He is called the Mediator of God and men" (3, q. 26, a. 2, ad 3). For emphasis on Christ as mediator, in response to N.T. Wright, see Alan Spence, "A Unified Theory of the Atonement," *International Journal of Systematic Theology* 6 (2004): 404–20.

[86] John Paul II teaches this view in *Novo millennio ineunte*, no. 26. The Catechism of the Catholic Church, quoting Maximus the Confessor, states,

> "The human nature of God's Son, not by itself but by its union with the Word, knew and showed forth in itself everything that pertains to God." Such is first of all the case with the intimate and immediate knowledge that the Son of God made man has of the Father . . . Jesus knew and loved each us and all during his life, his agony, and his Passion and gave himself up for each one of us: "The Son of God . . . loved me and gave himself for me." (nos. 473, 478)

[87] 3, q. 46, a. 6.

as ours is, by a lack of knowledge of the Good which sin repudiates.[88]
As Aquinas puts it,

> this grief in Christ surpassed all grief of every contrite heart,
> both because it flowed from a greater wisdom and charity,
> by which the pang of contrition is intensified, and because He
> grieved at the one time for all sins, according to Isa. liii.4: *Surely
> he hath carried our sorrows.*[89]

We can see, too, that the grief of a guilty person, who knows that the
suffering is in some way deserved, could in no way match the grief of
an innocent person, who endures completely undeserved suffering at the
hands of those who ought to be his friends.[90] Indeed, in Christ's case
this reality is intensified because of his knowledge of what a great gift
human beings are destroying by destroying his bodily life: the gift of none
other than God *incarnate*. The intensity of Christ's suffering, then,
flows also from his profound awareness of the gift of his bodily life as
the incarnate Son – now (on the Cross) being destroyed – the supreme
divine gift that only Christ himself, on earth, knows and experiences in
its unfathomable greatness.[91] Moreover, Christ grieved not only for the
sins of all, but also he grieved as does an innocent man whose friends
(the apostles) have betrayed him, and as does an innocent and just ruler
whose subjects (the Jews and indeed all humankind) have rejected him.
In all of these ways, Christ's sorrow attains a depth commensurate with
the guilt of all sins (all earthly separation from God), and he bears the
penalty for all sin by his unimaginable interior suffering. Christ does not
allow his supreme knowledge of God to weaken his suffering in any way;
on the contrary, his knowledge of God serves only to heighten his
awareness and interior experience of the emptiness and delusion of the
horrifying sins for which, by his suffering, he is satisfying in restoring
the order of justice between rational creatures – who owe to God the
radical gift of self – and Creator.[92] Yet his restoration of this due order
is itself a manifestation, not of God's entrapment in juridical models,
but of God's inexpressibly profound humility: it is God's *humility* in Christ
that most fully demonstrates, in reversing, the ungodliness of pride.[93]

---

[88] See 3, q. 46, a. 7.

[89] 3, q. 46, a. 6, ad 4.

[90] Ibid., ad 5.

[91] Ibid., ad 4.

[92] Cessario emphasizes that this disorder is on our side, not God's (Cessario, "Aquinas
on Christian Salvation," 128).

[93] 3, q. 1, a. 2. For further analysis of this profound Augustinian motif, appropriated by
Aquinas in his theology of Christ's Cross, see Deborah Wallace Ruddy, "The Humble
God: Healer, Mediator, and Sacrifice," *Logos* 7 (2004): 87–108.

Christ's suffering has the intensity, then, of a "dark night," in which the horror of the *darkness* of sin is finally and perfectly exposed in Christ's soul by contrast to the glorious light of the divine Goodness, which Christ also knows. It is only by contrast to this light that "darkness" is intelligible. Christ bears interiorly the darkness in his anguish over the sins of each one of us, but it is crucial to note that he can only bear this darkness fully because of his simultaneous "light" by which he knows God. He can only fully bear the anguish of the rejection of God, because he has not rejected God. In knowing God, he can know, and experience, the full reality of the anguish that is separation from God – in other words, the full reality of injustice. "Separation from God," after all, is metaphysically constituted not as a spatial reality, or even primarily as an emotional state, but as "injustice." Anguish over injustice can be experienced by the saint more profoundly than by the sinner to whom the injustice belongs. As Matthew Lamb has written:

> The higher the created consciousness, the greater will be the suffering. As a weak analogy might put it, someone with a finely tuned ear for music will suffer more intensely when someone sings off-key. Knowing and loving the Triune God both divinely and humanly, only Christ's human nature united hypostatically to the Word could take up into his human mind and heart each and every human being with all his and her sins and sufferings. Jesus Christ as the divine person of the Word incarnate suffered more than all the sufferings of human beings throughout history put together.[94]

Thus Aquinas's metaphysical anthropology allows him to avoid falling into a mythological account of Christ as "alienated" in the sense that sinners are. Christ experiences and suffers for their injustice, without undergoing the "hellish" alienation from the Father that von Balthasar describes. Such alienation that would be, in fact, less intensely sorrowful because sinners, precisely as unjust, do not fully experience the horror of their injustice.

Even so, why does not Christ have to undergo this ultimate penalty of sin, Hell itself, the everlasting and hopeless experience of punishment that is absolute rejection of the divine mercy? How can he pay the true penalty of sin without experiencing Hell?[95] Aquinas notes that:

---

[94] Matthew L. Lamb, "The Eschatology of St Thomas Aquinas," in *Aquinas on Doctrine*, 225–40, at 231–2. See also Benoît-Dominique de La Soujeole, O.P., "La présence dans les saints mystères," *Revue Thomiste* 104 (2004): 407.

[95] Hans Urs von Balthasar poses this question.

[t]he pain of a suffering, separated soul belongs to the state of future condemnation, which exceeds every evil of this life, just as the glory of the saints surpasses every good of the present life. Accordingly, when we say that Christ's pain was the greatest, we make no comparison between His and the pain of a separated soul.[96]

Simply put, Christ's suffering is, as "satisfactory" in restoring the order of justice, an act of perfect charity that restores the bond of love between humankind and God. Hell, understood in its deepest sense, is the profound absence of love. Christ's suffering, on the contrary, embodies the perfection of love. Christ sorrows for the injustice of all sins, and thereby "bears" and "expiates" them, precisely because of his love; and it is his suffering-in-love that accomplishes perfect justice.[97] In freely enduring suffering proportionate to the injustice of sinners in this life, he loves us "to the end" and reconciles all sinners to God. Christ suffers even for our sinful choice to remain in this state of injustice despite God's offer of mercy, but his suffering is of this world: he does not undergo the sufferings of the damned, because their suffering consists precisely in eternally rejecting his merciful suffering. As Aquinas puts it, drawing together Paul and Isaiah:

Two things are required for the perfect cleansing from sins, corresponding to the two things comprised in sin – namely, the stain of sin and the debt of punishment. The stain of sin is, indeed, blotted out by grace, by which the sinner's heart is turned to God: whereas the debt of punishment is entirely removed by the satisfaction that man offers to God. Now the priesthood of Christ produces both these effects. For by its virtue grace is given to us, by which our hearts are turned to God, according to Rom. iii. 24, 25: *Being justified freely by His grace, through the redemption that is in Christ Jesus, Whom God hath proposed to be a propitiation, through faith in His blood.* Moreover, He satisfied for us fully, inasmuch as *He hath borne our infirmities and carried our sorrows* (Isa. liii. 4). Wherefore it is clear that the priesthood of Christ has full power to expiate sins.[98]

In short, since Christ's heart is turned in perfect charity toward God, he can offer his bodily life as a sacrifice that restores the relational order

---

[96] 3, q. 46, a. 6, ad 3.
[97] Cessario emphasizes that Christ's charity constitutes his perfect worship (Cessario, "Aquinas on Christian Salvation," 125).
[98] 3, q. 22, a. 3. Cf. J. Ross Wagner, *Heralds of the Good News: Isaiah and Paul in Concert in the Letter to the Romans.*

of justice – now revealed by the God-man to be a deifying order of charity, in which human beings are called to share in the supreme relational life of the Trinity – between creature and Creator.

4 CHRIST'S SACRIFICE AND THE EUCHARIST

Aquinas's account of Christ's reconciling work cannot be fully described without discussing the sacraments.[99] Regarding the Eucharist, Aquinas remarks that "the attaining of glory is the effect of this sacrament."[100] To share Eucharistically in Christ's sacrificial Cross means to be drawn into communion, in the Mystical Body on earth, with the risen life of blessedness. It follows that for Aquinas "the whole mystery of our salvation is comprised in this sacrifice," that is, in the Eucharistic sacrifice.[101]

What kind of sacrifice, however, is the Eucharist? We have seen that in Israel's sacrifices or *korbanot*, expiation, purification, reparation, absolute self-giving, and covenantal feasting are united.[102] If Christ's self-offering on the Cross is the fulfillment and transformation of Israel's sacrificial liturgy, it is because all these elements are joined together perfectly (messianically). Commenting on Hebrews 10:5, Aquinas describes the sacrifices of Israel, including the burnt offering and the sin offering, and concludes, "Now the offering of Christ's body in the New Testament *corresponds to all of these*, because God was placated by the body of Christ, i.e., in offering Himself on the cross: 'When we were enemies, we were reconciled to God by the death of his Son' (Rom. 5:10)."[103] He makes the same point regarding the Christ's fulfillment of Israel's *korbanot* – the perfect expiation, thanksgiving, and praise – in the *Summa Theologiae* when discussing Christ's priesthood: "Therefore Christ himself, as man, was not only priest, but also a perfect victim, being at the same time victim for sin, victim for a peace-offering, and a holocaust."[104] In words that apply as well to Aquinas as to Eastern

---

[99] See Stump, "Atonement According to Aquinas," 75. Aquinas holds that the "form" of the sacrament of the Eucharist includes the reference to the Passion: see 3, q. 78, a. 3.

[100] 3, q. 79, a. 2, *sed contra*. See Nicholas Cabasilas, *The Life in Christ*, trans. Carmino J. deCatanzaro (Crestwood, NY: St Vladimir's Seminary Press, 1998): Book IV, pp. 141–8.

[101] 3, q. 83, a. 4.

[102] Cf. Berman, *The Temple*, 126–30 and Milgrom, *Leviticus 1–16*, 442–3.

[103] Thomas Aquinas, *Commentary on the Epistle to the Hebrews*, Ch. 10, lect. 1 (no. 486), emphasis added, unpublished translation by Fabian Larcher, O.P.

[104] 3, q. 22, a. 2. This passage follows upon references to Romans 4:25, Hebrews 5:9, and Hebrews 10:19. On this passage see also Leo J. Elders, S.V.D., "The Inner Life of Jesus in the Theology and Devotion of Saint Thomas Aquinas," in *Faith in Christ and the Worship of Christ*, ed. Leo Scheffczyk and trans. Graham Harrison (San Francisco: Ignatius Press, 1986): 74.

Orthodoxy, David Bentley Hart beautifully depicts the interrelationship, discerned through appreciation of Israel's *korbanot*, of these aspects of "sacrifice":

> Perhaps no word serves better to capture the intuition that governs the Orthodox tradition's reflections on sacrifice (whether in relation to the self-offering of Christ or the offering of bread and wine in the liturgy) than the Hebrew "*qurban*," with its connotation of "drawing nigh," or "coming into the Presence." I say this not only because of the prominence the Letter to the Hebrews has traditionally enjoyed in Orthodox texts as a heuristic of the eucharistic oblation, and the consequently frequent resort of Orthodox theologians to the language of Israel's Day of Atonement offering as part of their sacramental grammar, but because the word *qurban* (or *qurbana*, as Christians who worship in Syriac call the Eucharist) points to an understanding of sacrifice as not, obviously, a simple propitiation of the Divine (crudely conceived) or an attempt to importune God under the shelter of an ingratiating tribute, but as a miraculous reconciliation between God, who is the wellspring of all life, and his people, who are dead in sin. Sacrifice, in this sense, means a marvelous reparation of a shattered covenant, and an act wherein is accomplished, again and again, that divine indwelling, within the body of his people, that is God's purpose in shaping for himself a people to bear his glory. If it is indeed always the will of God to "tabernacle" upon the earth, indeed ultimately to make the whole earth his temple, then the atonement sacrifice is that moment when God restores to himself the body he has chosen to dwell within and so also makes of himself an abode for his creatures. When the blood of the people, so to speak, which is its life, now forfeited through sin, is brought into the ambit of the *Shekinah*, before the mercy seat, an exchange occurs in which the life's blood of those who were perishing is made pure again, infused with the life that flows from God, and the nuptial bond of this mutual indwelling – God in his creatures and they in him – is repaired.[105]

---

[105] David Bentley Hart, "'Thine Own of Thine Own': Eucharistic Sacrifice in Orthodox Tradition," in *Rediscovering the Eucharist: Ecumenical Conversations*, ed. Roch Kereszty, O. Cist. (New York: Paulist Press, 2003): 143; cf. the patristic texts he cites on 148–50, as well as his further evocation of this theme on 159. See also Hart, "A Gift Exceeding Every Debt: An Eastern Orthodox Appreciation of Anselm's *Cur Deus Homo*," *Pro Ecclesia* 7 (1998): 333–49.

In the suffering Lord, sacrifice brings us into God's presence; the dynamism of sacrificial charity unites reconciliation and indwelling (deification). Understanding "blood" as symbolic of the soul poured out to God (Heb. 9:13–14), we apprehend the full weight of Christ's cruciform charity in which we are "justified by his grace as a gift, through the redemption which is in Christ Jesus, whom God put forward as an expiation by his blood, to be received by faith" (Rom. 3:24–5).

If sacrifice and feasting, reconciliation and indwelling, belong together in the *korbanot* of Israel, the same is true for our sacramental sharing in Christ's sacrificial fulfillment, and radical transformation, of Israel's *korbanot*.[106] As Aquinas remarks, following Leo the Great, that "it was fitting that when the hour of the Passion was come, Christ should institute a new Sacrament after celebrating the old."[107] At the Last Supper, Christ offers his sacrifice to his disciples. As the letter to the Hebrews, appealing to the witness of the Holy Spirit in believers, says, "But when Christ had offered for all time a single sacrifice for sins, he sat down at the right hand of God, then to wait until his enemies should be made a stool for his feet. For by a single offering he has perfected for all time those who are sanctified" (Heb. 10:12–14; cf. Heb. 10:15). There is only one sacrifice, Christ's, through which human beings receive true communion in the forgiveness of sins. Christ makes clear to his disciples at the Last Supper that what he is offering is none other than "my body which is given for you" and "the new covenant in my blood" (Luke 22:19–20).[108] In offering his sacrificial body and blood to

---

[106] That the fulfillment described in 3, q. 22, a. 2 is of course a radical transformation in Christ is indicated in 1-2, q. 108, a. 3, ad 3, where Aquinas explains that Christ, who brings to an end the ceremonial precepts by fulfilling them,

> makes it clear that the entire bodily worship which was fixed by the Law, was to be changed into a spiritual worship: as is evident from Jo. iv. 21, 23, where He says: *The hour cometh when you shall neither on this mountain, nor in Jerusalem adore the Father . . . but . . . the true adorers shall adore the Father in spirit and in truth.*

The eucharistic worship is a sharing in the perfect *charity* of Christ's sacrificial worship on the Cross, which is the "advent of the reality" to which the ceremonial precepts pointed (1-2, q. 108, a. 3, ad 3).

[107] 3, q. 73, a. 5.

[108] Pope John Paul II observes,

> This aspect of the universal charity of the Eucharistic Sacrifice is based on the words of the Savior himself. In instituting it, he did not merely say: "This is my body," "this is my blood," but went on to add: "which is given for you," "which is poured out for you" (Luke 22:19–20) . . . "The Mass is at the same time, and inseparably, the sacrificial memorial in which the sacrifice of the Cross is perpetuated, and the sacred banquet of communion with the Lord's body and blood." (*Ecclesia de Eucharistia*, no. 12)

his disciples at the Last Supper, he witnesses to the sacramental mode in which he makes his sacrifice present to his Church.[109]

At the Last Supper Christ commands his disciples, "Do this in remembrance of me" (Luke 22:19). Thus he instructs the Church to perform a liturgical action: he gives the Church a share in his own fulfillment of Israel's liturgy, and indeed it is this share that makes the Church.[110] St Paul witnesses to the Church's (broken by sin, yet sustained by the Holy Spirit) obedience to this command: "The cup of blessing which we bless, is it not a participation [communion] in the blood of Christ? The bread which we break, is it not a participation in the body of Christ?" (1 Cor. 10:16). Urging his audience to "[c]onsider the practice of Israel" (1 Cor. 10:18), he reminds them that those who share in the sacrifices, as fulfilled by the sacrifice of the Messiah, are united in communion: "Because there is one bread, we who are many are one body, for we all partake of the one bread" (1 Cor. 10:17). The Eucharist makes the Church, and yet this *communion* ("one body") cannot be conceived outside the one *sacrifice* in which believers share. As Aquinas says, "the offering up of the true lamb, i.e. Christ, was the culminating sacrifice of all. Hence (Jo. i. 29) it is said: *Behold the Lamb of God, behold Him Who taketh away sins* (Vulg., – *sin*) *of the world.*"[111]

---

[109] In *Ecclesia de Eucharistia* John Paul II affirms that at the Last Supper, "Jesus did not simply state that what he was giving them to eat and drink was his body and his blood; he also expressed *its sacrificial meaning* and made sacramentally present his sacrifice which would soon be offered on the Cross for the salvation of all" (no. 12). See also 3, q. 81, aa. 1, 3, 4. In article 3, Aquinas corrects Hugh of St Victor's position that at the Last Supper Christ "gave His body in an impassible and immortal condition to His disciples." There is only one body and blood of Christ, and it exists under the sacramental species as it exists in his natural mode, which at the Last Supper would not have been impassible and immortal. For further analysis see chapter 4's discussion of transubstantiation.

[110] Durwood Foster, in his "A Response to Cardinal Avery Dulles on 'The Eucharist as Sacrifice'" (in *Rediscovering the Eucharist: Ecumenical Conversations*, ed. Roch Kereszty, O. Cist. [New York: Paulist Press, 2003]: 197), expresses the Protestant concern that this liturgical action, as the Church's offering of Christ's sacrifice, must be an additional sacrifice. Resolution of this concern depends upon an adequate understanding of participation.

[111] 3, q. 22, a. 3. Aquinas is here following Origen's commentary on John 1:29, which Origen connects with the morning and evening offering of a lamb prescribed in Numbers 38:3–4. Note that in 1-2, q. 101, a. 4 Aquinas distinguishes in the Old Law between "sacrifices" and "sacraments," both belonging to Israel's worship, and he suggests that the distinction indicates that sacramental fullness is not attained, but rather foreshadowed, in Israel's worship. In 3, q. 60, a. 2, obj. 2 and ad 2, Aquinas recalls this point ("not even all the ceremonies of the Law, were sacraments, but only in certain special cases") and specifies:

> Some things pertaining to the Old Testament signified the holiness of Christ considered as holy in Himself. Others signified His holiness considered as the cause of our holiness; thus the sacrifice of the Paschal lamb signified Christ's Sacrifice whereby we are made holy: and such like are properly styled sacraments of the Old Law. (ad 2)

Even so, in obeying Christ's command, *how* are we sharing in this sacrifice of the true Lamb of God? Do we "merely" receive his body and blood under the sacramental sign? If so the Eucharist would be a meal but not a sacrifice. Lacking the fullness in Christ of "the practice of Israel," the Eucharist would not be a truly *liturgical* action on the part of the Church – rather it would be a feasting without the inseparable element, given our sinful condition, of purifying *korban*.

Aquinas teaches that the Church becomes herself by means of obeying Christ's command through sacramental representation.[112] While we

---

To be a "sacrament," a sacrifice must be "a sign of a holy thing so far as it [the holy *res*] makes men holy" (1-2, q. 60, a. 2).

[112] For what follows on sacramental representation, see especially Anscar Vonier, O.S.B.'s classic *A Key to the Doctrine of the Eucharist* (Eugene, OR: Wipf and Stock, 2002 [1925]). In *The Eucharistic Mystery* (New York: Crossroad, 1997), David Power, O.M.I. suggests, mistakenly in my view, that the early-twentieth century work of Anscar Vonier and Louis Billot to retrieve "sign" in sacramental theology was completed a generation later by Schillebeeckx and Rahner. According to Power, Schillebeeckx and Rahner enter more deeply into the meaning of "sign" in its human context, rather than examining "sign" in relation to what is signified and thus in light of the mode of being of the sacrament. Analysis of human subjectivity and historicity displaces metaphysical analysis. In Power's view, sacramental representation should be investigated by analysis of the "modalities of symbolic expression and communication" (*The Eucharistic Mystery*, 318) rather than by attention either to the signifying power of the bread and wine – which Power finds to be "alien" to the event signified (319) – or to God's efficient causality working through Christ's passion and the sacraments. The investigation of "symbolic expression and communication" avoids the cultic, causal, and ontological affirmations of traditional sacramental theology, without denying the transformative power of sacramental life as a channel of interpersonal presence. As Power concludes:

> [sacramental r]epresentation comes about through the act of remembrance, as the event remembered passes into language anew, by a retrieval of forms and images and a weaving into the circle of gathering through the renewal of forms. The role of the presider has to be conceived in terms of how it serves the prayer of the community, its unity, its coherent ritual action, its relation to other communities, and its openness to the word that is proclaimed, gathers, invites, and promises. In summary, one may say that, as for memorial, representation is best understood in terms of presence *to*, or being present to another, *through* intermediary expression. (319)

As undefinable ontologically, the effect of this presence, what precisely is present, and how what is present is present, are all left thoroughly ambiguous. For Power, the ambiguity serves ecumenical and inter-religious purposes by relativizing the distinctively Catholic priesthood and cult, in addition to defending against onto-theological rationalizing which seeks to control the mystery for ideological or power purposes (319). Robert Sokolowski's *Eucharistic Presence* is particularly helpful in suggesting why such a dissociation of "disclosure" from metaphysical structures will not work. See also the excellent critique provided by Peter Casarella, who compares Power's linguistic theory with Jean-Luc Marion's understanding of the Eucharist as "hors texte" (Casarella, "Eucharist: Presence of a Gift," in *Rediscovering the Eucharist: Ecumenical Conversations*, ed. Roch Kereszty, O. Cist. [New York: Paulist Press, 2003]: 212).

will discuss the liturgy of the Eucharist further in chapter 5, here we should emphasize that for Aquinas, as for Paul, the "fruit" of Christ's sacrifice, in which Christ became an offering for sin (2 Cor. 5:21), is reconciliation and deification. The Church, the "new creation," is the body, in Christ the head, of reconciled humanity. As Paul says,

> Therefore, if any one is in Christ, he is a new creation; the old has passed away, behold, the new has come. All this is from God, who through Christ reconciled us to himself and gave us the ministry of reconciliation; that is, God was in Christ reconciling the world to himself, not counting their trespasses against them, and entrusting to us the message of reconciliation. (2 Cor. 5:17–18; cf. Eph. 2:14–22)

Since the Eucharist, as we have seen, contains for Aquinas the "whole mystery of our salvation,"[113] in the Eucharist the Church enacts the saving mystery of Christ's sacrifice that, by bringing about reconciliation, constitutes the Church in deifying charity.

David Bentley Hart has pointed out that for medieval Orthodox theologians, Christ's sacrifice has a threefold reality:

> the already accomplished historical mission of Christ, the eternal efficacy of this mission in the presence of God, and the real availability in the present of the reconciliation it effects (in both its creaturely and divine dimensions) in the tangible – and frangible – form of Christ's body and blood.[114]

For Aquinas, similarly, the reconciling power of Christ's sacrifice constitutes the Church ever anew not by repeating the sacrifice, but by drawing us into contact with it, a contact that eternally (eschatologically) mediates our communion with the Trinity.[115] Agreeing with Augustine,

---

[113] 3, q. 83, a. 4.

[114] Hart, "'Thine Own of Thine Own': Eucharistic Sacrifice in Orthodox Tradition," 145.

[115] The "end" of the sacrifice is not merely restoration or reconciliation, but eternal life (3, q. 22, a. 5). As Aquinas remarks in ad 1 of this article: "The Saints who will be in heaven will not need any further expiation by the priesthood of Christ, but having expiated, they will need consummation through Christ Himself, on Whom their glory depends, as is written (Apoc. xxi. 23): *The glory of God hath enlightened it* – that is, the city of the Saints – *and the Lamb is the lamp thereof*." Similarly, he points out in ad 2 (referencing Leviticus 16:11 as a "figure"), "Although Christ's passion and death are not to be repeated, yet the virtue of that Victim endures for ever, for, as it is written (Heb. x. 14), *by one oblation He hath perfected for ever them that are sanctified*." See also Denis Chardonnens, O.C.D., "Éternité du sacerdoce du Christ et effet eschatologique de l'eucharistie: La contribution de saint Thomas d'Aquin au thème de théologie sacramentaire," *Revue Thomiste* 99 (1999): 159–80. Geoffrey Wainwright's *Eucharist and Eschatology* (London: Epworth, 1971), with its marvelous citations from the Fathers, is

therefore, Aquinas affirms that Christ "is sacrificed daily in the sacrament."[116] He first appeals to the sacramental character of the eucharistic sacrifice. It is not a new sacrifice, but rather "an image representing Christ's Passion."[117] Thus, in describing Christ's priesthood, Aquinas states

> The Sacrifice which is offered every day in the Church is not distinct from that which Christ Himself offered, but is a commemoration thereof. Wherefore Augustine says (*De Civ. Dei* x. 20): *Christ Himself both is the priest who offers it and the victim: the sacred token of which He wished to be the daily Sacrifice of the Church.*[118]

Sacramental representation makes present, by liturgical action, what is signified. Aquinas explains that Christ gives his disciples, and those in every generation who receive the sacrament of orders to serve as priests *in persona Christi*[119] at the altar, "the power to consecrate the body and blood of Christ."[120] This priesthood is the fulfillment and transformation of Israel's priesthood rather than an extension of it, since Israel's priesthood participates in Christ's rather than the other way around:

> Now Christ is the fountain-head of the entire priesthood: for the priest of the Old Law was a figure of Him; while the priest of the New Law works in His person, according to 2 Cor. 2.10: *For what I have pardoned, if I have pardoned anything, for your sakes have I done it in the person of Christ.*[121]

Aquinas finds here the significance of Christ's priesthood "after the order of Melchizedek" (Heb. 5:10, cf. Ps. 110:4). Just as Abraham "paid tithes" to Melchizedek, so also Israel's priesthood is ordered to Christ's.[122]

---

the classic study of this theme. The eschatological aspect of the Eucharist is emphasized by M. Francis Mannion, "Rejoice, Heavenly Powers! The Renewal of Liturgical Doxology," *Pro Ecclesia* 12 (2003): 37–60. Mannion recognizes that the eschatological theme is found in Aquinas, but argues, I think incorrectly, that "eschatological consciousness" went into decline "soon after the patristic era" (43). For further reflection on the eschatology and the Eucharist, see *Ecclesia de Eucharistia*, nos. 18–20, and William T. Cavanaugh, *Torture and Eucharist: Theology, Politics, and the Body of Christ* (Oxford: Blackwell, 1998).

[116] 3, q. 83, a. 1, *sed contra.*
[117] 3, q. 83, a. 1.
[118] 3, q. 22, a. 3, ad 2.
[119] 3, q. 83, a. 1, ad 3.
[120] *Suppl.*, q. 37, a. 2; see Aquinas's *Commentary on the Sentences*, Book IV, dist. 24, q. 2, a. 1 q.1a 2. Aquinas states that "the sacrament of Order is directed to the sacrament of the Eucharist, which is the sacrament of sacraments, as Dionysius says (*Eccles. Hier.* iii)."
[121] 3, q. 22, a. 4.
[122] 3, q. 22, a. 6.

In consecrating the body and blood of Christ, the priests of the New Covenant cause the whole Christ, in his sacrificial mode, to be present in the sacrament. Aquinas states, "The Eucharist is the perfect sacrament of our Lord's Passion, as containing Christ crucified."[123] In this sacramental mode, facing east together with the congregation so as to represent sacramentally the offering of sacrifice, the priest offers up, *in persona Christi*, Christ's body and blood as a sacrificial offering. Participating in this offering (in sacrifice and in the sacrificial meal that makes our participation perfect), believers are configured to Christ's offering and thus *are offered* in Christ as his Body, sharing in his sacrificial justice. As Jean Danielou has shown with regard to the Fathers, the figure of the "paschal lamb" unites sacrifice and meal, so that "the Eucharist is seen to be the sacrament of the Passion."[124] In offering the Lamb (and receiving him in sacrificial feasting), believers partake in the reconciliation and deification, the radically new creation, won by the Lamb. David Bentley Hart depicts this graced union as "an exhaustion of our poverty, so to speak, to make way for the riches he pours into us."[125]

The sacrificial offering on the altar differs according to its mode from Christ's sacrifice on the Cross: it is a sacrament, a sign, and therefore unbloody.[126] It thus bears repeating that it is not a different sacrifice,

---

[123] 3, q. 73, a. 5, ad 2.

[124] Jean Danielou, S.J., *The Bible and the Liturgy* (Notre Dame, IN: University of Notre Dame Press, 1956): 172. Avery Dulles, S.J. has made the same point: "Since the Eucharist is by nature a sacrificial banquet, the reception of Holy Communion is no mere appendix. It pertains to the integrity of the sacrifice itself" (Dulles, "The Eucharist as Sacrifice," in *Rediscovering the Eucharist: Ecumenical Conversations*, ed. Roch Kereszty, O. Cist., 175–87, at 184).

[125] David Bentley Hart, "'Thine Own of Thine Own': Eucharistic Sacrifice in Orthodox Tradition," 150–1.

[126] In a useful survey of the development of Eucharistic theology during the first half of the 20th century, the Anglican theologian E.L. Mascall remarks that

> the general tendency of post-mediaeval Roman Catholic theologians down to our own time has been to think of the relation between the Eucharist and Calvary in terms of repetition, and this has led them almost inevitably to seek for some action in the Mass which can be considered as an equivalent of the slaying of our Lord which took place once for all on the Cross. (Mascall, *Corpus Christi: Essays on the Church and the Eucharist*, 2nd edn [London: Longmans, 1965]: 119–20)

In contrast, Mascall finds, the twentieth century has seen a movement away from this tendency in Roman Catholic Eucharistic theology due to the work of Maurice de la Taille, Anscar Vonier, O.S.B., Eùgene Masure, Charles Journet, and Odo Casel, O.S.B. For Mascall, despite his sympathy with Vonier, "It must, I think, be admitted that Vonier is inclined, in the mediaeval manner, to identify sacrifice too exclusively with death, but this is an emphasis which can easily be corrected without detriment to his [Vonier's] special contribution" (133). While not agreeing fully with Casel's position, therefore, Mascall

because what is represented in the sacramental action is Christ's Passion.[127] As Augustine says in a passage from Book X of *De Civitate Dei* cited by Aquinas, "The visible sacrifice is the sacrament, i.e. the sacred sign, of the invisible sacrifice."[128] In teaching human beings about eternal realities in accord with the manner of human knowing through sensible things, God works through the visible sign to make present the invisible reality.[129] By God's power, the sacramental sign of Christ's Passion makes present Christ in his sacrificial mode of separated body and blood. Aquinas addresses the mystery in this way:

---

writes, "The strong point of Casel's theory is, in my opinion, precisely his insistence that the Mass contains sacramentally the whole sweep of the Lord's incarnate life, and not merely an image of Redemption" (154). Mascall traces his own position on sacrifice to that of the Anglican F. C. N. Hicks, who argues in *The Fullness of Sacrifice* (1930):

> that in the Old-Testament sacrifices the essentially priestly and sacrificial act was not the slaying of the victim, which might in fact be performed by a lay person, but the offering upon the altar to God of the blood, which in Jewish thought was identical with, or was at least a divinely ordained symbol of, the victim's life. The slaying was merely an indispensable preliminary by which the life was set free to be offered. So . . . applying these considerations to the work of Christ, in whom all the Old-Testament types are fulfilled, "the Sacrifice is not the death alone; nor the pleading with the blood alone; nor the offering upon the altar "in heaven"; nor the act of Communion alone . . . Each stage is sacrificial. All together make the one Sacrifice. (Mascall, 126–7)

Although the death of the victim should not be separated from the intentional offering – and although of course Christ need not die again – it seems to me mistaken to set death to the side (cf. Wyschogrod). For explanation and critique of Casel's approach, see, e.g., Colman E. O'Neill, O.P., "The Mysteries of Christ and the Sacraments," *The Thomist* 25 (1962): 1–53; Jean Gaillard, O.S.B., "Chronique de liturgie. La théologie des mystères," *Revue Thomiste* 57 (1957): 510–51; Jean-Hervé Nicolas, "Réactualisation des mystères rédempteurs dans et par les sacrements," *Revue Thomiste* 58 (1958): 20–54.
[127] John Paul II states,

> The Church constantly draws her life from the redeeming sacrifice; she approaches it not only through faith-filled remembrance, but also through real contact, since *this sacrifice is made present ever anew*, sacramentally perpetuated, in every community which offers it at the hands of the consecrated minister . . . "The sacrifice of Christ and the sacrifice of the Eucharist are *one single sacrifice*." Saint John Chrysostom put it well: "We always offer the same Lamb, not one today and another tomorrow, but always the same one. For this reason the sacrifice is always only one . . . Even now we offer that victim who was once offered and who will never be consumed." The Mass makes present the sacrifice of the Cross; it does not add to that sacrifice nor does it multiply it. (*Ecclesia de Eucharistia*, no. 12)

[128] 3, q. 60, a. 1, *sed contra.*
[129] See 3, q. 61, a. 1.

But the fact that we offer the sacrifice every day seems to contradict the statement that it is not repeated. I answer that we do not offer something different from what Christ offered for us, namely, His blood; hence, it is not a distinct oblation, but a commemoration of that sacrifice which Christ offered: "Do this in commemoration of me" (Luke 22:19).[130]

The priest's consecration of the sacrament constitutes a sacrificial offering that is both Christ's sacrifice and the Church's sacramental-sacrificial sharing in Christ's sacrifice. Moreover, in the consecration of the Eucharist, the priest thus never acts alone but always in and with the mystical Body of those who possess faith and charity. The members of the Mystical Body, participating in the action of Christ the Head as represented by the priest, share by the common priesthood of baptism in the priest's sacramental offering of Christ's sacrifice and in the benefits that flow from Christ's sacrificial expiation, whose power is made present in the Eucharist.[131] As an expiatory sacrifice, the Eucharist not only provides for communicants the "daily bread" whose fruits cleanse us of our "daily defects,"[132] but also extends its salvific influence to all those who are united in Christ's Mystical Body.

Does the sacramental representation bring Christ's Passion into the present, or return Christ's glorified body to its state on the Cross? The

---

[130] Aquinas, *Commentary on the Epistle to the Hebrews*, ch. 10, lect. 1 (no. 482), unpublished translation by Fabian Larcher, O.P.

[131] On the congregation's participation in the priest's (*in persona Christi*) offering, see *Mediator Dei* nos. 80–111 and *Sacrosanctum Concilium* no. 48. See also Colman O'Neill, O.P., *Meeting Christ in the Sacraments*, rev. ed. Romanus Cessario, O.P. (New York: Alba House, 1991): 210–18. O'Neill observes:

> What the priest does at the altar makes available to the faithful a bodily, sacrificial expression for their praise, prayer, reparation and thanksgiving, offered in interior union with Christ. "The external rite of sacrifice must of its very nature be a sign of internal worship; and what is signified by the sacrifice of the New Law is that supreme homage by which Christ, the principal offerer, and with him and through him all his mystical members, pay due honor and veneration to God" (*Mediator Dei* #98). Only the baptized can offer this sacramental Victim with the priest. This is because it forms part of the visible structure of the Church and only those who are baptized are inserted into this structure and possess in their sacramental characters the power necessary for acting in this sphere. (213)

Cf. *Ecclesia de Eucharistia* no. 24, as well as Colman O'Neill, O.P., "St. Thomas on Membership of the Church," *The Thomist* 27 (1963): 121–4; idem, "The Role of the Recipient and Sacramental Signification," *The Thomist* 21 (1958): 257–301 and 508–40; Anscar Vonier, O.S.B., *A Key to the Doctrine of the Eucharist* (Eugene, OR: Wipf and Stock, 2002 [1925]): 223–40, especially 238–9.

[132] See 3, q. 79, a. 7.

answer is in both cases no. For Aquinas Christ's Passion remains an event in the past, and Christ's body remains unchanging in heaven. While we will discuss this aspect more fully in chapter 4, the important point for now is that Christ in the Eucharist is not drawn into the present, but rather draws the present into his heavenly reality. Even though we can rightly say that the consecration of the sacrament makes the whole Christ present to us in the sacrament, nonetheless it is we, not Christ, who are changed by the sacrament of the Eucharist. Thus in participating in Christ's sacrificial body and blood, we participate in the power or redemptive effect of his sacrifice – that is, the reconciling grace that accomplishes charity in us. We are thereby configured to the image of his cruciform love and share in the divine communion he enjoys. In this second way, Aquinas states, the Eucharist should also be called a sacrifice:

> by this sacrifice, we are made partakers of the fruit of our Lord's Passion. Hence in one of the Sunday *Secrets* (Ninth Sunday after Pentecost) we say: *Whenever the commemoration of this sacrifice is celebrated, the work of our redemption is enacted.*[133]

We share in his sacrifice sacramentally by becoming like him, thereby accomplishing God's purpose in Israel of forming a holy people in and through holy worship.

Aquinas sums up the inseparable union of sacrament and sacrifice in the Eucharist by remarking that:

> this sacrament is not only a sacrament, but also a sacrifice. For, it has the nature of a sacrifice inasmuch as in this sacrament Christ's Passion is represented, whereby Christ *offered Himself a Victim to God* (Eph. v. 2), and it has the nature of a sacrament inasmuch as invisible grace is bestowed in this sacrament under a visible species.[134]

In understanding the Cross and the Eucharist (as participating in the Cross) in terms of expiatory sacrifice, we illumine the wisdom and love of the Trinity's action in the world. Without minimizing in any way Christ's suffering for sin, we can recognize that Christ's obedient suffering – and ours when sacrificially united to his – flows from his fullness of active wisdom, his fulfillment of the wise law of love that constitutes the fabric and goal of the Trinity's plan for the world.[135] As the charitable

---

[133] 3, q. 83, a. 1.
[134] 3, q. 79, a. 7.
[135] Rather than from a "dark night" of radical unknowing experienced by Christ on the Cross, as von Balthasar and others suggest. For further discussion see, e.g., my "Balthasar on Christ's Consciousness on the Cross," *The Thomist* 65 (2001): 567–81.

act of Christ in his wisdom, the culmination of the entire pattern of his life[136] and the revelation of the meaning of human history, the Cross is a self-offering to God in which Christ has already at the Last Supper included the disciples, despite their weakness.

We are thus sacramentally caught up into the wisdom, the right ordering of all things to God, of Christ's sacrificial Cross. Christ, the "high priest" (Heb. 7:26), has given, in his wisdom, his disciples a priestly participation in his reconciling and uniting Cross, by which they may sacramentally follow him in his path of reconciliation. The Holy Spirit is thus profoundly at work here. Commenting on Hebrews 9:14, Aquinas observes that "the reason why Christ shed His blood" is "the Holy Spirit, through Whose movement and instinct, namely, by the love of God and neighbor" Christ in his humanity was moved to offer himself on the Cross.[137] The same Holy Spirit enables our full eucharistic participation in Christ's sacrifice.[138]

5 CONCLUSION

The created relational order of justice, fulfilled by the expiatory sacrifice to the Father of the incarnate Son inspired by the Spirit, becomes through our eucharistic inclusion in Christ's fulfillment of all justice none other than an eschatological order of resplendent love grounded in a divine wisdom whose humility is endless.[139] To move beyond

---

[136] Aquinas often affirms that "all Christ's actions and sufferings operate instrumentally in virtue of his Godhead for the salvation of men" (3, q. 48, a. 6). Far from isolating Christ's Cross, Aquinas finds salvific value in all of Christ's deeds. In this sense, Aquinas could agree with David Bentley Hart's remark,

> The whole course of Christ's life, as he recapitulates the human in himself and then makes it a pure offering of atonement, is his sacrifice, and the whole course of the liturgy is a progressive integration of worshipers into the journey of his life, into that wondrous exchange he brings about within the temple of his body, so that when at last the consecrated elements "scatter" him among his worshipers, his life has become theirs.

Although this image of "scattering" gives the wrong impression. See Hart, "'Thine Own of Thine Own': Eucharistic Sacrifice in Orthodox Tradition," 157.

[137] Thomas Aquinas, *Commentary on the Epistle to the Hebrews*, ch. 9, lect. 3 (no. 444), unpublished translation by Fr. Fabian Larcher, O.P.

[138] Cf. the optional communion prayer of the priest in the Catholic *Novus Ordo*:

> Lord Jesus Christ, Son of the living God, by the will of the Father and the work of the Holy Spirit your death brought life to the world. By your holy body and blood free me from all my sins and from every evil. Keep me faithful to your teaching and never let me be parted from you.

[139] See, for further discussion, Deborah Wallace Ruddy, "The Humble God: Healer, Mediator, and Sacrifice."

Eucharistic idealism does not mean denying that Christ's priesthood and his sacrifice flow from charity and are ordered eschatologically to charity. Aquinas affirms that "the power of the New Testament consists in charity, which is the fulfillment of the Law."[140] But avoiding an idealist account of the Eucharist does require recognizing, as the fulfillment of the "practice of Israel," the expiatory character of Christ's sacrifice within the created order constituted by relationships of justice. The Eucharist, as a sacramental-sacrificial participation in Christ's expiatory sacrifice, configures and nourishes Christ's Mystical Body in the charitable form of Christ's Cross. In and through Christ's sacrifice and our eucharistic participation in its offering through the Holy Spirit, the Father is accomplishing his will to establish a holy people dwelling eternally in the Trinity.[141] Attending to the practice of Israel, Aquinas illumines the mercy that liberates human beings from the state of sinful injustice which prevents us from enjoying fellowship in charity and thereby attaining, through the graced meriting that flows from our cruciform practices, our true selves.[142] Only when sharing in this cruciform charity in and through Christ's reconciling sacrifice, can we share, as the Body of Christ, in the eschatological "end" or goal of Christ's sacrifice, namely eternal life in and with the risen Christ. To this communion of cruciform charity, attained in and through the Christological and pneumatological participation that is the eucharistic sacrifice, we now turn.

---

[140] Aquinas, *Commentary on the Epistle to the Hebrews*, ch. 10, lect. 1 (no. 480), unpublished translation by Fabian Larcher, O.P.

[141] See Michael Dauphinais and Matthew Levering, *Holy People, Holy Land: A Theological Introduction to the Bible* (Grand Rapids, MI: Brazos Press, 2005).

[142] For a valuable ecumenical treatment of the theology of merit, see Michael Root, "Aquinas, Merit, and Reformation Theology after the *Joint Declaration on the Doctrine of Justification*," *Modern Theology* 20 (2004): 5–22.

3

The Eucharist and the Communion of Charity

In the dedication to his book *The Election of Israel*, the Jewish theologian David Novak observes:

> I do not remember just when the question of the election of Israel first presented itself to me. But I do remember who first taught me to appreciate election itself, the privilege of being one of the chosen people. This book, therefore, is dedicated to the memory of George and Clara Eller Krulewitch – Uncle George and Aunt Clara – who loved being Jews and at whose Seder table I received my first and best lessons in how to celebrate what God does for and with his people.[1]

Through the Passover, God establishes an elect communion, a people who are radically identified as a people *in relation to God*. For Novak, the Passover seder cannot be separated from the election, in history, of a people – from "what God does for and with his people." The privilege constituted by, and celebrated in, the Passover seder is the privilege of being a people *unto God*, a privilege that manifests itself around the family table.[2] I mention David Novak's story because when transposed into a Christian context in which Christ is the Pasch, the connection he implies between the Passover celebration and the historical communion of a people who gather (or are gathered) in love is central to understanding the Eucharist. The Eucharistic Pasch cannot be separated from the Mystical Body. As David Bentley Hart states, "Christian talk of divinization is essentially the christological radicalization of the language

[1] David Novak, *The Election of Israel: The Idea of the Chosen People* (Cambridge: Cambridge University Press, 1995): xiv–xv.
[2] For exploration of the Passover seder in terms of memory/memorial, or as he puts it *"zekher/zikharon* as the act of making the past present" (3), see David E. Stern, "Remembering and Redemption," in *Rediscovering the Eucharist: Ecumenical Conversations*, ed. Roch A. Kereszty, O. Cist (New York: Paulist Press, 2003): 1–15.

of indwelling that lies at the heart of the biblical account of God's election of Israel, and indeed of God's election of creation, for himself, from nothingness."[3] Such divine indwelling, radicalized in and mediated by the Incarnation and the Eucharist, makes – and is – the Church.

Drawing upon Henri de Lubac's *Corpus Mysticum*, however, Ephraim Radner has argued that insufficient attention has been paid to the Eucharist's fundamental reality as constitutive of a communion (in charity) of divine indwelling. Protestant and Catholic theologians since the Reformation have used arguments over the "how" of "the Eucharist's significatory character" to distance the Eucharist from its ecclesial referent as embodied in the (broken) history of the Church's love. After comparing Calvin's polemics with those of Calvin's Catholic counterparts, Radner remarks:

> The Eucharist, then, in its significatory function, had become a mark of distinction between ecclesial bodies, a tool of separatist justification. That the character of the Eucharistic presence should somehow be linked with the status of a church was not in itself, as we shall note, an untraditional notion. But that defining the Eucharistic presence should become an instrument for defining the Eucharistic community's status *as* Church indicated, in fact, a radically new task of theological and disciplinary discernment. For now, not simply a wedge, but a conceptual and realistic breakage between the thing called "Eucharist" and the thing called "Church" had occurred that made of each entity a logically distinct construct. The meaning of these two entities could be gleaned through independent avenues of analysis – one could ask what the Eucharist or the Church was without referring to the other *ab initio*. And their positive relationship one to another could now only be asserted as something existing between two discrete phenomena, separate signs that needed to be brought together through some externally imposed grammar if they were to make common sense. In the separative grammar of ecclesial division, the Eucharist was an indicator of the Church; but it was so in the manner of a "conventional" sign (to use Augustine's term), an artificially designated "mark" whose meaning either Scripture or tradition had linked with the independent reality of "Church" already asserted oppositionally by each side . . . [T]he Eucharist's first order reality could no longer "refer" to the Church directly,

---

[3] David Bentley Hart, "'Thine Own of Thine Own': Eucharistic Sacrifice in Orthodox Tradition," in *Rediscovering the Eucharist: Ecumenical Conversations*, ed. Roch Kereszty, O. Cist. (New York: Paulist Press, 2003): 158.

or "naturally," as something whose essential being was, even prior to its theological articulation, of one substance with the Church . . . Catholics asserted a mode of signification that pointed to something whose reality lies *within* the bounds of the true Church (the transubstantiated elements) but is not itself joined to it in a prior way.[4]

Radner's concern (following de Lubac) exposes the importance of understanding the Eucharist and the Church as a participation in Christ's Paschal mystery. At the center of Aquinas's Eucharistic theology lies our sacrificial participation in Christ's sacrifice. It is this participation, begun in baptism, that configures us to him as members of his Body the Church. The communion of charity comes about in and through the sacrifice. Thus, as Anscar Vonier and Gilles Emery have shown, for Aquinas – as for Radner and de Lubac, as well as *Lumen Gentium* and John Paul II's *Ecclesia de Eucharistia* – the Eucharist makes or builds the Church.[5] The Eucharistic body of Christ cannot be isolated

---

[4] Ephraim Radner, *The End of the Church: A Pneumatology of Christian Division in the West* (Grand Rapids, MI: Eerdmans, 1998): 208–10. Radner largely adopts de Lubac's thesis regarding the loss of the intrinsic ecclesial referent of the Eucharist. Radner shows, however, that de Lubac is wrong in locating the blame for this loss in the ninth-century debate between Paschasius Radbertus and Ratramnus and the eleventh-century debate between Lanfranc and Berengar. See Radner, *The End of the Church*, 228–39. Taking up de Lubac's thesis, Andrew Louth has pinned the blame on Augustine's "logic of inwardness," which for Louth, quite unfairly I think, stands as the key to pre-Reformation distortions of Christianity in the Latin West: Louth, "The Body in Western Catholic Christianity," in *Religion and the Body*, ed. Sarah Coakley (Cambridge: Cambridge University Press, 1997): 111–30. De Lubac's thesis receives similar appropriation, as regards the authority structures of the Church, in Michel de Certeau, *The Mystic Fable*, trans. Michael B. Smith (Chicago: University of Chicago Press, 1992) and John Milbank, *Being Reconciled: Ontology and Pardon* (New York: Routledge, 2003): 122–37. Milbank's work here merits careful response, which I hope to give it in a future study on the Church. See also Frank C. Senn, "The Eucharist and Ecumenical Inter-Communion: Reflections on *Ecclesia de Eucharistia*," *Pro Ecclesia* 13 (2004): 307–22. Following J.-M.-R. Tillard's analysis of St Paul and the Fathers, Senn remarks,

> The ecclesial body is formed by its individual members being bonded with Christ by sharing in the sacrament of the body and blood of Christ . . . The unanimous conviction of the ancient church is that the ecclesial body of Christ is formed, maintained, nourished and kept in union with the crucified and risen Christ by means of the sacramental body of Christ. (313)

[5] See *Lumen Gentium*, nos. 3, 11 and *Ecclesia de Eucharistia*, nos. 1, 21. Anscar Vonier, O.S.B. wrote in 1925 that for Aquinas, "Christ's sacramental Body makes Christ's mystical Body" (Vonier, *A Key to the Doctrine of the Eucharist* [Eugene, OR: Wipf and Stock, 2002]: 254). Gilles Emery, O.P. has shown that Aquinas's theology of the Eucharist illumines the "organic relationship between the Eucharist and the Church" (Emery, "The Ecclesial Fruit of the Eucharist in St. Thomas Aquinas," trans. Therese C. Scarpelli, *Nova*

from the ecclesial Body of Christ, since the latter is our cruciform sharing in the former.

It follows that in order to understand this relationship of the Eucharist and the Church in Aquinas's theology, one must learn what he means by calling the Eucharist the "sacrament of charity." By attending to Aquinas's *Commentary on John*, we will seek insight first into the (Christological) nature of charity, and second into the Eucharist in its relationship to the Church, understood in light of charity. Eucharistic charity exposes that the Church's unity is not triumphalist, but rather requires the particularity of a people formed in and through *cruciform* practices, the hierarchically ordered obedience and charitable suffering of the saints. The ecclesial unity achieved in Eucharistic charity likewise rules out imagining that the Church is, or could be, a production dependent upon sinful and weak human beings. Moreover, as we will see, Eucharistic charity constitutes the Mystical Body not only by sacramental eating but also by spiritual eating, thereby ruling out any inbuilt narrowness in God's saving plan. Understood as constituted by the Eucharist, ecclesial unity in charity is a divine gift – unity in *Christ's* sacrifice to God – and thereby a unity that takes up and encompasses, in Christ's mercy, our human neediness and sinful brokenness during our Exodus pilgrimage to the heavenly Jerusalem.

1 AQUINAS ON CHARITY

No greater depiction of "communion" is found in the New Testament than the lengthy discourse in the Gospel of John in which Jesus, after washing the disciples' feet, instructs his disciples at the Last Supper:

> As the Father has loved me, so I have loved you; abide in my love. If you keep my commandments, you will abide in my love, just as I have kept my Father's commandments and abide in

---

et Vetera 2 [2004]: 43–60, at 43). De Lubac argues in *Corpus Mysticum* that "the fact that the *Summa* readily says 'corpus Ecclesiae mysticum' in place of 'corpus Christi mysticum' indicates an advanced evolution" away from employing *corpus mysticum* in the context of Eucharist (I am indebted for this citation to Martin Morard, "Les expressions 'corpus mysticum' et 'persona mystica' dans l'œuvre de saint Thomas d'Aquin," *Revue Thomiste* 95 [1995]: 653–64, at 653). Using the Index Thomisticus to do an exhaustive search for the expression *corpus mysticum* in Aquinas's corpus, Morard has shown that de Lubac's charge is not validated by examination of the texts, a fact that has been generally ignored. Milbank is something of an exception in this regard. He writes, "As long as an essential relation between the three bodies remained however, strong traces of the older view persisted – for example in the thought of Bonaventure or of Thomas Aquinas. It remained the case that the historical body was mediated to the Church by the sacramental body" (*Being Reconciled*, 123).

his love. These things I have spoken to you, that my joy may be in you, and that your joy may be full. This is my commandment, that you love one another as I have loved you. Greater love has no man than this, that a man lay down his life for his friends. You are my friends if you do what I command you. No longer do I call you servants, for the servant does not know what his master is doing; but I have called you friends, for all that I have heard from my Father I have made known to you. You did not choose me, but I chose you and appointed you that you should go and bear fruit and that your fruit should abide; so that whatever you ask the Father in my name, he may give it to you. This I command you, to love one another. (John 15:9–17)

Commenting upon this passage, Aquinas begins by proposing Christ as our model. He states, "For just as the love which the Father has for him is the model or standard of Christ's love for us, so Christ wants his obedience to be the model of our obedience."[6] To abide in Christ's love, we must imitate his obedience to the Father's commandments. According to Aquinas, this means two things: submitting to death, and committing no sin. In other words, there must be in us no impediment to God's love. Sin constitutes such an impediment, as does prideful unwillingness to pay the due penalty of sin (death). Aquinas explains that Jesus says, "'I abide in his love,' because there is nothing in me, as a human being, opposed to his love."[7] Yet, how are we to share in Jesus' condition of having no impediment to God's love? As Aquinas notes in his commentary on Aristotle's *Nichomachean Ethics*, "Friendship is destroyed especially when one friend finds in the other something opposed to their friendship. But this is impossible in friendship between the virtuous."[8] How are we to share in the perfect virtue of Christ's charity?

Drawing upon the Old Testament, Aquinas first affirms an ontological reason for hope that we might share in Jesus' condition: namely, God's causal love, which overflows both in creation and new creation. The Trinity rejoices from eternity in the reality of being participated by human creatures:

---

[6] St Thomas Aquinas, *Commentary on the Gospel of St. John*, Part II, trans. James A. Weisheipl, O.P and Fabian Larcher, O.P. (Petersham, MA: St Bede's Publications, 1999): Chapter 15, Lecture 2, no. 2003 (p. 398).
[7] Ibid.
[8] Aquinas, *Commentary on Aristotle's Nicomachean Ethics*, trans. C.I. Litzinger, O.P. (Notre Dame, IN: Dumb Ox Books, 1993 [1964]): Book VIII, Lecture 4, no. 1592 (p. 490).

> Now love is the cause of joy, for everyone takes joy in what
> he loves. But God loves himself and creatures, especially
> rational creatures, to whom he grants an infinite good. So Christ
> rejoices in two things from all eternity: first, in his own good
> and that of the Father: "I was delighted every day, playing
> before him" [Prov. 8:30]; secondly, he delights in the good of
> the rational creature: "delighting in the sons of men" (Prov.
> 8:31), that is, in the fact that I am shared in by the children
> of men. He rejoices in these things from eternity: "As the bride-
> groom rejoices over the bride, so shall your God rejoice over
> you." (Isa. 62:5)[9]

Christ has joy in us. Indeed, as Aquinas later states, Christ has an "intense
desire for the salvation of the human race."[10] For Aquinas, Christ's words
from the Cross, "I thirst" (John 19:28), express this intense desire. In
urging his disciples to abide in his love, Christ refers to the joy he will
have in them if they obey: "that my joy may be in you, and that your
joy may be full" (John 15:11). As Aquinas says, "our Lord wants us to
become sharers of his joy by our observing his commandments."[11] God
wills to draw us into his trinitarian life of wisdom and love.

   On biblical grounds illumined metaphysically, then, Aquinas holds that
God wills to make us sharers of his joy. Christ's obedience is the model
for ours; in order to share in God's joy, we too must submit willingly
to death and be without sin. This sinless submission is possible for us
because of Christ's Cross. Aquinas states,

> Christ loved us in the correct order and efficaciously. His love
> was orderly because he loved nothing in us but God and in
> relation to God: "I am the mother of beautiful love" (Sir 24:18),
> and efficacious because he loved us so much that he delivered
> himself for us: "Christ loved us and gave himself up for us,
> a fragrant offering and sacrifice to God" (Eph. 5:2).[12]

Objectively speaking, Christ has removed the impediment to God's love
in us. He has restored a right relationship between human beings and
God, and all human beings can now travel this path in Christ. His
sacrificial charity opens the path of our charity. Yet, how can particular human beings share in his charity? How can we "abide" in him by
truly imitating his love as his friends?

---

[9] Aquinas, *Commentary on the Gospel of St. John*, no. 2004 (p. 398).
[10] Ibid., no. 2447 (p. 577).
[11] Ibid., no. 2004 (p. 398).
[12] Ibid., no. 2009 (p. 400).

It will be no surprise that, according to Aquinas, Christ makes possible our conversion (from servants to friends of God) by the grace of the Holy Spirit: "Servitude is opposed to friendship; and he rejects this by saying, 'No longer do I call you servants.' It is like saying: although you were formerly servants under the law, now you are free under grace: 'You have received the spirit of adoption' [Rom. 8:15]."[13] The efficacious sign of our reception of grace is that we come to share in God's wisdom, the wisdom of sacrificial love. Aquinas states:

> For the true sign of friendship is that a friend reveals the secrets of his heart to his friend . . . Now God reveals his secrets to us by letting us share in his wisdom: "In every generation she [Wisdom] passes into holy souls and makes them friends of God and prophets" (Wisd. 7:27).[14]

To abide in Christ – to be able as his friends to obey his commandments and imitate his sacrificial love – is thus a gift of grace whereby we receive the divine Wisdom, the Word of God, that enables us to know and to love as Christ knows and loves. Aquinas quotes Gregory the Great,

> All the things he has made known to his servants are the joys of interior love and the feasts of our heavenly fatherland, which he excites in our minds every day by the breath of his love. For as long as we love the sublime heavenly things we have heard, we already know what we love, because the love itself is knowledge.[15]

In receiving the Wisdom of God, we discover that true wisdom is love. This is so, as Aquinas has remarked earlier in the *Commentary*, because the Word of God is not a mere word, but a Word that "breathes forth love."[16] The hearer of this Word truly learns when he or she hears with

---

[13] Ibid., no. 2014 (p. 402). Nicholas Cabasilas likewise places "the reality of our adoption as sons," which occurs through the Eucharist, at the forefront of his theology. See *The Life in Christ*, trans. Carmino J. deCatanzaro (Crestwood, NY: St Vladimir's Seminary Press, 1998): Book IV, pp. 126–9, 137–9, as well as *Ecclesia de Eucharistia* #34. See also Luc-Thomas Somme, *Fils adoptifs de Dieu par Jésus Christ* (Paris: Vrin, 1997).

[14] Aquinas, *Commentary on the Gospel of St. John*, no. 2016 (p. 403). Colman O'Neill, O.P. comments on our suffering as a sharing in Christ's (understood as the transformative activity of divine love) in *Sacramental Realism* (Wilmington, DE: Michael Glazier, 1983): 49.

[15] Ibid., no. 2018 (p. 404). The quotation is from Homily 27. See also *Catena Aurea*, Vol. 4, Part II (St John) (Albany, NY: Preserving Christian Publications, 1995 [1842]), p. 486.

[16] Aquinas, *Commentary on the Gospel of St. John*, Part I, trans. James A. Weisheipl, O.P. and Fabian Larcher, O.P. (Albany, NY: Magi Books, 1980): Chapter 6, Lecture 5, no. 946 (p. 376).

love: "For that person learns the word who grasps it according to the meaning of the speaker."[17]

The goal of this receptive learning of the Word, possible only in the Holy Spirit, consists in our bearing the ecclesial fruit of the eternal life of the community of the blessed. Aquinas interprets Christ's wish "that that your fruit should abide" (John 15:16) to mean "that the society of the faithful would be led into eternal life and their spiritual fruit flourish: 'He gathers fruit for eternal life' (John 4:36)."[18] Christ desires eternal life for us, and so he gives us his Wisdom – that is, himself – that inspires love. He does this in two ways: through the gift of faith, and through the sacrament of the Eucharist. As Aquinas remarks in his *Commentary on John* as regards the Eucharist, "whatever is an effect of our Lord's passion is also an effect of this sacrament. For this sacrament is nothing other than the application of our Lord's passion to us."[19] Christ's gift of himself in the Eucharist flows from his desire to unite human beings to himself; he enables us to "love one another as I have loved you" by enabling us to share Eucharistically in the self-giving love of his sacrifice on the Cross. The Eucharist enables us to abide in the divine Wisdom of his Pasch. Abiding in and with him, in the joy of the life of the Trinity, we accomplish his intense desire, his thirst, that "my joy may be in you, and that your joy may be full" (John 15:11).

Returning to biblical exposition, therefore, we can say that in calling us to enjoy the communion of friendship with the Trinity, Christ in the Gospel of John teaches that we must "love one another as I have loved you" (John 15:12). Such love is sacrificial, as Christ makes explicit: "Greater love has no man than this, that a man lay down his life for his friends" (John 15:13). Commenting upon Ephesians 5:2, Louis Bouyer has observed that "Paul seems to regard love, *agape*, and sacrifice as identical in Christ. Perhaps it would be better to say that sacrifice appears here as the consummation of love."[20] This sacrificial love is, for both St John and St Paul, the "love" in which we must "abide." If we do so, we become no longer Jesus' servants, but his friends. Jesus contrasts the servant, who "does not know what his master is doing" with Jesus' disciples who are now his friends because he has revealed to them what their divine Master "is doing," that is to say, God's *self-giving love*. We can love as Christ loved because the Eucharist inflames our charity and enables us radically to offer our lives to God in Christ, thereby sharing in Christ's (cultic) justice. In his communion with us in his Eucharistic

---

[17] Ibid.

[18] Aquinas, *Commentary on the Gospel of St. John*, Part II, no. 2027 (p. 407).

[19] Aquinas, *Commentary on the Gospel of St. John*, Part I, no. 963 (p. 382).

[20] Louis Bouyer, *The Christian Mystery: From Pagan Myth to Christian Mysticism*, trans. Illtyd Trethowan (Edinburgh: T. & T. Clark, 1990): 287.

sacrifice, Jesus enables us bear the fruit of sacrificial love, a community of self-giving love in Christ (John 15:16).[21]

Aquinas's theology of charity – further unfolded in the *Summa theologiae* – ultimately reduces to a simple claim.[22] This claim is not specific to Aquinas, but finds expression also in the words of the Methodist exegete Ben Witherington III commenting on John 13:34:

> Notice here that love is commanded. Jesus is not referring to a warm mushy feeling, he is referring to an action. In particular he is referring to the sort of loving self-sacrificial action that is foreshadowed in the foot washing and preeminently modeled in Jesus' death for others.[23]

Charity and sacrifice are one. Through such sacrificial charity, a community, with Christ as its Head, is built.

2 CHARITY AND THE EUCHARIST

Aquinas's theology of charity, as would be expected, informs his doctrine of the Eucharist, and vice versa. In the *Summa Theologiae*'s general discussion of the sacraments (questions 60–5 of the *tertia pars*), Aquinas thinks in Abrahamic terms: Jesus, on the Cross, takes up Israel's sacrificial posture before God and perfectly fulfills, in cruciform *charity*, the sacrificial intentionality that belongs to Israel's communion with God.

When Enrico Mazza charges Aquinas with prioritizing Christ over the Church, therefore, Mazza fails to grasp the Christological character of the Church's charity.[24] Mazza states:

> Early documents speak of the Eucharist as a sacrament of the unity of the Church. In the medieval approach the Eucharist changes from sacrament of unity (of the Church) to sacrament of union (of the believer with Christ). This fact, which is coextensive with the entire medieval period, takes on a special importance when it comes to the ontological approach which Thomas takes to the Sacrament of the Eucharist.[25]

---

[21] See John Yocum, "Sacraments in Aquinas," inThomas Weinandy, Daniel Keating, and John Yocum, eds., *Aquinas on Doctrine* (New York: T. & T. Clark, 2004): 168.

[22] For further discussion of Aquinas's theology of charity, see Michael Sherwin, O.P., *"By Knowledge and by Love": Charity and Knowledge in the Moral Theology of St. Thomas Aquinas* (Washington, DC: Catholic University of America Press, 2005).

[23] Ben Witherington, III, *John's Wisdom: A Commentary on the Fourth Gospel* (Louisville, KY: Westminster John Knox Press, 1995): 247–8.

[24] As well as Aquinas's understanding of the *res tantum* of the sacrament of the Eucharist, as we will see.

[25] Mazza, *The Celebration of the Eucharist*, trans. Matthew J. O'Connell (Collegeville, MN: Liturgical Press, 1999): 208.

Mazza envisions an emerging individualism because he does not grasp Aquinas's account of the Eucharist constituting the Church in and through our sacramental-sacrificial participation in Christ's sacrifice, in other words in and through our divinely given pedagogy in the practice of charity. For Aquinas, we share in Christ's sacrifice not individualistically, but in the communion of his mystical Body. Following Augustine, Aquinas states, "In the Sacrament of the Altar, two things are signified, viz. Christ's true body, and Christ's mystical body; as Augustine says (*Liber Sent. Prosper.*)."[26] The "mystical Body" is the continuing historical enactment of Christ's love – his cruciform communion – as manifested on the Cross at Calvary (his "true body"). By sharing in the sacrifice of his "true body," we are united to him in his "mystical Body" and live out in our own lives the cruciform communion with God and neighbor that the Holy Spirit makes possible.[27]

Christ's "true body" and his "mystical Body" are thus not divided in the sacramental signification. Rather, by the power of the Holy Spirit, the sacraments unite us with the holiness of Christ's passion (his "true body") and thus sanctify us as his mystical Body, sharing in his holiness through grace and the virtues and ultimately through the consummation of grace in heavenly glory. Sanctification comes about by sharing in Christ's passion as a member of his mystical Body. The sacraments, therefore, are not mere culturally constructed forms but rather are divinely appointed modes of union with Christ's "true body" in his "mystical Body." As such, the sacraments belong to Christ's personal communication of the effects of his sacrifice on the Cross by drawing us into communion in and with his sacrificial humanity.[28] Aquinas notes that "the sacraments of the Church derive their power specially from

---

[26] 3, q. 60, a. 3, *sed contra*. The *sed contra* derives not from Augustine but from Lanfranc, as Wayne Hankey has clarified in his "Reading Augustine through Dionysius: Aquinas's Correction of One Platonism by Another," forthcoming in Michael Dauphinais, Barry David, and Matthew Levering, eds., *Aquinas the Augustinian*.

[27] After noting the Augustinian roots of Aquinas's view, Gilles Emery, O.P. states:

> The effect proper to the Eucharist, as Thomas expresses it, is the transformation (*transformatio*) of man into Christ by love, the transmutation (*transmutatio*) of the one who eats into the food which is eaten, our *conversio* into Christ, a union or *adunatio* of man to Christ: in other words, incorporation into Christ. Such is the meaning of the *communio* or *synaxis*, which characterizes the Eucharist. (Emery, "The Ecclesial Fruit of the Eucharist," 47)

Agreeing with St John Damascene, Aquinas holds that we are transformed not only into a sharing in his humanity, but also his divinity. For the spirituality of graced *imitatio Christi* at work here, see Jean-Pierre Torrell, O.P., *St. Thomas Aquinas*, vol. 2: *Spiritual Master*, trans. Robert Royal (Washington, DC: Catholic University of America Press, 2003): 101–224.

[28] 3, q. 62, a. 6; cf. q. 64, a. 3.

Christ's Passion, the virtue [power] of which is in a manner united to us by our receiving the sacraments."[29] The power of causing grace flows from Christ's cruciform humanity because it is by the Cross that Christ frees us from sin, bestowing upon us cruciformity rather than pride and thereby renewing our communion of love.

When treating of the Eucharist as a sacrifice, Aquinas notes that the discussion has two aspects: "in the celebration of this mystery, we must take into consideration the representation of our Lord's Passion, and the participation of its fruits."[30] The "representation of our Lord's Passion" is the sacrifice, and the "participation of its fruits" is our communion in charity with Christ and each other. As the note of "participation" makes clear, charitable communion with God (and each other) in Christ through the Holy Spirit cannot be separated from Christ's sacrifice. It is our offering of Christ's sacrifice that enables, in the sacrament of the Eucharist, our sharing in its fruits of ecclesial unity and communion.

The Church's offering of Christ's sacrifice, her sharing in Christ's holy sacrificial act, culminates in her reception of, or communion in, the sacrifice. Arguing that the priest who consecrates the sacrament of the Eucharist must also receive the sacrament, Aquinas states, "Now whoever offers sacrifice must be a sharer in the sacrifice, because the outward sacrifice he offers is a sign of the inner sacrifice whereby he offers himself to God, as Augustine says (*De Civ. Dei* x)."[31] Indeed, Aquinas goes on to say that "it is by partaking of the sacrifice that he has a share in it, as the Apostle says (1 Cor. x. 18)."[32] When the Church sacramentally represents Christ's sacrifice, she receives what she has sacramentally represented. Our stature as "participators in His sacrifice"[33] is fully attained when "through the Eucharist we eat Christ."[34] In the celebration of the Eucharist we do not only represent Christ; by communing in the sacrificial meal, we are transformed into the Christic image that we have

---

[29] 3, q. 62, a. 6.

[30] 3, q. 83, a. 2.

[31] 3, q. 82, a. 4.

[32] Ibid.

[33] 3, q. 22, a. 3, ad 2.

[34] 3, q. 73, a. 5, ad 1. Alvin Kimel's "Eating Christ: Recovering the Language of Real Identification," *Pro Ecclesia* 13 (2004): 82–100 argues that Aquinas and many others posit an unfortunate dualism between the sacramental species and Christ's body and blood in the theology of the Eucharist, a dualism that contrasts with Berengar's forced confession (1059) that the body and blood of Jesus are chewed by the faithful. For similar views, see Gary Macy, *Treasures from the Storeroom: Medieval Religion and the Eucharist* (Collegeville, MN: Liturgical Press, 1999): 26f. and, from a moderately critical position, Enrico Mazza, *The Celebration of the Eucharist: The Origin of the Rite and the Development of Its Interpretation*, trans. Matthew J. O'Connell (Collegeville, MN: Liturgical Press, 1999): 202–4. Mazza states, "In Thomas's system there is no room for a corporeal presence of Christ in the Eucharist" (202) – a claim that is patently false unless "corporeal" for Mazza means that Christ must appear as over five feet tall and so forth.

taken on by our sacramental act of representation and become fully his mystical Body. Aquinas explains that "the Eucharist is the sacrament of Christ's Passion according as a man is made perfect in union with Christ who suffered."[35] Note that the union accomplished by the sacrament of the Eucharist is not simply with "Christ," but with "Christ who suffered." Our union with Christ is found in union with Christ's sacrifice.

The Eucharist thereby presses us forward in the imitation of Christ's love. Recalling John Damascene's comparison of the Eucharist to Isaiah's burning coal (Isa. 6) and Gregory the Great's observation that God's love is continually working great things, Aquinas argues that "through this sacrament, as far as its power is concerned, not only is the habit of grace and of virtue bestowed, but it is furthermore aroused to act, according to 2 Cor. v. 14: *The charity of Christ presseth us.*"[36] In the sacrament of the Eucharist, we are conformed to Christ both externally, through sacramental representation, and internally, through charity aroused to act – active self-giving love.[37] This active self-giving love, restoring the relationship of justice between humankind and God, makes Christ's sacrificial death pleasing before God. As Aquinas notes, Christ's "voluntary enduring of the Passion was most acceptable to God, as coming from charity."[38]

But perhaps the charity that marks Christ's body (his "true body" and his "mystical Body") is above all a sharing not in a sacrifice but in "resurrection life"?[39] Has not Aquinas's focus on the Cross caused him to bind the sacramental sharing of "resurrection life" too strictly to the sacraments of the Church that communicate the effects of the *Cross*? Indeed, this concern is recorded by Aquinas himself as the third objection in his article devoted to the question of whether the power of the sacraments comes from Christ's Passion. In answer, Aquinas notes that far from neglecting the salvific power of Christ's Resurrection, he is simply affirming that there is no "resurrection life" without the Cross. Aquinas states, "Justification is ascribed to the Resurrection by reason of the term *whither*, which is newness of life through grace. But it is ascribed to the Passion by reason of the term *whence*, i.e. in regard to the forgiveness of sin."[40] "Resurrection life," the life of charity, is made possible because of the charity of Christ's Cross, and indeed the (cruciform) self-giving of the Cross characterizes the historical enactment of "resurrection life."

---

[35] 3, q. 73, a. 3, ad 3.
[36] 3, q. 79, a. 1, ad 2.
[37] See also 3, q. 79, a. 4, and numerous similar texts.
[38] 3, q. 48, a. 3.
[39] As Edward Schillebeeckx, Joseph Martos and others argue.
[40] Ibid., ad 3.

Aquinas consistently depicts the Eucharist, therefore, in terms of the sacrifice and communion of persons that characterize the charity of both Christ's "true body" and his "mystical Body," the Church. In cruciform charity, nourished by its offering of Christ's sacrifice in the sacrifice of the Eucharist, the Church manifests Christ's body in the history of the world. Quoting Pseudo-Dionysius's statement that the Eucharist is "the end and consummation of all the sacraments," Aquinas notes that "the Eucharist belongs to the Divine worship, for the Divine worship consists principally therein, so far as it is the sacrifice of the Church."[41] The purpose of all the sacraments is that human beings be "incorporated with Christ."[42] Sharing in Christ's sacrifice by means of the sacrament of the Eucharist – the sacrifice of the Church, in which the Church sacramentally offers up Christ's sacrificial body and blood and thereby partakes in Christ's cruciform charity – conduces to the formation of a visible communion of believers incorporated into Christ.

Why would a mere invisible communion of believers in charity not suffice? Once Christ has offered his life for sins, it seems that there would be no need for a visible offering. Aquinas explains that without the visible sacramental sign the Church would be hard pressed to sustain the communion of persons in charity:

> man is prone to direct his activity chiefly toward material things. Lest, therefore, it should be too hard for man to be drawn away entirely from bodily actions, bodily exercise was offered to him in the sacraments, by which he might be trained to avoid superstitious practices, consisting in the worship of demons, and all manner of harmful action, consisting in sinful deeds.[43]

The activity of offering and participating in the sacrifice of the Eucharist, on this wonderfully practical view, meets the human need for charity to be embodied.[44] Without such embodied practices, "religion" would lose its concreteness and its adherents would drift inevitably, due to sin, into idolatrous practices. Right worship shapes all aspects of our lives. Indeed, Augustine (quoted by Aquinas) denies that human beings can sustain unity in a religion (*nomen religionis*), whether true or false,

---

[41] 3, q. 63, a. 6. The quotation is from Pseudo-Dionysius's *The Ecclesiastical Hierarchy*, ch. 3.

[42] 3, q. 62, a. 1.

[43] 3, q. 61, a. 1. See also Liam G. Walsh, O.P., "The Divine and the Human in St. Thomas's Theology of Sacraments," in *Ordo sapientiae et amoris*, ed. C.-J. Pinto de Oliveira, O.P. (Fribourg: Éditions universitaires, 1993): 321–52.

[44] Gilles Emery points out that Aquinas does not conceive of the Eucharist's ecclesial effect as divided from the Eucharist's effect in procuring charity. The two are the same effect. Emery goes on to note that this unity (ecclesial and personal) is particularly well articulated by Cajetan. See Emery, "The Ecclesial Fruit of the Eucharist," 49.

without such visible signs or sacraments, which are unitive simply at the level of communal actions.[45] Although Christ's Cross accomplishes human salvation, believers, in God's wise plan, participate in this salvation through sacramentally sharing in Christ's Cross, and thereby constitute a visible community of embodied cruciform charity.

Rather than separate the Eucharist from the other sacraments, Aquinas speaks of the seven sacraments as a sacramental organism, similar to the life of the body. Here he compares the Eucharist to the food that nourishes and strengthens the body, with the difference that the Eucharist nourishes and strengthens the body unto *eternal* life (cf. John 6) or "final perfection."[46] Eternal life is the fullness of our sharing in Christ's life, and the Eucharist, as the greatest sacrament, nourishes and strengthens this in three ways. First, the Eucharist "contains Christ Himself substantially."[47] By consuming Christ's body and blood offered in sacrifice, we share in his resurrected life. Second, the whole sacramental organism, as we have already noted, is ordered to the Eucharist as its consummation. Aquinas explains,

> For it is manifest that the sacrament of Order is ordained to the consecration of the Eucharist: and the sacrament of Baptism to the reception of the Eucharist: while a man is perfected by Confirmation, so as not to fear to abstain from this sacrament. By Penance and Extreme Unction man is prepared to receive the Body of Christ worthily. And Matrimony, at least in its signification, touches this sacrament; in so far as it signifies the union of Christ with the Church, of which union the Eucharist is a figure: hence the Apostle says (Eph. v. 32): *This is a great sacrament: but I speak in Christ and in the Church.*[48]

Each sacrament of the Church prepares for and points to our full sharing in Christ, which occurs in the sacrament of the Eucharist. The Eucharist thus shares Christ's "true body" in a way that constitutes fully his "mystical Body." As a third reason for the preeminence of the Eucharist, Aquinas mentions that most of the other sacraments terminate in the celebration of the Eucharist, as, for example, a Catholic wedding ends with the Eucharist. In the Eucharist, in short, the sacramental organism that is the Church takes on its true form, configured

---

[45] 3, q. 61, a. 1, *sed contra.*
[46] 3, q. 65, a. 1; q. 65, a. 2. For further discussion of this important theme, with its eschatological implications, see Martin Morard, "L'eucharistie, clé de voûte de l'organisme sacramental chez saint Thomas d'Aquin", *Revue Thomiste* 95 (1995): 217–50.
[47] 3, q. 65, a. 3.
[48] Ibid.

to Christ's crucified and risen "true body." The whole sacramental organism – that is to say, the whole Church – enacts in history a fundamentally cruciform (Eucharistic) communion.

Aquinas thus notes that the Eucharist, as one sacrament, efficaciously signifies the unity of the Church, a unity with the one saving God, who comes to us in the one Messiah: "The Apostle says (1 Cor. x. 17): *For we, being many, are one bread, one body, all that partake of one bread*: from which it is clear that the Eucharist is the sacrament of the Church's unity."[49] The unity or communion with God and neighbor of the Church is achieved through the "spiritual food and spiritual drink" or "spiritual refreshment" of the Eucharist.[50] Aquinas quotes John 6:55: "For my flesh is food indeed, and my blood is drink indeed."[51] The Eucharist is thus the sacrament of the Church's unity because it is a participation in Christ's sacrifice: true communion is found in sacrificial self-giving.[52]

Is this communion possible without actually consuming the sacrament? Yes, because by faith (in the case of infants and the mentally handicapped, the Church's faith) and baptism, and even simply by faith, believers are united to Christ's mystical Body. What, then, about Jesus' statement in the Gospel of John, cited by Aquinas in an objection, "Except you eat the flesh of the Son of Man, and drink his blood, you shall not have life in you"?[53] Given the need to distinguish between the visible sign, the sacrament in its integral fullness, and the sacrament's effects, Aquinas draws a distinction between the *sacramentum tantum* or "sacramental sign alone" (the bread and wine), the *res et sacramentum* or the "sacramental sign containing and causing what it signifies" (Christ's true body), and the *res tantum* or "sacramental grace alone" (the grace of unity, the mystical Body, the bond of charity).[54] For the sacrament of the Eucharist, as Aquinas states, the *res tantum* or "the reality of the sacrament" is "the unity of the mystical body, without which there can

---

[49] 3, q. 73, a. 2, *sed contra*.

[50] 3, q. 73, a. 2.

[51] Ibid.

[52] See Michael J. Gorman, *Cruciformity: Paul's Narrative Spirituality of the Cross* (Grand Rapids, MI: Eerdmans, 2001). See also the biblical and patristic analysis in Tillard's *Flesh of the Church, Flesh of Christ: At the Source of the Ecclesiology of Communion*, trans. Madeleine Beaumont (Collegeville, MN: Liturgical Press, 2001). Tillard concludes that "the Christian sacrifice . . . is precisely where this living flesh of mutual love and communion is restored" (138).

[53] 3, q. 73, a. 3, obj. 1. See Tillard, "Le 'votum Eucharistiae': L'Eucharistie dans la rencontre des chrétiens," in *Miscellanea Liturgica in onore di S. E. il Cardinale Giacomo Lercaro*, vol. 2 (Paris: Desclée, 1967): 143–94.

[54] See 3, q. 73, a. 6. On the relationship of the *res* – the indissoluble union of Christ and his Church – with Aquinas's understanding of the sacrament of marriage, and thus with the nuptial imagery of Scripture, see Martin Morard, "L'eucharistie, clé de voûte de l'organisme sacramentel chez saint Thomas d'Aquin," *Revue Thomiste* 95 (1995): 230f.

be no salvation."[55] This "reality of the sacrament," the Mystical Body itself, can be received through spiritual desire. Aquinas affirms that through baptism one already, by spiritual desire, receives a share in the "reality of the sacrament," even if one is never able to consume the sacrament.[56]

Aquinas points out that in this way spiritual food – the Eucharist – differs from material food. Unlike material food, which is consumed and changed into oneself, "spiritual food changes man into itself, according to that saying of Augustine (*Conf.* vii), that he heard the voice of Christ as it were saying to him: *Nor shalt thou change Me into thyself, as food of thy flesh, but thou shalt be changed into Me.* But one can be changed into Christ, and be incorporated in Him by mental desire, even without receiving this sacrament."[57] Aquinas also emphasizes that the Eucharist perfects the person's configuration to Christ, as "the sacrament of Charity, which is *the bond of perfection* (Col. iii. 14)."[58] Baptism incorporates a person into Christ and thereby initiates the movement of configuration to Christ, whereas the Eucharist, "the consummation of the spiritual life, and the end of all the sacraments," fully brings about what baptism initiates.[59] This radical communion is what it means to be "made perfect in union with Christ Who suffered."[60]

Aquinas thus recognizes that it is Christ's sacrificial fulfillment and transformation of Israel's *korbanot* that mediate graced communion with God and with neighbor. The communion with God and neighbor in charity that is the "mystical Body," initiated by baptism and consummated in the Eucharist, requires that we actually "be changed into Christ" and be "made perfect in union with Christ Who suffered." This is a radical requirement. To be changed into Christ, and not simply Christ in his resurrected life but *Christ crucified*, involves a profound work of conversion from the idolatrous practices and sinful acts about which

---

[55] 3, q. 73, a. 3. Thus, as Joseph Wawrykow remarks, "A rich ecclesiology underlies III 73–83 and renders possible the analysis of the eucharist" (Wawrykow, "Luther and the Spirituality of Thomas Aquinas," Consensus 19 [1993]: 92). See also Frederick Christian Bauerschmidt, " 'That the Faithful Become the Temple of God': The Church Militant in Aquinas's Commentary on John," in *Reading John with St. Thomas Aquinas*, ed. Michael Dauphinais and Matthew Levering (Washington, DC: Catholic University of America Press, forthcoming).

[56] 3, q. 73, a. 3 and ad 1. Pierre-Marie Gy, O.P. points out that the citation of Augustine in ad 1 (regarding John 6:54) results from a misattribution to Augustine of a text from Fulgentius. See Gy, "Avancées du traité de l'eucharistie de S. Thomas dans la *Somme* par rapport aux *Sentences*," *Revue des sciences philosophiques et théologiques* 77 (1993): 219–28, at 221.

[57] 3, q. 73, a. 3, ad 2.

[58] Ibid., ad 3.

[59] 3, q. 73, a. 3. See also Nicholas Cabasilas, *The Life in Christ*, trans. Carmino J. deCatanzaro (Crestwood, NY: St Vladimir's Seminary Press, 1998): Book IV, pp. 125–6.

[60] Ibid., ad 3. See also Wawrykow's discussion of this point in "Luther and the Spirituality of Thomas Aquinas," 93–4.

Aquinas warns in article 1 of question 61. The Eucharist teaches us, by transforming us, how to worship God in a cruciform communion. Just as Christ is God's gift of salvation to us, so also we receive this communion in cruciformity as God's gift. It is the Eucharist that brings about in us the extraordinary conversion of cruciformity, even if God can stimulate this desire – ultimately *for the Eucharist* – in those who cannot bodily receive the sacrament in which Christ gives himself to us.

The radical gift-character of the Eucharist becomes clear only in light of the election of Israel and her corresponding sacrificial desire for communion with God. Aquinas's discussion of the sacrament of the Eucharist in question 73 culminates with an examination of the Old Testament "figures" of the sacrament of the Eucharist. Among these "figures," or signs of Israel's Abrahamic sacrificial desire for perfect communion with God, Aquinas includes Melchizedek's priestly offering of bread and wine (cf. Heb. 5:6); the priestly sacrifices of the Old Law, especially those of Yom Kippur, the Day of Atonement (cf. Heb. 9); the manna by which God nourished Israel in the desert (cf. John 6); and the Paschal lamb of the Exodus and the feast of Passover.[61] Each of these "figures" of sacrificial communion Aquinas finds significant for the Eucharist. Melchizedek's priestly offering signifies the *sacramentum tantum*, the bread and wine of the Eucharistic offering. The priestly sacrifices, especially Yom Kippur's "sacrifice of expiation," signify the *res et sacramentum*, Christ crucified. The manna, which refreshed the Israelites in the desert and strengthened them in their passage into the promised land of dwelling with God (union), signifies the *res tantum*, the spiritual effect of the sacrament, which "refreshes the soul in all respects."[62]

The greatest figure, however, is the Paschal lamb. The Paschal lamb prefigures the Eucharist in all three ways. Having quoted 1 Corinthians 5:7–8, "Christ our Pasch is sacrificed; therefore let us feast . . . with the unleavened bread of sincerity and truth," Aquinas explains how the Paschal lamb represents the sacrament of the Eucharist understood as *sacramentum tantum*, *sacramentum et res*, and *res tantum*:

> First of all, because it was eaten with unleavened loaves, according to Exod. xii. 8: *They shall eat flesh . . . and unleavened bread*. As to the second, because it was immolated by the entire multitude of the children of Israel on the fourteenth day of the moon; and this was a figure of the Passion of Christ, Who is called the Lamb on account of His innocence. As to the effect, because by the blood of the Paschal Lamb the

---

[61] 3, q. 73, a. 6. See Denis Chardonnens, O.C.D., "Éternité du sacerdoce du Christ et effet eschatologique de l'eucharistie," *Revue Thomiste* 99 (1999): 159–80.
[62] Ibid.

children of Israel were preserved from the destroying Angel,
and brought from the Egyptian captivity.[63]

Once these figures of sacrificial communion, belonging to the heart of
Israel's election, are understood, then one can see how Christ, the
Messiah of Israel, fulfills the desire of Israel by means of the sacrificial
communion that he enacts upon the Cross. When we come to share
in the divinely given desire of Israel by means of our sharing
Eucharistically in Christ's Cross, we become members of God's people,
the mystical Body of Israel's Messiah. We are preserved from death, freed
from slavery, and brought into the dwelling place of God through the
blood of the One who, through his holy sacrifice of himself out of
perfect charity, restores the path of sacrificial love (lost by human pride
and selfish love) that configures and unites humankind to the to the God
who is self-giving love.

Keeping in mind Israel as a sacrificial people, we can understand the
names given to the Eucharist. Aquinas emphasizes three: "sacrifice,"
"communion," and "Eucharist," which correspond to the past, present,
and future as *united* in the sacrament of the Eucharist.[64] As "sacrifice,"
the sacrament of the Eucharist unites us to the salvific past, "inasmuch
as it is commemorative of our Lord's Passion, which was a true
sacrifice."[65] As "communion," the Eucharist makes the Church.
Aquinas states, "With regard to the present it [the sacrament of the
Eucharist] has another meaning, namely, that of Ecclesiastical unity,
in which men are aggregated *through the Sacrament.*"[66] He draws
together "communion" and "sacrifice" through a quotation from St John
Damascene, who emphasizes that "communication" in the Church comes
about through sharing in Christ's sacrificial flesh:

> For Damascene says (*De Fide Orthod.* iv) that *it is called
> Communion because we communicate with Christ through it,
> both because we partake of His flesh and Godhead, and
> because we communicate with and are united to one another
> through it.*

We learn to "communicate" when we become cruciform.

The name "Eucharist," Aquinas suggests, displays the future aspect
because of its meaning of "good grace" or grateful thanksgiving. The

---

[63] Ibid.
[64] See Robert Sokolowski, *Eucharistic Presence* (Washington, DC: Catholic University of America Press, 1993): 103. One finds in Aquinas's approach affinities with Sokolowski's description of "theology of disclosure."
[65] 3, q. 73, a. 4.
[66] Ibid., emphasis added.

sacrament of the Eucharist "foreshadows the Divine fruition, which shall come to pass in heaven," and so the name "Eucharist" – like the names "Viaticum" and "Assumption" (deification), which Aquinas also mentions here – reflects this future grace, "because *the grace of God is life everlasting* (Rom. vi. 23); or because it [the sacrament] really contains Christ, Who is *full of grace.*"[67] The mystical Body's cruciform communion, the fruit of the grace of the Holy Spirit uniting us to Christ crucified and risen, draws believers into the incarnate Son's eternal life of self-giving love and wisdom, in other words accomplishes the great Exodus.

For Aquinas, this reality of a cruciform communion in Christ that draws believers into eternal (resurrection) life explains the institution of the sacrament at the Last Supper. Christ chose this time because "last words, chiefly such as are spoken by departing friends, are committed most deeply to memory; since then especially affection for friends is more enkindled, and the things which affect us most are impressed the deepest on the soul."[68] Because Christ left his disciples the mystery of the perfect sacrifice – here Aquinas quotes Augustine and Pope Alexander I – Christ impressed this upon them during his final hours, in order to deepen their communion with him. Similarly, Christ instituted the sacrament at that time so that his communion with his disciples would not come to an end, but would continue under the sacramental species. This communion would be a sacrificial one in accord with the sacrificial mode of our salvation: "without faith in the Passion there could never be any salvation, according to Rom. iii. 25: *Whom God hath proposed to be a propitiation, through faith in His blood.* It was necessary accordingly that there should be at all times among men something to show forth our Lord's Passion."[69] Just as the Passover, with its sacrifice of the Paschal lamb, was a sacrament that prefigured Christ to come, so likewise once Christ has come, it is fitting that he institute a new sacrament that manifests and contains his salvific sacrifice. In our sacrificial communion in this sacrament as his friends, filled with charity for him and for those for whom he has died, we offer true worship that nourishes the bonds of love.

3 CONCLUSION

In Aquinas's theology, the insights of St Paul and St John – insights which express the fulfillment of Israel's desire – regarding "cruciform communion" find systematic theological expression. Aquinas exposes the Eucharist as the true sacrament of charity, which communicates Christ's

---

[67] Ibid.
[68] 3, q. 73, a. 5.
[69] Ibid.

sacrifice to us and thereby establishes our communication, or communion, with God and neighbor as Christ's mystical Body, marked by the communication of self-giving, cruciform love. By the sacrament of the Eucharist, which signifies and is his "true body" and which signifies his "mystical Body," Christ gives us his "true body" that makes us into his "mystical Body," by the power of his Spirit.

Without narrowing Eucharistic consummation to those who are able to consume the sacrament visibly, Aquinas insists that Christ, through the Eucharistic manifestation of his sacrificial love, continues to instruct us in the radical practices of cruciformity, Christic love. Such practices both continue the work of healing our brokenness – thus enabling us not to despair in the efficaciousness of the Eucharist – and remind us that charity, as founded upon divine gift, comes about through historically particular communion. Recall how for Novak the seder table became a pedagogy in God's love. In a similar way, the particularity of the ecclesially mediated sacrament of the Eucharist, a participation in the sacrificial Cross of Jesus of Nazareth, shapes us by divine gift in the cruciform "love" expressed through the vast array of human relationships and experiences. We are nourished spiritually so that, no longer cleaving to the idolatrous and sinful practices of our own construction, we are changed into what we eat and sacrificially cleave to God. In the particularity of the Messiah of Israel, we find the (sacrificial) healing from sin and the corresponding glorious communion with God and neighbor for which Israel longed.

Christ's radical invitation to us to share in his sacrifice hinges upon the extraordinary gift of his sacramental bodiliness in the Eucharist. What this statement – which belongs to the truth that our communion is to be a communion in and through Christ's sacrifice – means must now be investigated.

4

Transubstantiation

The importance of the "olive tree" of Israel for Christian theology should not obscure the differences between Jewish and Christian understandings; rather, in light of the centrality and irreducibility of Israel in Christian theology, the differences take on their proper theological value. Awareness of the differences provides insight into why the Christian tradition teaches as it does. A case in point is the doctrine of transubstantiation. This doctrine, far from being an unwarranted importation of (even radically transposed) Aristotelian metaphysics,[1] in fact bears significantly upon the dialogue between Christians and Jews. It does so because it clarifies how Christians are inserted into Christ's sacrifice.

That this is an issue for Jewish thinkers, as well as Christian ones, becomes clear in the great thirteenth-century compendium of Jewish-Christian polemic, the *Nizzahon Vetus*. There, Jewish thinkers press upon their Christian counterparts two related sets of questions. First, after quoting the institution narrative in Mark 14:22, the *Nizzahon Vetus* challenges the intelligibility of Jesus' words:

---

[1] Michael Dummett does away with the "metaphysical baggage" (241), without much effort to rummage through it, of substance-accidents in his account from an analytic perspective of transubstantiation: Dummett, "The Intelligibility of Eucharistic Doctrine," in *The Rationality of Religious Belief: Essays in Honor of Basil Mitchell*, ed. William J. Abraham and Steven W. Holzer (Oxford: Clarendon Press, 1987): 231–61. In discussing Aquinas's theology of the Eucharist, P.J. FitzPatrick tends not to grasp Aquinas's perspective, in part due to the differences between his analytic framework and Aquinas's metaphysical theology. See P.J. FitzPatrick, *In Breaking of Bread: The Eucharist and Ritual* (Cambridge: Cambridge University Press, 1993). For a sympathetic reading of transubstantiation, see G.E.M. Anscombe, "On Transubstantiation," in *Ethics, Religion and Politics*, vol. 3 of *The Collected Philosophical Papers of G.E.M. Anscombe* (Oxford: Blackwell, 1981): 107–12. Fergus Kerr has commented on the Wittgensteinian aspects of Anscombe's account: see Kerr, "Transubstantiation after Wittgenstein," in *Catholicism and Catholicity: Eucharistic Communities in Historical and Contemporary Perspectives*, ed. Sarah Beckwith (Oxford: Blackwell, 1999): 3–18.

In what sense was it his body that they ate and drank? Did he cut a piece off his body which he gave to them, or did his body first become bread and wine and he gave them pieces of it? Moreover, where did that body which they ate and drank descend? Did it go on its way separately or was it mixed up in the stomach with all the other food?[2]

This set of questions makes clear that Christians will have to account for the claim that Jesus, at the Last Supper, could give his "body." Is his "body" cut to pieces, or is his "body" transformed into bread and wine?

The second set of questions has to do with the issue of sacrifice. Having noted that Christians claim to offer sacrifice in the mass, the *Nizzahon Vetus* draws upon Deuteronomy and the Psalms to remark: "Respond by pointing out that sacrifices and burnt offerings should not be brought here but only in Jerusalem."[3] As long as Jerusalem "is destroyed and we are not in it," sacrifices should not, in accordance with God's revealed word, be brought.[4] Those who do continue to offer any sacrifices other than spiritual ones are disobeying God's teaching. Moreover, in daring to offer sacrifice during the time of Jerusalem's "destruction," Christians have ignored the clear words of the prophets – e.g. Isaiah 60:7 and Malachi 3:1–4 – that explicitly foretell a time when the Temple will be rebuilt in Jerusalem and animal sacrifice renewed there. In other words, even assuming for the sake of argument that Christians truly offer Christ's body and blood in sacrifice, the question remains as to whether such a sacrifice could be acceptable, since the Church's sacrifice, it would seem, is offered outside Jerusalem and presumptuously acts without waiting for the fulfillment of the prophecies about the restoration of Jerusalem and her Temple. Christians are thus called to explain the relationship of their sacrifice to the sacrifices in the Temple in Jerusalem.

The Jewish contributors to the *Nizzahon Vetus* thus move straight to the issues that the doctrine of transubstantiation seeks to address. By means of the doctrine of transubstantiation, Christian respondents can account for the facts that his Eucharistic body can be present at many places, is not segmented into parts, is not related by "transformation" to the bread and wine, and does not remain present through the process of digestion – all of which facts, if not properly explained, would derail Christian claims about the Eucharist. Even more importantly, the

---

[2] *The Jewish-Christian Debate in the High Middle Ages: A Critical Edition of the Nizzahon Vetus*, translation and commentary by David Berger (Northvale, NJ: Jason Aronson, 1996): 185.

[3] Ibid., 207.

[4] Ibid., 207–8.

doctrine of transubstantiation enables Christians to affirm the radical insertion of believers into Christ's sacrifice. By insisting upon the sacramental bodiliness of Christ's sacrificial presence in the Eucharist, the doctrine of transubstantiation upholds the absolute unity of the sacrifice. This sacrifice, precisely because of its historical character in Israel and thus its intelligible (even if disputed) claim to fulfill the Temple sacrifices, can be offered on altars outside Jerusalem without displacing the role of Jerusalem, and can embody the renewal of Israel's worship foretold by the prophets without displacing the role of sacrifice – although all is of course transformed in Christ.

I have suggested in the previous two chapters that the Eucharist makes the Church because the Eucharist's sacramental constitution provides for humankind's embodied sharing in Christ's own sacrifice, in Christ's holy fulfillment of Israel's Torah and Temple. In offering up Christ's sacrifice in the sacrament of the Eucharist, we fulfill in and with him all justice and become God's holy Temple. As Charles Journet, investigating the "why" of transubstantiation, has observed, God wills "to invite all men to a *visible and cultural* participation in the sacrifice of the Cross, a participation in no way destined to dismiss faith or love, but rather to draw their unitive capabilities to the highest degrees."[5] Journet goes on to say: " 'The Lord's Banquet,' yes, but one calculated to immerse us actively in 'the Lord's Sacrifice.'"[6] This active immersion becomes intelligible once one grasps the radical conversion, not transformation, of the elements of bread and wine.[7] Aquinas's conversion theory sustains our sacramental-sacrificial participation, or immersion, in Christ's sacrifice, and thereby makes possible a response to the combined sets of questions proposed in the *Nizzahon Vetus*.

In order to identify the central marks of Aquinas's conversion theory, I will explore Aquinas's approach in light of an important alternative posed by the early twentieth-century Russian Orthodox theologian Sergius Bulgakov and further developed by Alexander Schmemann. This alternative to transubstantiation has become increasingly influential as other theories such as transignification, debunked by Jean-Luc Marion and others, wane.[8] After presenting the alternative posed by

---

[5] Charles Journet, "Transubstantiation," *The Thomist* 38 (1974): 734–46, at 735.
[6] Ibid., 736.
[7] Stephen L. Brock, "St. Thomas and Eucharistic Conversion," *The Thomist* 65 (2001): 529–65. I am indebted to Brock's luminous presentation, written as a response to concerns posed by Germain Grisez in "An Alternative Theology of Jesus' Substantial Presence in the Eucharist," *Irish Theological Quarterly* 65 (2000): 111–31.
[8] In presenting a devastating critique of theories of transignification (Schillebeeckx et al.) as constituting an idolatry of the community's self-consciousness (Marion, *God without Being*, trans. Thomas A. Carlson [Chicago: University of Chicago Press, 1991]: 165f.), Jean Luc-Marion has drawn attention to Hegel, who "saw precisely in this eucharistic consciousness without real mediation the great superiority of Lutheranism over

Bulgakov and Schmemann, I will turn to Aquinas's account of transubstantiation in the *Summa Theologiae*. I will attempt to show that Aquinas's conversion-theory of the Eucharistic change addresses Orthodox concerns about sacramental bodiliness. In so doing, it offers a framework from which to respond to the key difficulties that the

---

Catholicism" (169). Quoting Hegel's *Encyclopaedia* (sec. 552), and citing as well Hegel's *Philosophy of History, Philosophy of Religion,* and *History of Philosophy* in order to demonstrate the importance of the theme, Marion remarks,

> Hence nothing better than his [Hegel's] reproach can allow us to understand, *a contrario,* how real presence (guaranteed by a thing independent of consciousness) alone avoids the highest idolatry: "And yet in Catholicism this spirit of all truth [that is to say, God] is in actuality set in rigid opposition to the self-conscious spirit. And, first of all, God is in the 'host' presented to religious adoration as an *external thing.* (In the Lutheran Church, on the contrary, the host as such is not at first consecrated, but in the moment *of enjoyment,* i.e. in the annihilation of its externality, and in the act of *faith,* i.e. in the free self-certain spirit: only then is it consecrated and exalted to be present God.)'" What the consecrated host imposes, or rather permits, is the irreducible exteriority of the present that Christ makes us of himself in this thing that to him becomes sacramental body. That this exteriority, far from forbidding intimacy, renders it possible in sparing it from foundering in idolatry, can be misunderstood only by those who do not want to open themselves to *distance.* Only distance, in maintaining a distinct separation of terms (of persons), renders communion possible, and immediately mediates the relation. Here again, between the idol and distance, one must choose. (169; cf. 176–7)

In describing this "highest idolatry," Marion marvelously grasps the link between Hegel and Schillebeeckx; cf. Robert Barron, "The Liturgy as Display of God's Justice," *Antiphon* 4 (1999): 19–24, at 23. Schillebeeckx reads transubstantiation as fatally "physicalist" (Aristotelian substance/accident) rather than attentive to the anthropological and interpersonal dimensions of the sign. See Edward Schillebeeckx, O.P., *The Eucharist,* trans. N.D. Smith (New York: Sheed and Ward, 1968 [1967 Dutch edition]): 98–9. As the evangelical theologian, Alister McGrath, has insightfully (and approvingly) remarked,

> There is, for Schillebeeckx, no need to invoke the notion of a physical change of substance of the bread and wine. Christ's intention was not to alter the metaphysics of the bread and wine, but to ensure that these pointed to his continuing presence within the church, as the community of the faithful . . . The parallels with Zwingli's position, though not noted by Schillebeeckx himself, can hardly be overlooked. (McGrath, *The Reenchantment of Nature* [New York: Doubleday, 2002]: 146)

For criticism of "transignification" as found in the sacramental theologies of Louis-Marie Chauvet and John Macquarrie, see Laurence Paul Hemming, "After Heidegger: Transubstantiation," *Heythrop Journal* 41 (2000): 170–86, at 176. See also on this topic Joseph Ratzinger, "Das Problem der Transsubstantiation und die Frage nach dem Sinn der Eucharistie," *Theologische Quartalschrift* 147 (1967): 129–58, as well as Horst Seidl's survey of German scholarship, including Ratzinger's article, in "Zum Substanzbegriff der katholischen Transubstantiationslehre: Erkenntnistheoretische und metaphysische Erörterungen," *Forum Katholische Theologie* 11 (1995): 1–16.

Nizzahon Vetus brings to light regarding what is offered in the Eucharistic sacrifice and whether it is offered properly.

1 THE RUSSIAN ORTHODOX CRITIQUE

I will begin by outlining Bulgakov's position on the Eucharistic change, which he terms "transmutation." Bulgakov rejects any distinction in Eucharistic theology between "substance" and "accidents."[9] The whole bread and wine are "transmuted." He explains:

> It is, however, precisely the bread and wine that are transmuted, that is, not the qualityless, abstract matter of this world ("earth"), which does not even exist, but a specific type of this matter, with qualities, namely bread and wine, which, as materials of this world, do not change but now belong not to themselves and not to this world but to Christ's glorified, spiritual body.[10]

As materials of the world, the bread and wine remain, after the transmutation, simply what they were: bread and wine. Now, however, they are not merely materials of this world. In the transmutation, Christ, by means of his glorified body's absolute power over material things, makes the bread and wine his body and blood.[11]

---

[9] Sergius Bulgakov, *The Holy Grail and the Eucharist*, trans. Boris Jakim (Hudson, NY: Lindisfarne Books, 1997): 109. For the Hegelian influence upon Bulgakov's theology, see Boris Jakim's introductions to *The Holy Grail and the Eucharist* and *The Bride of the Lamb* as well as Paul Valliere, *Modern Russian Theology: Bukharev, Soloviev, Bulgakov: Orthodox Theology in a New Key* (Grand Rapids, MI: Eerdmans, 2000).

[10] Bulgakov, *The Holy Grail and the Eucharist*, 109. See also the discussion in David Bentley Hart, "'Thine Own of Thine Own': Eucharistic Sacrifice in Orthodox Tradition," in *Rediscovering the Eucharist: Ecumenical Conversations*, ed. Roch Kereszty, O. Cist. (New York: Paulist, 2003): 150–3. Citing John Meyendorff's *Byzantine Theology* (New York: Fordham University Press, 1974): 204–5, Hart defends a doctrine of consubstantiation: "John Meyendorff is simply conventionally Byzantine when he asserts the importance of the fact that the *prosphora* and *antidoron* consumed during and after the Divine Liturgy is true, consubstantial bread, rather than ethereal (and nutriently vapid) azymes . . ." (151). Hart reviews the history of Byzantine acceptance of the doctrine of transubstantiation during the fifteenth to eighteenth centuries, and then treats Bulgakov's criticism of transubstantiation, while noting that "whether Bulgakov has quite done justice to the theology of transubstantiation is debatable" (153).

[11] For diametrically opposed reasons, Terence Nichols and Alvin Kimel adopt Bulgakov's understanding of Christ's glorified body as taking on the "divine relationship to creation" so that the world is "one place" for Christ's glorified humanity (Kimel, 96). See Nichols, "Transubstantiation and Eucharistic Presence," *Pro Ecclesia* 11 (2002): 57–75, especially 74 and Kimel, "Eating Christ: Recovering the Language of Real Identification," *Pro Ecclesia* 13 (2004): 82–100. Bulgakov's concept of Christ's glorified "body" does away with any concept of material bodily specificity. See also, for perspectives that flow from Luther's notion of "ubiquity," Robert Jenson's "The Sacraments," in *The Christian Dogmatics*,

Attention to Bulgakov's theological anthropology is required here. For Bulgakov, Christ's glorified body is identical to his earthly body, and yet takes on, as indicated by the Ascension, a different relation to the material cosmos. Prior to the Ascension, Christ's body belonged to the world (although Bulgakov's sophiological doctrine is quite complicated as regards the status of bodies in this world[12]); after the Ascension, Christ's body is "supramundane, metacosmic."[13] Bulgakov states:

> The ascended body of the Lord, glorified and spiritual, is, in itself, free, of course, from the "earth," from the matter of this world, but it retains the power to manifest itself through the matter of this world, and it thereby becomes the body and blood of the Lord.[14]

Christ's glorified body is still a "body" in the sense that all material things are created to manifest spirit. Christ's body is "metacosmic," therefore, because his spirit can manifest itself in any matter and thereby unite such matter with his glorified "body," making the matter to *be* his glorified body. The bread and wine manifest and are the glorified Lord. In terms of this world, the bread and wine are not changed; but in terms of the heavenly realm they are deified. As Bulgakov affirms:

> Things that belong to different realms of being can only be *transmuted* the one into the other, while preserving their own mode of being in their *own* realm. The body of Christ, being manifested in the bread and wine, does not cease being a spiritual body, abiding above this world.[15]

---

ed. Carl E. Braaten and Robert W. Jenson, vol. 2 (Philadelphia, PA: Fortress Press, 1984): 359–60; Allen G. Jorgenson, "Luther on Ubiquity and a Theology of the Public," *International Journal of Systematic Theology* 6 (2004): 351–68. Jorgenson notes that "ubiquity" is more "aesthetics" than "metaphysics," and I would agree that rather than attempt metaphysical explanation of "ubiquity," one would do better to give up the attempt to explain how Christ's presence in the Eucharist could be a bodily presence in this world.

[12] Bulgakov writes, "The Lord, in receiving human flesh, unites His Divine corporeality, Sophia, Glory, with human creaturely corporeality" (*The Holy Grail and the Eucharist*, 131). For Bulgakov's ecclesiology, which posits on the basis of the theory of "divine-humanity" an essential (prophetic and royal) "Church" *prior to* the visibly hierarchical Church, see *The Bride of the Lamb*, trans. Boris Jakim (Grand Rapids, MI: Eerdmans, 2002): especially 292–4. The Eucharist constitutes the "fount" of "divine-humanity." For an effort to present an ecclesiology that addresses the relationship of "Spirit and institution" without dislodging one from the other in sophiological fashion, see Hans Urs von Balthasar's "Spirit and Institution" in *Explorations in Theology*, vol. 4: *Spirit and Institution*, trans. Edward T. Oakes, S.J. (San Francisco: Ignatius Press, 1995 [1974]): 209–43.

[13] Bulgakov, *The Holy Grail and the Eucharist*, 91.

[14] Ibid., 108–9.

[15] Ibid., 110.

Christ's spiritual "body," which is not material in any way but which can freely manifest itself in matter, gives him the ability to manifest his "body" in many places at once: "The Lord with His spiritual body is not present in any particular place, because in His supraspatiality He is, in general, above all places; but, by His will, He can enter into space and then manifest Himself in a definite place."[16] To possess a spiritual "body," for Bulgakov, means to move from the limitations of material existence to freedom constituted by a new relation to materiality, namely the ability to manifest one's spirit in the matter of the world, which thereby becomes, on another plane of being, one's "body." Bulgakov thus remarks:

> In the future age, spiritual bodies, clothed in incorruption, will become capable of maintaining their form, and all the matter of the world will become the common matter, the body for all of humankind. (Through this, spatial fragmentedness, impenetrability, and separation will be overcome.)[17]

---

[16] Ibid., 106; cf. 105. See also Paul Evdokimov's "The Eucharist – Mystery of the Church," in *In the World, of the Church*, ed. and trans. Michael Plekon and Alexis Vinogradov (Crestwood, NY: St Vladimir's Seminary Press, 2001), as well as the recent articles by Nichols and Kimel.

[17] Ibid., 100. Nichols, in "Transubstantiation and Eucharistic Presence," seems to adopt a similar position. He proposes that Christ's glorified body incorporates, in a way comparable to the hypostatic union, the material elements of bread and wine, so that the bread and wine no longer subsist on their own but instead subsist in Christ's glorified body, to which they now directly "owe their being" (75). The comparison with the hypostatic union, also employed by Alvin Kimel, does not work metaphysically unless one imagines that the glorified body is no longer matter, but rather is divine. Scotus takes a similar position with regard to the "time" of the risen Christ, holding that the Eucharist could have existed before the Incarnation. See R. Trent Pomplun, "Israel and the Eucharist: A Scotist Perspective," *Pro Ecclesia* 11 [2002]: 272–94, at 284. With regard to Scotus, in "The Doctrine of Transubstantiation from Berengar through Trent: The Point at Issue," *Harvard Theological Review* 61 (1968): 385–430, James F. McCue argues that numerous medieval theologians, among them Scotus and Ockham, advocated positions that suggested the logical preferability of consubstantiation. He observes, "It is with Scotus that the important change comes, because with Scotus the doctrine of transubstantiation comes to be more a question of the authority of the post-apostolic Church than of the understanding of the eucharist" (403). For Scotus,

> Scripture does not favor transubstantiation over consubstantiation, and on philosophical grounds cons. would be more plausible. The theologian, if left to his own devices, would come down in favor of cons.; but in light of the Church's formal definition to the contrary, he will hold transubstantiation. (403)

During the same time period, McCue was also beginning to doubt the Church's understanding of priesthood: see his "Bishops, Presbyters, and Priests in Ignatius of Antioch," *Theological Studies* 28 (1967): 828–34. See also the discussion in Richard Cross, *Duns Scotus* (Oxford: Oxford University Press, 1999): 139–42.

Transmutation brings about this future world by establishing a new relation of Christ's glorified body to the bread and wine on the altar.[18]

Given this understanding of transmutation as not changing the bread and wine in their status in this world, but rather as changing the bread and wine by giving them a relation (of identity through iconic manifestation) to Christ's glorified "body," it is not surprising that Bulgakov faults Catholic and Protestant theology for an obsession with the "how" of the Eucharistic change. He describes this obsession as "Catholic cosmism," and attributes it to undue reliance upon Aristotle rather than Scripture.[19] In an important passage, he writes,

> And so, what does the Eucharistic problem consist in? Does it consist in *how* the bread and wine physically change into the body and blood of Christ, how the one is replaced by the other (that is how Catholic theology has seen this problem since time immemorial)? Or does Orthodox theology need here to "depart out of that . . . city" (Matt. 10:14), to effect a *metabasis eis allo genos*, to reject the Catholic understanding of the problem, and to establish that such a question does not exist, and that to an ill-posed question false answers are inevitably given? Western theology, in both its orthodox and heretical doctrines, in both Berengarius and Aquinas and the Protestant doctrines, has been more concerned with demonstrating the *real presence* of Christ in the bread and wine, His indwelling in them, than with showing that, in the bread and wine, Christ's true body and blood are offered to the *communicants*, and that, through this communion, they are united with Christ bodily and spiritually.[20]

The bread and wine do not change as things in this world, but they do change by being iconically caught up into the glorified body of Christ. In other words, they change as regards their capacity for communion. They become Christ's "body" by Christ's will to communicate or manifest himself through them; and, furthermore, they make such

---

[18] Bulgakov, 90.

[19] Ibid., 82.

[20] Ibid., 83–4. See the similar view, though less imbued with sophiological tenets, of Alexander Schmemann in *The Eucharist: Sacrament of the Kingdom*, trans. Paul Kachur (Crestwood, NY: St Vladimir's Seminary Press, 1988): 226. Schmemann charges Catholic sacramental theology, particularly as concerning eucharistic adoration, with rationalism in *Great Lent: Journey to Pascha* (New York: St Vladimir's Seminary Press, 1974 [rev. edn]): 59. As Robert Sokolowski has shown, however, eucharistic adoration belongs to a spirituality of the (ongoing) Incarnation that lies at the heart of Eucharistic communion (*Eucharistic Presence* [Washington, DC: Catholic University of America Press, 1993]: 99–100).

communion possible for us. Bulgakov suggests that Catholic theology, preoccupied with the alleged "substantial" change of the bread and wine, focuses upon the this-worldly "how" of Christ's new mode of being present, rather than upon the purpose of that presence. In Catholic theology, he argues,

> the transmutation of the bread and wine is not discussed as being *for* communion, in direct connection with communion. Rather, it is discussed in itself, and communion is considered as only *one* of the consequences of the transmutation, not the sole, and not even the most important, consequence.[21]

Catholic theology would not make this mistake if it possessed a proper doctrine of transmutation, in which the bread and wine are seen to be deified, rather than transubstantiated, and thus become "the offering of divine food, which is the body and blood of the Lord."[22] As divine food, the transmuted bread and wine enable the partaker of the Eucharist, similarly, to be deified, that is, to manifest and be Christ's glorified "body" on earth, in the communion of the Eucharist.

By focusing upon the "how" of the change instead of upon the deifying communion in the divine food, "Western eucharistic theology," according to Bulgakov, remains at the this-worldly level and fails to apprehend the iconic role of the bread and wine in signifying the ultimate transformation of everything material into the Body of Christ. Placing the blame for this situation upon Aquinas's Aristotelian theory of transubstantiation, "canonized" by Trent and constituting the basis for the Reformers' own mistaken Eucharistic doctrines, Bulgakov describes the Western position as "cosmological immanentism, an attempt to interpret the sacrament within the limits of this world."[23] He admits that Aquinas's position has been in the past broadly accepted by many Eastern theologians, but argues that this influence "must be completely overcome."[24] Experiential evidence, Bulgakov points out, testifies to the

---

[21] Bulgakov, 84.

[22] Ibid.

[23] Ibid., 68–9.

[24] Ibid., 69. In his introduction to the English translation of Bulgakov's study, Robert Slesinski, a Catholic priest, notes that Bulgakov's rejection of "transubstantiation" contrasts with the positions of "such Orthodox hierarchs and theologians as Metropolitan Peter Mogila of Kiev (d. 1646), Patriarch Dositheus of Jerusalem (d. 1707), and Metropolitan Filaret of Moscow (d. 1867)" (17). See Frank Gavin, *Some Aspects of Contemporary Greek Orthodox Thought* (Milwaukee: Morehouse, 1923). Alexander Schmemann speaks of the Orthodox East's "school teaching on the sacraments – which took hold in the Orthodox East in the 'dark ages' of the Church's western 'captivity'" (*The Eucharist: Sacrament of the Kingdom*, 27). Schmemann has in mind, in particular, "the authoritative *Longer Catechism* of Metropolitan Filaret (Drozdov) of Moscow, which was accepted by the entire Orthodox East" (ibid., 28).

fact that the bread and wine, as regards their this-worldly condition, do not change in the consecration. To look for a this-worldly change is entirely, on this view, to miss the point. He argues that Aquinas's careful efforts to articulate a this-worldly change in the bread and wine are thus profoundly counter-productive. Locked into the "cosmological" perspective, Aquinas cannot see that what occurs in the consecration is the inbreaking of an entirely distinct dimension of reality. The result is to turn Eucharistic theology into "sacramental natural-science, so to speak."[25] The glorified Christ, and communion with him, no longer stand at the center of such Eucharistic theology. Without a true appreciation of the realm of spirit, "materialism" reigns in Catholic Eucharistic theology, and Protestant Eucharistic theology responds with an exaggerated spiritualism that similarly fails to understand the iconic truth of Christ's statement that the bread and wine are his body and blood.

For these reasons, Bulgakov rejects Aquinas's substance-accident argumentation as another form of the heresy of "impanation." By means of his account of the "accidents" of the bread and wine, Aquinas tries to draw together what are for Bulgakov the two radically distinct levels of Eucharistic reality. As Bulgakov notes, Aquinas insists that "[e]ven though they are mutually foreign to one another, the substance of Christ's body and blood and the accidents of the bread and wine are united in the sacrament so inseparably that the substantial presence ceases if the accidents are destroyed."[26] Yet, if the accidents have any reality, how does this resulting conglomeration (substance of Christ's body and blood, accidents of bread and wine) escape impanation? If "substance," furthermore, has a metaphysical rather than merely logical meaning, how is it that "transubstantiation" is not occurring everywhere in the world at all times? As Bulgakov, interpreting transubstantiation as a transformation theory, puts it,

> the number of things fluctuates constantly, because things perish and arise, and constantly merge into one another, and their substance with them, so that an unceasing *transsubstantiatio* occurs in the world . . . In short, the world is a stream of substances and their unceasing dance, a kind of infinite *trans*.[27]

He rightly rejects such a theory as philosophically "crude," although he does so on the grounds that idealist philosophers such as Hegel and Kant have moved philosophy beyond this Aristotelian theory of substance.

[25] Bulgakov, 70.
[26] Ibid., 74.
[27] Ibid., 77. Cf. 69: "As we have said before, in the West the eucharistic problem has focused on the question of the transformation of the eucharistic matter, and thus the Eucharist acquired a reified character."

For Bulgakov, then, the key problem with the theory of transubstantiation is its aspect of *transformation*, which, in his view, cannot be avoided once "substance" and "accidents" are split and (as it were) re-combined. Instead of deification produced by the freedom and power over matter of Christ's spiritual body, as envisioned by his theory of transmutation, transubstantiation as he understands it unites the two distinct levels of reality in ways that do violence to the unchanging – untransformable – character of Christ's glorified body. Even if the "substance" of Christ's body and blood does not move spatially, as Bulgakov acknowledges to be Aquinas's doctrine,[28] nevertheless the "substance" is united to the material "accidents" of bread and wine and in a real sense tabernacles under "breadness" and "wineness."[29] This means not only that Christ's glorified body and blood are separated in substance from their accidents, but also that

> Christ's body and blood that abide in heaven are drawn into a series of earthly things and share the basic destiny of these things, changeability: earth, grain, flour and water, bread, the body of Christ, the human body (into which the body of Christ enters during the partaking), again the earth, and so on.[30]

Such changeability conflates radically distinct levels of reality and thus leads Eucharistic theology into a fatal "cosmological immanentism." Rather than material elements of this world coming to share in the deified state of Christ, Christ's glorified body comes to share in the changeable state of material elements in this world, thereby denying the theological meaning of the Ascension.[31] Such a "communion" could not be salvific, because it turns the truth of reality upside-down. The material governs the spiritual.[32] This is even so in the case of Christ's soul and divinity, which in Aquinas's theology of the Eucharist are made present, by concomitance, by the substance of the material body and blood of Christ.[33] Cosmological materialism replaces divinization: "The [glorified] body of the Lord is placed in the same series with and in direct relation to things of this world."[34] Christ's glorified body is thus reified as a "thing" in the world in the Eucharist, rather than manifesting (and making present) iconically the deifying communion in which the entire material realm

---

[28] Ibid., 73.
[29] Ibid., 80.
[30] Ibid., 79.
[31] Ibid., 81.
[32] The seriousness of such "materialism," in which God is relegated to a secondary position, is expressed by Alexander Schmemann in *The Eucharist: Sacrament of the Kingdom*, 9–10.
[33] Bulgakov, 80.
[34] Ibid.

will one day share. Bulgakov sums up his criticism of Aquinas's doctrine by affirming that given "the reifying cosmism of the theory of transubstantiation," the Reformers were correct to seek "a way out of the dead end of diphysitism that characterizes the doctrine of *transsubstantiatio* – a diphysitism that rejects true transmutation," even though the Reformers' solutions were themselves caught up in this diphysitism.

Alexander Schmemann, the Russian Orthodox theologian who died in 1983, takes up this criticism of Western Eucharistic theology as locked in the this-worldly realm. For Schmemann, the "cosmological immanentism" described by Bulgakov as regards the doctrine of transubstantiation has its roots in a failure, on the part of Western scholastic theologians, to understand the cosmos. Referring to the conclusion of Dom Anscar Vonier's *A Key to the Doctrine of the Eucharist*, which Schmemann rightly takes to be representative of the classical Western Eucharistic tradition, Schmemann remarks,

> When Dom Vonier writes that "Neither in heaven nor on earth is there anything like the sacraments," does he not indicate above all that, although the sacraments in any event depend on creation and its nature for their accomplishment, of this nature they do not reveal, witness or manifest anything?[35]

For the West, in other words, the sacraments are God's radically gratuitous intervention in the world, and thus radically extrinsic to the world. The sacraments, on this view, reveal nothing about the world. Thus, when Western theologians talk about the sacraments as events in this world, they can only speak of a this-worldly mechanism (e.g., transubstantiation). They have no sense, as Bulgakov emphasized, of the iconic character of the material world. This is so because Western theology proceeds abstractly, rather than from the liturgical experience of believers, in which the iconic aspect of material creation is paramount.[36]

In Schmemann's view, therefore, Vonier's position that the sacraments are metaphysically distinct both from God and from normal created realities (because they directly convey divine grace) becomes a marker of how the West, lacking the iconic sense of creation, has separated (rather than merely distinguished) God and creation. Schmemann argues:

> This doctrine of the sacraments is alien to the Orthodox because in the Orthodox ecclesial experience and tradition a sacrament is understood primarily as a revelation of the

---

[35] Schmemann, *The Eucharist: Sacrament of the Kingdom*, 33.
[36] Anscar Vonier emphasizes that in the mode of being that belongs to the sacrament of the Eucharist, the change is never cut off from the historical sign, from the historical realm. See Vonier, *A Key to the Doctrine of the Eucharist*, 99–100.

genuine *nature* of creation, of the world, which, however much it has fallen as "this world," will remain God's world, awaiting salvation, redemption, healing and transfiguration in a new earth and a new heaven. In other words, in the Orthodox experience a sacrament is primarily a revelation of the *sacramentality* of creation itself, for the world was created and given to man for conversion of creaturely life into participation in divine life.[37]

Each sacrament does not merely mechanistically employ nature; on the contrary, each sacrament manifests the fulfillment of the purpose of nature, namely the spiritualization of the material world by participation in the divine.[38] The cosmos is not locked in upon itself, and what is important about the sacrament is not the intra-cosmic mechanism. Rather, what is important is the manifestation of the divine in the created realm, which fulfills the very *telos* of the created realm. As Schmemann puts it:

> A sacrament is both cosmic and eschatological. It refers at the same time to God's world as he first created it and to its fulfillment in the kingdom of God. It is cosmic in that it embraces all of creation, it returns it to God as God's own . . . and in and by itself it manifests the victory of Christ. But it is to the same degree eschatological, oriented toward *the kingdom which is to come.*[39]

The mechanistic "cosmological immanentism" of the West, with the resulting effort to understand the Eucharist in terms of this-worldly mechanisms, stems from a forgetting of the true nature of the cosmos, whose *telos* is and always has been spiritualization, the manifestation of the divine.[40] Given this *telos*, one can understand that the created realm is

---

[37] Schmemann, *The Eucharist: Sacrament of the Kingdom*, 33–4. One can see here a source, with shared antecedents in German idealism, for mainstream contemporary Catholic sacramental theology.

[38] For an evaluation of Aquinas's theology in light of such concerns, see A.N. Williams, "Mystical Theology Redux: The Pattern of Aquinas' *Summa Theologiae*," *Modern Theology* 13 (1997): 53–74.

[39] Schmemann, *The Eucharist: Sacrament of the Kingdom*, 34.

[40] Schmemann argues further that the Eucharist is the sacrament of the Last Supper, not the Cross, because it is the Last Supper rather than the Cross that manifests the glorious communion of the Kingdom of God. For sympathetic but ultimately critical comment on this position, see Robert Sokolowski, *Eucharistic Presence: A Theology of Disclosure* (Washington, DC: Catholic University of America Press, 1993): 79–80. Without reducing the Last Supper to a merely instrumental preparation for the Cross, one can acknowledge the principal place that the Cross (vis-à-vis the Last Supper) enjoys as, according to the consistent witness of the New Testament, the central locus of Christ's saving action.

and always has been imbued with "sacramentality," with symbolic meaning that testifies to its goal and rids Eucharistic theology of any sense of radical extrinsicism.

David Fagerberg has addressed such concerns recently from a Catholic perspective in a brief article. Appealing to *Unitatis Redintegratio*'s call for Catholic theologians to appropriate more deeply the riches of the Eastern Fathers, Fagerberg notes:

> Our Eastern Orthodox colleagues offer a criticism of the Western doctrine of transubstantiation which bears all the marks, it seems to me, of a good, true, and valid criticism: it is accurate, it stings slightly, and it contains what is needed to improve the thing criticized.[41]

The criticism, as we have seen in Schmemann, is that Western theologians have separated the cosmos from its iconic status. As a result, the material bread and wine seem to have no real role, and matter (created reality) does not seem to be truly taken up in the Eucharist. As Fagerberg says, "Transubstantiation appears basically to be the process of removing something from the realm of nature into the realm of supernature, or turning natural stuff into super-stuff, under the suspicion that the natural world cannot function sacramentally."[42] A focus on the radical change involved in transubstantiation seems to evacuate the symbolic meaning, and *telos* of deification, that created reality possesses: "When the West began exalting the change, it was only too easy to turn the sacrament into nature's exception instead of nature's perfection."[43] Furthermore, a focus on the mechanism of transubstantiation tends to make the miracle itself (understood philosophically rather than theologically, i.e., without apprehending the role of the Holy Spirit) the center of attention, rather than placing the emphasis where it should be, namely the deifying communion to which transubstantiation is ordered.

Fagerberg's solution to these difficulties is not to do away with the doctrine of transubstantiation. Rather, he proposes a twofold development. First, transubstantiation needs to be re-contextualized within an incarnational and sacramental understanding of the cosmos. In this view, "the world exists to be the cradle of the God-man," and thus possesses an "incarnational and sacramental potency."[44] Against such heresies as monophysitism and docetism, which sought to radically separate the created realm from the divine, Fagerberg notes that the Incarnation,

---

[41] David W. Fagerberg, "Translating Transubstantiation," *Antiphon* 6 (2001): 9–13, at 9.
[42] Ibid.
[43] Ibid.
[44] Ibid., 10.

as the basis for the sacraments, shows that "[g]race perfects nature; redemption consummates creation; the spiritual climaxes the material; the divine fulfills the human."[45] He draws from this incarnational understanding of the cosmos the conclusion that "material objects were made in order to be seen in the light of the spiritual sun with spiritual eyes and experienced as sacrament."[46] Once this is understood, then one recognizes that in the Eucharist, nature attains its spiritual *telos* by working sacramentally, by manifesting or communicating the divine. Viewing the material object with spiritual eyes, one recognizes the "substance" or "truth" of the Eucharist as "the body of a man in whom human and divine commingled, and creation came to completion."[47] Were one only to see with bodily eyes, one would see in the Eucharist nothing but the "accidents," which, as "breadness," "remains bread."[48]

Having reclaimed this iconic cosmology, Fagerberg moves to his second point: the "accidents" should no longer be minimized. Lacking a cosmology that recognized the iconic status of created things, Western theologians have tended to interpret the Eucharist in a "monophysite" fashion, focusing entirely upon the body and blood of the Lord. Fagerberg points out:

> The accidents of bread and wine on the altar are something of an embarrassment to such an interpretation, and various strategies (theological, mythical, gestural, achitectural, devotional) were devised to persuade us that the accidents are as unimportant and insignificant as the Monophysites thought Jesus' human nature was.[49]

The substance of Christ does not make the natural "accidents" of the bread and wine meaningless. Fagerberg here appeals to Aquinas, noting that Aquinas insists upon the positive status of the accidents by the divine power even after (*contra* Aristotle) the substance of the bread and wine is changed. As Fagerberg states, reviewing question 77 of the *tertia pars*,

---

[45] Ibid., 11. A similar point is made by Terence Nichols, "Transubstantiation and Eucharistic Presence," *Pro Ecclesia* 11 (2002): 57–75, at 66–7, 72–3.

[46] Fagerberg, 11.

[47] Ibid.

[48] Ibid. Terence Nichols goes farther than Fagerberg and argues that "transubstantiation" need not mean that the bread and wine, in themselves, actually change at all. Nichols holds that modern science makes unintelligible Aquinas's view of a "substance" that could be converted without its "accidents" being likewise converted. Nichols suggests that "substance," in the sense of the "essential reality" of the thing, must ultimately be an empirically describable reality – e.g., "proto-energy" (Nichols, "Transubstantiation and Eucharistic Presence," 65) – if the term "substance" is to have meaning. For the opposite view, see Richard J. Connell, "Substance and Transubstantiation," *Angelicum* 69 (1992): 3–37.

[49] Fagerberg, 11.

"We cannot speak of the accidents as unearthly or ethereal since Thomas says, 'they retain every action which they had while the substance of the bread and wine remained' (a 3), and will suffer corruption (a 4), and can nourish the human body by digestion (a 6), just as they did when the substance of the bread was present."[50] Aquinas's positive theology of the accidents suggests to Fagerberg that the doctrine of transubstantiation is not so much about the mechanism of the change (which is a divine miracle), but rather about how the accidents remain. In short, Aquinas devotes serious attention to the accidents, thus recognizing in the bread and wine an important iconic significance. Aquinas does not slight the Eucharistic "sign," or "sacramentum."[51]

In making this point, Fagerberg emphasizes the character of transubstantiation as a transformation. He writes:

> Transubstantiation affirms that matter is totally suffused with grace in the Eucharist, in fulfillment of creation's purpose and as a prophetic sign of creation's eschatological end. Transubstantiation involves (or should involve) a positive theology of accidents. Transubstantiation means just what it says: the substance is transformed, not supplanted, not duplicated, and not evacuated by pneumatic suction and pumped full of an alien substance. Instead, the matter of this earth communicates the very body of Christ.[52]

For Fagerberg, the key is that transubstantiation describes the change of the matter of the bread and wine into the matter of the body and blood of Christ: "the matter of this earth communicates the very body of Christ." The same matter that once was bread and wine now is Jesus'

---

[50] Ibid., 12.
[51] Indeed, Dom Anscar Vonier, O.S.B. observes:

> If the priest at the altar brought down Christ from heaven in his natural state as a full-grown man, this would not be a sacrament in the least, as it would lack the very essence of the sacrament, representative signification . . . At no time do we deal in the Eucharist with Christ in his natural condition, *in propria specie*. It might almost be said that if at any moment Christ in his natural condition were to step into the sacramental *processus*, the sacrament at once would be made meaningless. He must be there *in specie aliena* in order to safeguard the veracity of the sacrament as a sign" (*A Key to the Doctrine of the Eucharist*, 32; cf. 70–1)

As Vonier remarks elsewhere, "It is the main scope of this little book to make this idea clear, that in dealing with the Eucharist in all its aspects we are still dealing with a sacrament" (59). Thomas Merton's *The Living Bread* (New York: Farrar, Straus & Giroux, 1956) nicely popularizes Vonier's approach in this regard.
[52] Fagerberg, 12.

body and blood, fulfilling the iconic capacity and *telos* of deification that the material creation possesses. Fagerberg quotes Cardinal Joseph Ratzinger to a similar effect. For Ratzinger, Fagerberg notes, "the transubstantiated host is 'the anticipation of the transformation and divinization of matter in the christological "fullness"'" (29). The Eucharist is the action of God that

> is the real "action" for which all of creation is in expectation. The elements of the earth are transubstantiated, pulled, so to speak, from their creaturely anchorage, grasped at the deepest ground of their being, and changed into the Body and Blood of the Lord.[53]

For Fagerberg, transubstantiation, as a transformation and divinization of material elements, bespeaks the eschatological New Creation; transubstantiation is a fundamentally eschatological doctrine that makes manifest the iconic sacramentality of the cosmos. Thus the "accidents," understood in terms of the doctrine of transubstantiation, have a crucial signifying role that avoids the charge of "cosmological immanentism." The accidents display the reality that matter, in the transubstantiation, has been transformed and deified. They thus display the eschatological reality that Christ will be "all in all" (Eph. 1:23).

Yet, this position seems to attend to Schmemann's criticism without addressing the deeper problematic that Bulgakov poses. Bulgakov's position, it is true, verges on what one might call "Nestorian" in his care to preserve distinctions between the material and spiritual realms. Yet, these distinctions are quite important. In his understanding of the deification of the material realm, Bulgakov is careful to make clear that the unchanging realm of the divine, the spiritual, shines through the created and material. Christ's glorified body, as glorified, belongs to this divine, spiritual realm. Christ's glorified body does not change; rather, it manifests itself through, and makes completely its own, the iconic materiality of the bread and wine. Given the status of Christ's glorified body, it makes no sense to speak of the matter of the bread and wine being transformed into the matter of Christ's (glorified) body. The "matter" of Christ's glorified body is unchanging, after all.

The theory of transformation, as Bulgakov recognizes, encounters a crucial problem here. How can the matter of the bread and wine be

---

[53] Ibid., quoting Cardinal Joseph Ratzinger, *The Spirit of the Liturgy*, trans. John Saward (San Francisco: Ignatius Press, 2000): 29 and 173. Ratzinger, it should be noted, does not here adopt a transformation-theory of transubstantiation. Like Fagerberg, Terence Nichols emphasizes the need for the bread and wine to be transformed, rather than transubstantiated, so as to model our deification (Nichols, "Transubstantiation and Eucharistic Presence," 67).

transformed into Christ's body and blood without thereby composing a material body quite distinct from the "material body" that the living, glorified Christ possesses in a completely unchanging mode in heaven? It would seem that the theory of transubstantiation as a transformation of the material realm does not account for the unchanging reality of glorification, and thereby conflates the two realms in a way that does not do justice to the state of glory. As Bulgakov puts it, the danger is that "[t]he [glorified] body of the Lord is placed in the same series with and in direct relation to things of this world."[54] Christ's glorified body would thereby be "reified," as Bulgakov notes, by becoming itself a changing thing still on the same metaphysical level as the bread and wine. Thus, Christ's glorified body in the Eucharist would not in fact be able to manifest iconically the deifying communion that is the destiny of the created realm, because Christ's glorified body would appear as simply another changeable thing, capable of literally taking into itself and transforming the matter of bread and wine into itself, as in the temporal process of digestion. By conflating the state of glory with the condition of material things in the world and thereby undermining the metaphysical distinctiveness of the state of glory, the understanding of transubstantiation as transformation, despite its attention to the iconic character of created reality, seems to fall into what Bulgakov terms "cosmological immanentism."

Nonetheless, neither is Bulgakov's own position satisfactory. It is not surprising that Schmemann, for his part, does not adopt it, preferring instead to approximate Bulgakov's view by affirming that the Eucharistic change is a mystery that can only be known in faith by the inspiration of the Holy Spirit: "Nothing is explained, nothing is defined, nothing has changed in 'this world.'"[55] Schmemann's refusal to explain or define the change stands against Bulgakov's explanation that, as regards their status in this world, the bread and wine are completely unchanged by the Eucharistic consecration – even though Schmemann leaves room for Bulgakov's explanation by affirming also that "nothing has changed in 'this world.'" Fagerberg adapts Schmemann's view to the discourse of transubstantiation by noting that worldly eyes, as opposed to spiritual eyes, cannot see the change, cannot see the "substance" or "truth" of the consecrated host, but instead can only see the "accidents." Indeed, as we have seen, Fagerberg goes so far as to state that "the part seen by the physical light" actually "remains bread"; yet Fagerberg makes clear that he does not mean this in a "Zwinglian" sense. Neither Fagerberg nor Schmemann wish to adopt Bulgakov's radical position, which seems to involve a radical separation of the divine and human realms that does not accord with a full sense of the Incarnation.

---

[54] Bulgakov, *The Holy Grail and the Eucharist*, 80.
[55] Schmemann, *The Eucharist: Sacrament of the Kingdom*, 226.

Is Schmemann's position on the Eucharistic conversion – neither Fagerberg's "transformation," nor Bulgakov's absence of this-worldly change, nor Aquinas's and Trent's "transubstantiation" as explaining too much – perhaps the best one for accounting for the deifying communion accomplished in the Eucharist (manifested by the fulfillment of creation's iconic status) without falling into rationalistic explanations? An answer will require analysis of Aquinas's doctrine of transubstantiation.[56] For Aquinas, the eucharistic conversion is a miraculous this-worldly change, not an eschatological event. Although the change occurs in this world, it does not constitute an "immanentism" or "cosmism," because the change belongs to the movement whereby God makes earth present to heaven and inaugurates our deification.[57] Jean-Pierre Torrell beautifully depicts this sacramental movement:

---

[56] For a discussion of Aquinas's eucharistic theology in relation to late medieval theology, see John L. Farthing, *Thomas Aquinas and Gabriel Biel: Interpretations of St. Thomas Aquinas in German Nominalism on the Eve of the Reformation* (Durham, NC: Duke University Press, 1988): 103–49; David Burr, *Eucharistic Presence and Conversion in Late Thirteenth-Century Franciscan Thought* (Philadelphia, PA: American Philosophical Society, 1984). In dialogue with Burr's work, Gary Macy has argued that Albert the Great marks the shift toward metaphysics:

> In a distinct departure from his predecessors, and in a more thorough manner than even Thomas, Albert placed eucharistic conversion at the heart of his theology, emphasizing the role of metaphysics over that of theology. Thomas would enthusiastically follow the lead of his teacher, while Bonaventure would accept Albert's theology only up to a point. (54)

According to Macy, this metaphysical shift resulted in an ecclesial narrowing of the mediation of sacramental grace:

> As long as presence [Christ in the Eucharist] depended upon intention, at last to some extent, the Eucharist did not so much produce salvation as it celebrated a salvation already attained through a union of faith and love between the individual believer and the risen Lord. (66)

Macy's point that the Reformers' positions were already present in the medieval period is well taken, but in deploying "metaphysics" against "theology" (cf. 65) he fails to see what Aquinas understands to be at stake in the metaphysical discussion, namely the theological reality of our eucharistic sharing in Christ's sacrificial Cross. See Gary Macy, "A Re-evaluation of the Contribution of Thomas Aquinas to the Thirteenth-Century Theology of the Eucharist," in *The Intellectual Climate of the Early University*, ed. Nancy Van Deusen (Kalamazoo, MI: Medieval Institute, 1997): 53–72.

[57] The sense of "this-worldly" is different from that criticized in passing by Peter Casarella, because Aquinas has recourse to an understanding of "substance" that goes beyond the chemical. Casarella argues that "substantial presence signifies that in the Eucharist a real transformation takes place. The transformation is not a this-worldly one, as if the priest had access to a special ecclesiastical chemistry. The transformation partakes even now of the messianic banquet that is still to come" (Casarella, "Eucharist: Presence of a Gift," in *Rediscovering the Eucharist: Ecumenical Conversations*, ed. Roch Kereszty, O. Cist. [New York: Paulist Press, 2003]: 207). Were the change not "this-worldly," then the bread and wine would remain, as regards this world, bread and wine; but in fact they are changed precisely as realities of this world.

The historical Christ, today glorified, touches us by each of the acts of his earthly life, which is thus the bearer of a divinizing life and energy. As to the concrete manner in which everything that the Savior did and suffered in the flesh reaches us even today, it suffices to reply with Thomas: "*spiritually* through faith and *bodily* through the sacraments, for Christ's humanity is simultaneously spirit and body in order that we might be able to receive into ourselves [we who are spirit and body] the effect of the sanctification that comes to us through Christ."[58]

Not as an eschatological absorption of the world into divinity, but instead through a this-worldly making present and offering of the body and blood of Calvary, can the eucharistic sacrifice truly embody a participation in Christ's salvific Cross and thus in his heavenly communion. As Aquinas observes in commenting on John 6,

since this is the sacrament of our Lord's passion, it contains in itself the Christ who suffered. Thus, whatever is an effect of our Lord's passion is also an effect of this sacrament. For this sacrament is nothing other than the application of our Lord's passion to us.[59]

We become, as Bernhard Blankenhorn has remarked, "icons of Christ, signs of the Passion."[60]

2 AQUINAS ON TRANSUBSTANTIATION

With regard to transubstantiation, Aquinas undertakes three inquiries in his theological account of the Eucharist in the *Summa Theologiae*: the nature of the change of the bread and wine into the body and blood of Christ (III, q. 75); the manner in which Christ exists in the sacrament

---

[58] Jean-Pierre Torrell, O.P., *Saint Thomas Aquinas*, vol. 2: *Spiritual Master*, trans. Robert Royal (Washington, DC: Catholic University of America Press, 2003): 139; cf. 220. Torrell discusses Aquinas's eucharistic spirituality in a more sustained fashion in vol. 1: *The Person and His Work*, trans. Robert Royal (Washington, DC: Catholic University of America Press, 1996): 129–36, 286–7. He examines in particular Aquinas's composition of the Office for the Feast of Corpus Christi and his hymn *Adoro Te*, whose authenticity has been strongly defended by Robert Wielockx, "Poetry and Theology in the *Adoro te deuote*: Thomas Aquinas on the Eucharist and Christ's Uniqueness," in *Christ among the Medieval Dominicans*, ed. Kent Emery and Joseph Wawrykow (Notre Dame, IN: University of Notre Dame Press, 1998): 157–74.

[59] Aquinas, *Commentary on the Gospel of St. John*, Part I, trans. Fabian Larcher, O.P. and James Weisheipl, O.P. (Albany, NY: Magi Books, 1980): ch. 6, lect. 6, no. 963 (p. 382).

[60] From correspondence with Bernhard Blankenhorn, O.P.

of the Eucharist (q. 76); how the accidents remain in the sacrament (q. 77).[61]

Question 75, article 1: theological parameters

The first article of question 75 gives the student Aquinas's purpose in developing a theory of transubstantiation. It therefore deserves our careful attention. The article opens with four objections. First, it would seem that Christ's body and blood are not in the Eucharist in a literal sense, because after Jesus has instructed his disciples on the necessity of eating his flesh and drinking his blood, Jesus goes on to clarify to his murmuring disciples, "It is the spirit that gives life, the flesh is of no avail; the words that I have spoken to you are spirit and life" (John 6:63).[62] Second, the risen Jesus promises to be with the disciples until the end of the world (Matt. 28:20), but in fact Jesus is in heaven, and so his presence is rightly interpreted as a spiritual presence. Third, Jesus' body is in heaven, and it cannot be in more than one place. Fourth, attachment to Jesus' bodily presence prevents a disciple from true faith, through the Holy Spirit, in his divinity. In each case, what is at stake is not "presence" in an abstract sense. Rather what is sought is personal contact with Jesus of Nazareth, the incarnate Son of God. Each of the objections, however, makes the point that such Jesus has made such personal contact available spiritually, through faith. Indeed, faith gives the proper personal contact. Only faith, as spiritual contact with Jesus' divinity, "gives life." His body is in heaven precisely for this reason: otherwise people would cleave to his humanity and not raise their minds to his divinity, as the third and fourth objections, drawing upon John 16:7, together suggest. Contact with Jesus' physical body and blood would seem to be unnecessary and unfitting, now that Jesus has led the way to heaven.

Yet, as Aquinas points out in the *sed contra*, the Fathers – here represented by St Hilary of Poitiers and St Ambrose, and in the *respondeo* by St Cyril of Jerusalem and Pseudo-Dionysius – attest to Christ's bodily presence in the sacrament of the Eucharist, and Jesus' words in the Gospels argue the same. The question then becomes, Why is contact with Jesus' body and blood important? Aquinas's answer holds the key to the entire discussion of transubstantiation. In his *respondeo*, he turns to the history of sacrifice:

---

[61] Joseph Wawrykow has argued that "Thomas's way of proceeding may be termed 'therapeutic' in the sense that he at once advances an account of presence and sharpens our sense of the pitfalls of less sophisticated positions, thus helping us secure our own grasp of the truth" (Wawrykow, "Luther and the Spirituality of Thomas Aquinas," *Consensus* 19 [1993]: 91).

[62] Cf. Michel Corbin, "Le pain de la vie: La lecture de Jean VI par S. Thomas d'Aquin," *Recherches de Science Religieuse* 65 (1977): 107–38.

the sacrifices of the Old Law contained only in figure that true sacrifice of Christ's Passion, according to Heb. x. 1: *For the law having a shadow of the good things to come, not the very image of the things*. And therefore it was necessary that the sacrifice of the New Law instituted by Christ should have something more, namely, that it should contain Christ Himself crucified, not merely in signification or figure, but also in truth.[63]

Bodily contact with Jesus is necessary because "the perfection of the New Law"[64] requires a sharing of his sacrifice that goes beyond offering him up in faith – as was possible in Israel's sacrifices – and achieves actual bodily sharing in his sacrifice, true offering up of Jesus in and with him. Such a sacrificial offering, the "sacrifice of the New Law," could not take place without the bodily presence of "Christ Himself crucified."[65]

Some clarification of Aquinas's use of these theological expressions will assist us. Christ's one sacrifice, and it alone, is the "sacrifice of the New Law," the sacrifice that fulfills the Old Law by establishing perfect justice and reconciling human beings to God. The New Law in believers

---

[63] 3, q. 75, a. 1. Between the *Commentary on the Sentences* and the *Summa Theologiae*, Aquinas in his eucharistic theology deepened his use of biblical quotations and thereby illumined more profoundly the unity of salvation history. See Ronald Zawilla, *The Biblical Sources of the Historiae Corporis Christi Attributed to Thomas Aquinas* (Doctoral Dissertation, University of Toronto, 1985), whose theses are summarized in Pierre-Marie Gy, O.P., "Avancées du traité de l'eucharistie de S. Thomas dans la *Somme* par rapport aux *Sentences*," *Revue des sciences philosophiques et théologiques* 77 (1993): 219–28, at 221–2. On the basis of Zawilla's research, Gy suggests that Aquinas's Office for the Feast of Corpus Christi marks an important transition in Aquinas's eucharistic theology.

[64] 3, q. 75, a. 1. As O'Neill affirms, "the one acceptable sign of union with God is the broken body of Calvary" (*Meeting Christ in the Sacraments*, 165).

[65] Here compare Edward Kilmartin's statement regarding Cajetan's doctrine of Eucharistic sacrifice: "Cajetan is influenced by the static concept of the somatic real presence fostered by the doctrine of transubstantiation, which tended to obscure the more dynamic patristic teaching about the presence of the salvation reality of Christ and his redemptive sacrifice" (Kilmartin, *The Eucharist in the West*, ed. Robert Daly, S.J. [Collegeville, MN: Liturgical Press, 1998]: 164; cf. 149–50 for similar reflections on transubstantiation). Kilmartin notes with disapprobation that "all the Catholic theologians [during and after Trent], whether favorable to Cajetan or to the Scotus – Biel synthesis, ground the sacrifice of the Mass on the identity of the victim of cross and Mass, and the proof of the sacrifice of the Mass on the fact that the priest offers the divine victim in the Mass" (165). For the impact of Eucharistic idealism in the mid-1960s on Catholic theologies of the Eucharistic change – a shift that had been in preparation since the 1930s and even before (as Catholic theologians of Schillebeeckx's and Rahner's generation sought to come to grips with Kant and Hegel) – compare also the shift that occurs in the work of E. Gutwenger: "Substanz und Akzidenz in der Eucharistielehre," *Zeitschrift für katholische Theologie* 83 (1961): 257–306 and then "Das Geheimnis der Gegenwart Christi in der Eucharistie," *Zeitschrift für katholische Theologie* 88 (1966): 185–97.

is our participation, through the grace of the Holy Spirit, in Christ's fulfillment of the Old Law. The "perfection" of the New Law goes beyond that made possible by faith in his offering. Israel, according to Aquinas, displayed such faith in her divinely commanded offering of animal sacrifices, but the perfect sacrifice, as the letter to the Hebrews makes clear, is now here. The perfection of the New Law means that believers, as the people of God (not merely as individuals), offer the perfect sacrifice to God. Israel offered animal sacrifices that prefigured Christ's sacrifice; the people of God that God gathers around Christ offer Christ's sacrifice. After Christ's coming and his establishment of the New Law on the Cross, believers do not offer this sacrifice only spiritually, as Israel did. Rather the "perfection" of the New Law consists precisely in bodily offering Christ's sacrifice in and with Christ. It is this offering of Christ's sacrifice that constitutes the people of God as Christ's Mystical Body.[66] Offering in union with him the sacrifice of his body, believers become the sacrificial Body of their Head. Were Christ not bodily present, believers could not offer up Christ's sacrificial body, and the New Law would not attain "perfection," but would instead remain at the figural level, a level already attained through Israel's sacrificial worship.[67] To attain perfection means to share in Christ's bodily sacrifice in and through which justice – true interpersonal communion – is attained. Such a "Law" constitutes a "perfect" community. Our "perfection" comes in sharing in this Law of love by sharing in its accomplishment.

The second and third steps of Aquinas's *respondeo* fill out this picture. The community of sharers in Christ's reconciling sacrifice is led by their Head, Christ. But since this is a community of love, the Head does not play an aloof or domineering role. Rather, the communion in his sacrifice is marked by the profoundest friendship. This community of friendship would be sorely lacking were Christ, in and with whose love we are friends of God and of each other, absent. Christ's bodily presence in the sacrament does not "solely" guarantee our ability to share in his saving sacrifice; his bodily presence also consummates his sacrifice in the goal of all sacrifice, namely interpersonal communion in love with God – a friendship that fulfills and perfects the natural friendship described by Aristotle. As Aquinas states, Christ's bodily presence in the sacrament

---

[66] Gilles Emery's remark is crucial: "Ecclesial realism appears deeply rooted in eucharistic realism" (Emery, "The Ecclesial Fruit of the Eucharist in St. Thomas Aquinas," trans. Therese Scarpelli, *Nova et Vetera* 2 [2004]: 47).

[67] In "Eating Christ: Recovering the Language of Real Identification," Kimel states, "Does the nature of the risen body therefore rule out the possiblity of our physical consumption of Christ? St. Thomas certainly thought so" (100). For Aquinas, however, we certainly do consume the very body and blood of Christ.

belongs to Christ's love, out of which for our salvation He assumed a true body of our nature. And because it is the special feature of friendship to live together with friends, as the Philosopher says (*Ethic.* ix), He promises us His bodily presence as a reward, saying (Matth. xxiv. 28): *Where the body is there shall the eagles be gathered together.* Yet meanwhile in our pilgrimage He does not deprive us of His bodily presence, but unites us with Himself in this sacrament through the truth of His body and blood. Hence (John vi. 57) he says: *He that eateth My flesh, and drinketh My blood, abideth in Me, and I in him.* Hence this sacrament is the sign of supreme charity, and the uplifter of our hope, from such familiar union of Christ with us.[68]

Our sacramental sharing in Christ's sacrifice thus also constitutes the most perfect friendship or communion of persons. Christ's profoundly intimate union with us, as St John's Gospel makes clear, constitutes "supreme charity," our sharing (through Christ's sacrifice) in Trinitarian communion. His bodily presence, which enables us to share in his sacrifice and attain communion with him, stimulates our hope to gain the fullness of this self-giving life in the state of glory.

A comparison with the position of the liturgical theologian David Power might be helpful here. Power rejects the language of "efficient causality" and "substantial change" and instead prefers to envision the Eucharist as God's special presence mediated through language and ritual.[69] He thus describes the "transformation" of the bread and wine:

The acknowledgment of a gracious and gratuitous presence in the midst of the people is what is expressed in thanksgiving and ritual sharing. Such acknowledgment is meant to find its focal point in the bread and wine set on the table in the middle of the assembly. In the bread and wine of the people there is the presence of a God who is revealed by being veiled under these symbols, just as the divine love continues to be revealed under the veil of Christ's suffering. The gratuity of God's presence at the heart of creation, the gratuity of God's advent in Jesus Christ, and the gratuity of the Spirit dwelling in the hearts of the people who convene as one are expressed in thanksgiving over these realities of daily life and in the communion of a common table that knows of no discrimination. All this is summed up in the symbolic reality of their transformation into the gift of Christ's body and blood.[70]

---

[68] 3, q. 75, a. 1.
[69] Cf. David Power, *The Eucharistic Mystery* [New York: Crossroad, 1997]: 320–4.
[70] Ibid., 324.

Aquinas, in contrast, places the emphasis upon *Christ's* friendship with us.[71] Christ's charity, as manifested by his bodily presence in the Eucharist, fuels our faith, hope, and love. Christ accomplishes the work of salvation; in Christ's Body we are made lovers of God and of each other. Without Christ, we would still be in our sins. Only radical dependence upon Christ as our Savior – a self-giving that is accomplished through knowing him in faith as the God-man, a knowing that (since there is no absolutely demonstrative proof) requires an act of will – enables us to participate in what he has accomplished for us. Both our sacrificial sharing in his sacrifice and our communion of friendship with him require faith in Christ.[72]

In preparing to explicate transubstantiation, Aquinas must therefore remark upon a third element of Christ's bodily presence in the sacrament of the Eucharist. Namely, Jesus' bodily presence in the sacrament assists the believer in entering into Jesus' sacrifice and the communion established in and through that sacrifice. As a bodily presence that, despite its bodiliness, is radically undetectable by empirical (natural-scientific) analysis, Christ's bodily presence in the sacrament aids in "the perfection of faith."[73] As the letter to the Hebrews points out, faith is "of things unseen" (Heb. 11:1). Yet, faith does not simply concern Christ's invisible divinity; since his divinity is inseparably united to his humanity, faith concerns Christ's humanity as well (here Aquinas cites John 14:1). Therefore, the empirical undetectability of Christ's bodily presence in the sacrament constitutes an important aspect of how the Eucharist enables our sharing in Christ's sacrifice and in the communion of his Mystical Body. As Aquinas affirms, "since faith is of things unseen, as Christ shows us His Godhead invisibly, so also in this sacrament He shows us His flesh in an invisible manner."[74] In short, the sacrament of the Eucharist is a sacrificial participation in Christ's sacrifice that achieves its end when we participate with faith, hope, and love, all of which are stimulated by Christ's bodily presence in the sacrament.

As this exposition of the first article regarding the change of bread and wine into Christ's body and blood indicates, everything in Aquinas's account of transubstantiation aims at establishing sapientially what is

---

[71] Romanus Cessario, O.P., affirms that "every sacramental mediation that God offers to the world begins with the gift of His Truth. Indeed, this Truth appears preeminently in the Person of Jesus Christ, who Himself embodies divine Truth itself" (Cessario, "The Sacramental Mediation of Divine Friendship and Communion," *Faith and Reason* 27[2002]: 7–41, at 8).

[72] Anscar Vonier, O.S.B. grounds his theology of the Eucharist in the believer's search for existential union with Christ. See the opening section of Vonier, *A Key to the Doctrine of the Eucharist.* Just as faith establishes spiritual communion with Christ in accord with the existential need to know our Redeemer, so also the sacraments unite us to Christ in ways befitting the existential condition of believers.

[73] 3, q. 75, a. 1.

[74] Ibid.

necessary for our revealed sharing in the "perfection of the New Law" by participating in Christ's sacrifice. Transubstantiation cannot be understood outside of its Christological grounding. In Aquinas's hands, the doctrine of transubstantiation is intended to illumine the revealed mystery that in the Eucharist we sacrificially offer, in and with Christ (a unity requiring faith and charity), the one and only body and blood of Jesus Christ to the Father – and thereby fulfill the Law of love that constitutes us in justice as Christ's Body. Certain requirements are clear at the outset. The body and blood we offer Eucharistically in and with Christ must be Christ's body and blood, and not another or a newly made "body and blood"; and therefore it must be the same body and blood that is now alive at the right hand of the Father. It must be present to us in a way that enables us to share in his once-and-for-all historical enactment of sacrificial offering on the Cross; it cannot be a new sacrifice, but rather must be the Church's sharing in his definitive sacrifice. Finally, it must be present to us in a way consistent with, or conducive to, our human mode of offering sacrificial gifts; it must be present on altars throughout the world, must be able to be handled and eaten, and so forth.

In the first article of question 75, these requirements are brought out in Aquinas's answers to the four objections. The replies to the objections contain Aquinas's response to questions surrounding Augustine's interpretation of the Eucharist. In Aquinas's view, and my own, Augustine's reading of John 6 – a reading which rules out cannibalism – "means not to exclude the truth of Christ's body, but that it was not to be eaten in this species in which it was seen by them."[75] The key point is the differentiation of the natural "species" or natural mode of being of Christ, in which Christ's body occupies spatial dimensions and so forth, from the sacramental species or sacramental mode of being. Since the Eucharist appears as bread and wine, common sense suffices to infer that if it really is Christ's body and blood, it must be Christ's body and blood in a different mode of being from what the disciples saw and touched in Jerusalem and its environs.

Augustine rightly points out, Aquinas notes, that Jesus' words in John 6 were not intended to suggest that his hearers were to eat his limbs after taking him down from the Cross, or to drink the blood that spilled from his sacred body during the crucifixion. Such an interpretation would be a horrible mistake. Rather, Jesus' words in John 6 are life-giving only when understood in the Spirit, that is, only when understood as referring to the mystical sacramental mode in which Jesus will make us fully sharers in his perfect sacrificial offering. This mystical sacramental mode will convey his true bodily presence. Having exposed the theological

---

[75] 3, q. 75, a. 1, ad 1.

significance of Christ's bodily presence in the Eucharist in his *respondeo*, Aquinas thus focuses the answers to the objections upon the central problem that will occupy him in his account of transubstantiation: exposing sapientially the way that our participation in Christ's sacrifice and communion depends upon acknowledging a sacramental mode of bodiliness. This exposition of a sacramental mode of bodiliness is the task of the doctrine of "transubstantiation." This task does not involve "defining" the mysterious action of God, as if one was speaking of a this-worldly *mechanism* (rather than a this-worldly bodiliness). Rather, Aquinas's teaching on the aspects of the Eucharistic conversion seeks to identify the intellectual paths that conduce to affirming Christ's sacramental bodiliness (and thus to affirming our sacrificial sharing in his sacrifice, that is, our communion with him) as opposed to those that would curtail or render impossible his sacramental bodiliness by which we are enabled to share fully in the Law of love that he has established.

The conversion of the elements: clarifications

Article 1 sets the theological parameters of the discussion. The remaining articles of question 75, often read outside of these theological parameters, discuss the change or conversion of the bread and wine into the body and blood of Christ, in order to affirm Christ's sacramental bodiliness in what appears to be, to the senses, a mere offering of bread and wine. The second article, anticipating Luther, asks whether the substance of the bread and wine remains, along with the substance of Christ's body and blood, in the sacrament of the Eucharist. Given (as is clear to faith) that a conversion or change occurs in the consecration of the sacrament, Aquinas's *respondeo* hinges upon the denial (with Bulgakov!) that Christ's glorified body materially changes. Christ's glorified body neither moves into a place, nor changes in any other material way. In the conversion, what then does change? If the two terms of the conversion are Christ's body and blood, and bread and wine, then it is the second term that must change. God changes the bread and wine into Christ's body and blood.

Yet, what kind of change is this? Article 3 asks whether the substance of the bread and wine is changed by being annihilated. Does the substance of the bread and wine become nothing, zapped, as it were, from existence? No, answers Aquinas, because this would be to deprive the change of its term. Were the substance of the bread and wine to become nothing, it could not be changed into Christ's body and blood – because it (the substance of the bread and wine) would not be there. Were that the case, then it would again be Christ's glorified body that would change, which has already been rightly ruled out.

If God changes the bread and wine, and they are not annihilated, it would seem that Aquinas is depicting, with Fagerberg, the transformation of the material elements. But this is not the case. The change, as Aquinas states in article 4 (following Ambrose and Chrysostom), "is not like natural changes." Every natural change involves the transformation of some matter from one form to another: "diverse forms succeed each other in the same subject." But God, in contrast to natural agents, can change the entire being of one thing to the being of another thing, thereby bypassing material transformation.

Granted that God can do this, why should God do this in the sacrament? The reason is that Christ's glorified body and blood already exist and are alive at the right hand of the Father, and the goal of the sacramental change is to make this unique body and blood present for the soteriological purposes outlined above. Thus the matter of the bread and wine cannot simply lose one form (bread and wine) and gain another (Jesus Christ). This would be, at best, to involve Christ's glorified body and blood in a process of material change, and at worst to imagine a constant stream of new material Jesus Christs with every new Mass. The Church, followed by Aquinas, gives the sacramental change of the substance of the bread and wine into the body and blood of Christ the name "transubstantiation"[76] precisely for the reason that it is a unique kind of change, unlike the continual "transformations" that, as Bulgakov rightly noted (even while believing that he was describing transubstantiation), go on unceasingly throughout the material world. The sacramental change occurs instantaneously by God's power (article 7).

Two problems arise here. The first problem is how, if the change is from one being to another, one can say that the bread and wine actually have a real role.[77] In other words, it would seem that Schmemann's concern that created nature plays no role in Western Eucharistic theology

---

[76] Pierre-Marie Gy, O.P. notes that Aquinas uses the phrase "substantial conversion" more in the *Summa Theologiae*, whereas the *Commentary on the Sentences* relies upon "transsubstantiatio." According to Gy, this shift indicates simply Aquinas's growing appreciation of Aristotelian terminology, not a theological shift. See Gy, "Avancées du traité de l'eucharistie de S. Thomas dans la *Somme* par rapport aux *Sentences*," 223. For an introduction to early medieval theologies of the Eucharist, with an emphasis on eucharistic pluralism, see Gary Macy, *The Theologies of the Eucharist in the Early Scholastic Period: A Study of the Salvific Function of the Sacrament according to the Theologians c. 1080–c. 1220* (Oxford: Clarendon Press, 1984). I find Macy's emphasis to be exaggerated, since despite evident difficulties in finding adequate modes of expression for the eucharistic mystery, the medievals generally agreed as regards conclusions. See, e.g., the debate over Abelard's understanding of the eucharistic accidents. As Macy's *Treasures from the Storeroom: Medieval Religion and the Eucharist* (Collegeville, MN: Liturgical Press, 1999) makes clear on p. 184 and elsewhere, his reading of the history is shaped by a profound ambivalence toward Trent. See also, for an application to a popular audience, his *The Banquet's Wisdom: A Short History of the Theologies of the Lord's Supper* (New York: Paulist Press, 1992).

[77] This is Germain Grisez's concern, to which Stephen Brock eloquently responds in "St. Thomas and the Eucharistic Conversion."

is borne out by Aquinas's claim that transubstantiation is not trans-formation. In article 8, Aquinas grants that transubstantiation bears a likeness to creation, in that in both transubstantiation and creation *ex nihilo* the two terms of the change (e.g. bread and Christ's body) do not have a common subject or substrate. In the same article he explains at length, however, that transubstantiation possesses a more important twofold likeness to natural change, even though in both cases one finds dissimilarity as well. As we have seen, in transubstantiation – as in natural change – one term changes into the other. Transubstantiation simply carries this out more radically, as a change of being rather than of matter, in order to make present the unique body and blood of Christ. Transubstantiation also includes the aspect, present in natural change, of something that remains the same through the change. In natural change, this is the matter; whereas in transubstantiation it is the accidents of the bread and wine. These points make clear that the created thing retains a crucial iconic role in the Eucharistic conversion. The bread and wine are truly changed into the body and blood of Christ, thus drawing out the incarnational dimension of the Eucharistic conversion: Christ's body and blood, like the bread and wine, are created material realities that are iconic to higher realities. It is in and through such created real-ities that our deification will be accomplished, in a way that radically changes us but does not do away with our creatureliness or materiality.

The accidents of the bread and wine remain through the change and thereby continue to *signify* the unseen reality, both Christ's bodily pres-ence and our graced spiritual nourishment in charity.[78] Our sacrificial sharing in the sacrifice remains a *sacrament*, a sign. The accidents of the bread and wine thus play the iconic signifying role upon which the

---

[78] Since these "accidents" continue to subsist without their "substance," Aristotelian metaphysics is used to depict a reality that would be impossible and unthinkable within a closed Aristotelian system: see Herbert McCabe, O.P., "The Involvement of God," in *God Matters* (London: Geoffrey Chapman, 1987): 39–51, at 43. For further discussion of the medieval debate about the subsisting of the accidents and about the use of Aristotle in eucharistic theology, see Rüdi Imbach, "Le traité de l'eucharistie de Thomas d'Aquin et les Averroïstes," *Revue des sciences philosophiques et théologiques* 77 (1993): 175–94. Imbach presents Aquinas's position as mediating between two later positions represented, on the one side, by the Dominican Thierry of Freiburg who rejected Aquinas's account of the accidents as absolutely impossible even for God, and on the other side by Ockham who argued that the accidents display God's power completely to overturn philoso-phical reasoning. The Neoplatonic *Liber de causis* contains the suggestion, adopted by Aquinas, that God could "suspend the influence of the secondary cause and intervene directly" (Imbach, 178). Among the 219 articles condemned in 1277 by Archbishop Tempier of Paris, four involve the argument that accidents cannot exist without a subject (Imbach, 175–6). For a comparison of Aquinas, Giles of Rome, and Ockham, see Marilyn McCord Adams, "Aristotle and the Sacrament of the Altar: A Crisis in Medieval Aristotelianism," *Canadian Journal of Philosophy*, supplementary vol. 17 (1992): 195–249.

meaning of sacraments, as manifestations of the fulfillment of created reality by God's grace in the Body of Christ, depends.[79] In short, Aquinas would agree with Schmemann's insistence upon the iconic role of the created things – as Fagerberg, in his brief survey of question 77, suggests. So long as one does not imagine that transubstantiation consists in a transformation of the matter, one may say that the body of Christ is "made out of" bread, in the sense that the bread is the first term of the change, and that underlying the selfsame accidents of the bread one finds first bread and then the body of Christ.

The second problem is why, if God changes the entire being or whole substance of the bread and wine into the whole substance of Christ's body and blood, do the consecrated elements continue to appear, to our senses, to be bread and wine? It would seem that such a radical change would result in a change in the empirical appearances as well. As Aquinas states in article 5, however, the "accidents" of the bread and wine – including quantity, quality, place, position, condition, action, passion – remain, though no longer under the "substantial form" of the bread (cf. article 6).[80] One needs little persuasion that the accidents of the bread and wine remain in the consecrated elements. Similarly, we can easily agree that God is wise, in changing the whole substance, to retain the accidents of bread and wine in the sacrament. Were Christ's body and blood to appear in the sacrament in their own proper species, with their accidents (such as quantity), our sharing in Christ's sacrifice would be, as Aquinas points out, a horrible act of cannibalism and rightly repudiated by unbelievers (article 5).

Substance and accidents

Even so, what are we to make of "accidents" that are present without a "substance"? Aquinas turns to a more concentrated investigation of this problem in questions 76 (on the mode in which Christ is present in the sacrament) and 77 (on the accidents of the bread and wine). In these two questions, Aquinas goes deeper into the issues that, in question 75's outline of the nature of the change itself, he had laid the groundwork for addressing. Before seeking answers to such problems, however, we cannot avoid what here becomes an ever more pressing concern: perhaps Aristotelian categories are impinging too far into a divine mystery. In raising this concern, Bulgakov gives a superb summary of the difficulty:

---

[79] Although, as Kimel points out and as the Second Council of Nicea defined, the Eucharist is not an "icon" of Christ but rather is Christ.
[80] The distinction between "substance" and "accidents" originates in Aristotle, *Categories* iv.

There appears to be an inherent strangeness in such a degree of dependence of the core of this dogma [transubstantiation] on the purely philosophical doctrine of some philosopher, and especially a pagan one. To be sure, it is impossible to deny the connection of Christian theology with Greek philosophy, which in its concepts developed ready terms and logical limits for the expression of dogmas. Such concepts as *ousia* (essence), *hupostasis* (hypostasis), *energeia* (energy), *phusis* (nature), concepts that are the building blocks of the dogmatic definitions, belong to the Greek philosophical lexicon. However, by introducing these concepts, dogmatics does not introduce into church teaching any purely philosophical doctrine, be it that of Plato, Aristotle, the Stoics, or the Neoplatonists. Instead, it employs concepts developed by these philosophers, using these concepts in its own way and sometimes substantially changing their original meaning (consider, for example, the use of *hupostasis* in the trinitarian definitions). The dogmatic definitions of the Church lay the foundation for wholly new doctrines of Christian philosophy (both in the patristic and in the modern period), which is based on, but by no means repeats, ancient philosophy. But the situation is reversed in the doctrine of transubstantiation, where philosophy does not serve theology but theology is a slave to philosophy: theology recognizes but a single one of philosophy's doctrines to be true and makes the whole of eucharistic theology dependent upon this doctrine, considering eucharistic theology to be a particular case of the general relation between substance and accidents.[81]

Could it be that Schmemann's rejection of any explanatory attempts (including Bulgakov's) for the Eucharistic conversion is the right approach?

I would suggest that a twofold consideration is required. As a first step, the use of metaphysical analysis in describing theological mysteries should not be despised *a priori*, as Bulgakov makes quite clear with regard to such distinctions as person/nature in Trinitarian theology. When undertaken in a sapiential mode as a spiritual exercise, metaphysical analysis serves to rule out possible distortions that would impinge upon, and reduce, the fullness of the mystery.[82] In the case of the Eucharist, what

---

[81] Bulgakov, *The Holy Grail and the Eucharist*, 75–6.
[82] For further discussion of this point, drawing upon Gabriel Marcel, see Thomas Weinandy, O.F.M. Cap., *Does God Suffer?* (Notre Dame, IN: University of Notre Dame Press, 2000): 27–39.

is at stake is the problem of bodiliness. Here a second step is necessary, in conjunction with the first: one must recall the theological parameters of the theology of the Eucharist as outlined in the first article of question 75, which provides the theological rationale for Aquinas's procedure in these three questions on transubstantiation. Believers are called to fulfill the Law with Christ, in other words to share in his justice or holiness (the universal call to holiness). The perfection of the "New Law," then, requires that believers receive a real participation in the perfect sacrifice of Christ on the Cross, in and through which the communion of persons – the fullness of true *friendship* – constituted by justice, reconciliation, and forgiveness is attained. This union with Christ's body and blood, in sacrifice and in communion, constitutes the fullness of Christian life. The union must be a this-worldly, bodily contact, despite the fact that Christ's glorified body is now in heaven.

These parameters of faith, of course, have a "necessity" imposed only by Christ's gracious will to make himself present to believers in this bodily way. Citing Luke 22:19 as well as various patristic commentaries, Aquinas points out that "[t]he presence of Christ's true body and blood in this sacrament cannot be detected by sense, nor understanding, but by faith alone, which rests upon Divine authority."[83] Once Jesus has given his promise at the Last Supper (as confirmed elsewhere in Scripture, as well as in Tradition) the Eucharistic question is then one of bodiliness. The Eucharistic conversion has to do with the bodily presence of Christ in this world, in the Church's sacrifice and communion with his friends. Once the issue is clearly seen as having to do with bodily presence in this world, then metaphysical reflection upon bodily presence is necessary in order to proclaim the mystery, precisely as a mystery of bodily presence.

Such metaphysical reflection serves to accomplish two tasks, both necessary for the proclamation of Eucharistic faith. First, it assists in ruling out errors that either falsely conceive this bodily presence in the sacrament – by underestimating the role of the sacramental sign, by undercutting the uniqueness of Christ's body alive and glorified in heaven, and so forth – or lead to a denial of the bodily presence. Second, it affirms boldly the central truth about this mystery of faith, namely that Christ's presence in the sacrament truly is bodily. Bodily realities require a metaphysics that accounts for both continuity and change.[84]

---

[83] 3, q. 75, a. 1.

[84] A helpful philosophical survey of the issues at stake in the doctrine of transubstantiation is found in Joseph Bobik, *Aquinas on Divine Truth* (South Bend, IN: St Augustine's Press, 2001): 167–94; see also Stephen Brock, "St. Thomas and the Eucharistic Conversion." That a "metaphysics" will be present in any account of the Eucharist is made clear by Charles Sanders Peirce's dismissal of Eucharistic controversies in light of his own metaphysical positions. According to Peirce,

The metaphysics of substance and accidents provides such an account, in explanatory categories whose complexity is proportionate to the complexity of reality, of the continuity and change of a thing. "Accidents" describe a thing empirically; "substance" describes a thing insofar as it is a whole, not dependent for its wholeness on any particular "accident." My "quantity," for instance, can change radically. The tiny embryo was none other than me; to kill the embryo would have been to kill me. Yet the embryo lacked many crucial aspects that now characterize "me" and possessed many aspects that now do not belong to "me." Something has radically stayed the same, while other things have radically changed. "Substance" does no more than name the reality, empirically describable in terms of its "accidents," that remains the same through a change in "accidental" characteristics.[85]

[W]e can consequently mean nothing by wine but what has certain effects, direct or indirect, upon our senses; and to talk of something as having all the sensible characters of wine, yet being in reality blood, is senseless jargon. Now, it is not my object to pursue the theological question; and having used it as a logical example I drop it, without caring to anticipate the theologian's reply. I only desire to point out how impossible it is that we should have an idea in our minds which relates to anything but conceived sensible effects of things. Our idea of anything *is* our idea of its sensible effects; and if we fancy that we have any other we deceive ourselves, and mistake a mere sensation accompanying the thought for a part of the thought itself. It is absurd to say that thought has any meaning unrelated to its only funciton. It is foolish for Catholics and Protestants to fancy themselves in disagreement about the elements of the sacrament, if they agree in regard to all their sensible effects, here and hereafter. (Peirce, *The Collected Papers of Charles Sanders Peirce*, vol. 5: *Pragmatism and Pragmaticism*, eds. Charles Hartshorne and Paul Weiss [Cambridge, MA: Harvard University Press, 1934]: 401–2; cf. 541–2 in the same volume)

[85] In modern science, as Terence Nichols has pointed out, the notion of "substantial form" is often rejected. Drawing upon Robert Sokolowski's "Formal and Material Causality in Science," *Proceedings of the American Catholic Philosophical Association* 69 (1995), John Goyette has shown that this rejection flows from a misunderstanding of what "substantial form" accounts for. See John Goyette, "Substantial Form and the Recovery of an Aristotelian Natural Science," *The Thomist* 66 (2002): 519–33; Terence L. Nichols, "Aquinas's Concept of Substantial Form and Modern Science," *International Philosophical Quarterly* 36 (1996): 303–18. Nichols's proposal for a revised notion of substantial form does not adequately understand, in my view, Aristotle's conception of form. For further analysis of substantial form, see Ric Machuga, *In Defense of the Soul: What It Means to Be Human* (Grand Rapids, MI: Brazos Press, 2002): 27–32, which distinguishes between "form" and "shape." See also the profound, lengthy discussion of the metaphysics of substance and accident in John F. Wippel, *The Metaphysical Thought of Thomas Aquinas: From Finite Being to Uncreated Being* (Washington, DC: Catholic University of America Press, 2000): 197–375, as well as shorter discussions in Leo J. Elders, S.V.D., *The Metaphysics of Being of St. Thomas Aquinas in Historical Perspective* (Leiden: Brill, 1993): 239–8 and W. Norris Clarke, S.J., *The One and the Many: A Contemporary Thomistic Metaphysics* (Notre Dame, IN: University of Notre Dame Press, 2001): 123–49.

As categories descriptive of everyday bodily changes, "substance" and "accidents" express the bodily character of the Eucharistic conversion. The same categories also are able to convey the mysterious character of the sacramental bodily change in the Eucharist. The bread and wine become Christ's body and blood while continuing to appear to be in every way the same bread and wine, and in no way like Christ's body and blood. Complicating things even more, Christ's body and blood appears on many altars and in many hosts and chalices, while being none other than the same body and blood now physically alive in the state of glory.

The sacrament of the Eucharist, in short, involves a change radically unlike any other change. Yet, this change is a bodily change whose structure still belongs recognizably within the basic patterns in which we locate "bodily changes." The doctrine of transubstantiation assists in preserving the Eucharistic conversion against tendencies to make the conversion totally like (rationalizing the mystery, e.g. transformation theories) or totally unlike (mystifying the mystery, e.g. placing the conversion entirely outside the explanatory realm of bodily change) the bodily changes that we know.

These two aspects – the uniqueness of the eucharistic conversion, and its status as a bodily change – guide Aquinas's metaphysical exploration of the sacrament of the Eucharist. The first article of question 76 raises the issue of whether the "whole Christ" is contained in the sacrament. Jesus says "This is my body" and "This is my blood" (Matt. 26:26–7). God's power in the sacramental conversion changes the bread and wine into the body and blood of Christ. This change, as we have said, is a bodily one: material substance is changed into material substance. As Aquinas's first objection points out, however, "Christ exists in three substances, namely, the Godhead, soul and body." Clearly even were the change not bodily, God could not change matter into Godhead. When added to Jesus' own reference simply to his body and blood, how the change involves Jesus' soul and divinity becomes problematic.

On the one hand, the theological affirmation of the hypostatic union, and the union of Jesus' body and soul (broken only during the three days of descent among the dead), means that when his living body and blood are made present, his soul and divinity are present as well. On the other hand, the Eucharistic conversion itself does not make his soul and divinity present. The Eucharistic conversion, as such, is a bodily conversion that, as we recall, is ordered to our sacrificial sharing in Christ's bodily death as his friends. The bread and wine are not converted into Christ's divinity. Yet, the body and blood of Christ are radically inseparable from his divinity. So as to understand properly Christ's words at the Last Supper, Aquinas therefore employs a metaphysical distinction to help clarify the precise nature of the Eucharistic conversion. The "power of the sacrament" changes the bread and wine into the body and blood;

what Aquinas calls "natural concomitance" requires that all that which is united to the living body and blood is present in the consecrated elements as well.[86] Similarly, the "power of the sacrament" changes, as Jesus says in his twofold consecration, bread into body and wine into blood; yet by "natural concomitance" the blood is present with the body, and the body with the blood.[87] The "power of the sacrament" thus effectively signifies the theological mystery of Christ's Pasch, in which his blood was (by his own free will, in perfect love) sacrificially spilled, separated, from his body.[88] The "power of the sacrament," in short, as a signifying causality, remains at the level of bodily change in a way that emphasizes that it is our union (communion) with Christ's sacrifice that is at stake.

The answer to the third objection in article 1 of question 76 then probes perhaps the most commonly troubling questions regarding the Eucharistic conversion. By affirming the truth that the conversion is a bodily conversion, as emphasized by the *respondeo*, one only heightens the serious difficulty, in the objector's words, that "a body of greater quantity cannot be contained under the measure of a lesser. But the measure of the bread and wine is much smaller than the measure of Christ's body." If it is a bodily change, then it should abide by bodily rules. Bodily rules include quantity as well as the other "accidents." Simply put, one cannot imagine a body without such bodily attributes. What kind of "body" would it be that had no bodily attributes? It would seem to be more a ghost than a body.[89]

Yet, in this sacramental bodily change – if we are to accept Christ's words – bodily rules do not seem to apply. For many, including many biblical exegetes, this philosophical point constitutes sufficient grounds for interpreting Christ's words in another way. Aquinas, however, has

---

[86] The Council of Trent also adopts this language of "concomitance." See Session 13, ch. 3; English translation in *Decrees of the Ecumenical Councils*, Vol. II, ed. Norman P. Tanner, S.J. (Washington, DC: Georgetown University Press, 1990): 694. Pierre-Marie Gy remarks that the concept of "natural" or "real" concomitance is an "Avicennian innovation of Thomas in eucharistic theology" (Gy, "Avancées du traité de l'eucharistie, 223; cf. his *La Liturgie dans l'Histoire* [Paris: 1990]: 264).

[87] 3, q. 76, a. 2.

[88] 3, q. 76, a. 2, ad 1.

[89] Catherine Pickstock asks, "Does one not rather have a fideistic denigration of vision and taste, and of the reliability of sensory evidence as indicators of truth? It might seem so, since there is discontinuity and rupture between the bread and the Body, or between the wine and Blood" (Pickstock, "Truth and Language," in *Truth in Aquinas*, 94). She answers: "[T]he appearance of bread and wine are not disowned as mere illusions. To the contrary, it is allowed that they remain as accidents, and indeed as accidents which convey with symbolic appropriateness their new underlying substance of Body and Blood" (94). See also Herbert McCabe, O.P., "Eucharistic Change," in *God Still Matters*, ed. Brian Davies, O.P. (New York: Continuum, 2002): 115–22.

already emphasized that to take such an exegetical route would, in addition to contradicting many of the Fathers and the tradition of the Church, fail to apprehend the salvific reality that the communion of Christ's people is, in its fullness, those who share in Christ's Law (the New Law, the perfect fulfillment of Israel's Law of justice) by sharing in the one sacrifice in and through which the Law's justice is restored – sharing not only by faith and sacrificial acts, as the holy Israelites and holy men and women of every time and place have done, but rather sharing in a "perfect" way by sacrificially partaking in Christ's Pasch. To take such an exegetical route, in other words, would be to fail to realize that the communion of the people of God gathered by Christ attains its "perfection" by fulfilling the Law with him, and thereby experiences the hope of Israel, becoming "a kingdom of priests" (Exod. 19:6) in the King who is the eschatological Temple of Ezekiel.

But is there another route by which to make sense of (without rationalizing by claiming to know the mode of God's power) this conversion precisely as a sacramental bodily change? Aquinas traces a route of metaphysical *ascesis*, in which we follow the path of bodily change but purify our minds of attachment to our imagistic understanding of "bodily." As we have argued, there must be something that underlies changes in quantity. Yet, this reality cannot be empirically describable, since empirical description inevitably employs the terms of changeable accidents. This underlying reality that constitutes a thing's continuity is, as we noted above, called "substance." Under normal bodily rules, a "substance" is present in the world "by way of," or according to the empirical mode of, its "accidents."

The metaphysical *ascesis* which we are undertaking in order to speak theologically about the Eucharist, however, enables us to recognize that the "substance" *could* be present, by God's power, according to its *own* mode. In such a situation, the "accidents" would be sublated under the mode of the "substance," rather than the other way around. This possibility, without losing its mystery as a sacramental mode of being, would describe a bodily change. By way of affirming the theological truth that Christ is entirely present in the consecrated elements, we can affirm that just such a reversal has occurred within the Eucharistic conversion. The substance of Christ's body and blood is present, and yet cannot be empirically recognized because it is present sacramentally according to the "mode" of substance.

Does this mean, however, that the "accidents" that characterize his living body in heaven are somehow separated from his "substance," to which direct access is then given? No. Such a situation would mean that the whole Christ, his whole body and blood, were not made present, and thus that our salvific participation in his Cross, the very purpose of the sacrament, could not be full and real. Rather, as Aquinas says, "it is clear that the body of Christ is in this sacrament *by way of substance,* and not by way of quantity."[90] He goes on to explain that substance can be fully present in any quantity: "the proper totality of substance is contained indifferently in a small or large quantity; as the whole nature of air in a great or small amount of air, and the whole nature of a man in a big or small individual."[91] The accidents of Christ's living body and blood are not thereby "cut off" from his body and blood, however. The "power of the sacrament" makes present the substance of Christ's body and blood. The accidents are present by way of concomitance. It cannot be emphasized enough that they are in fact truly present; the "substance" of Christ's body and blood is not cut off from the "accidents." We receive the whole Christ. Yet, they are present not according to their own mode, but according to the empirically undetectable mode of the substance, "whose nature it is for the whole to be in the whole, and the whole in every part."[92] Apprehending this mode constitutes the metaphysical *ascesis* necessary for learning how to speak of the Eucharist in its theological richness.

The fact that Christ's body and blood are not present according to the mode of dimensive quantity makes intelligible, on the level of bodily change, how Christ can be entirely under every part of the sacramental species or consecrated elements.[93] In article 3 of question 76 the objector argues that Christ is not entirely under every part because "an organic body . . . has parts determinately distant," as that of eye from ear, and also because "Christ's body always retains the true nature of a body, nor is it ever changed into a spirit. Now it is the nature of a body for it to be *quantity having position (Predic.* iv)."[94] Christ's body and blood, Aquinas grants, are indeed "under dimensions" – the dimensions of the bread and wine, which remain in the consecrated elements – but not under dimensions according to the mode of dimensions. Rather, they are under dimensions sacramentally according to the mode of substance. As Aquinas notes once again, "it is evident that the whole nature of a substance is under every part of the dimensions under which it is contained; just as the entire nature of air is under every part of air, and the entire nature of bread under every part of bread."[95]

---

[90] 3, q. 76, a. 1, ad 3. See also Joseph Ratzinger, *God Is Near Us: The Eucharist, the Heart of Life*, ed. Stephan Otto Horn and Vinzenz Pfnür, trans. Henry Taylor (San Francisco: Ignatius Press, 2003): 85f., although Ratzinger seeks to explain this reality in terms of radical transformation rather than by employing metaphysical precisions.

[91] 3, q. 76, a. 1, ad 3.

[92] 3, q. 76, a. 4, ad 1; cf. ad 2.

[93] For further discussion, see David Burr, "Quantity and Eucharistic Presence: The Debate from Olivi through Ockham," *Collectanea Franciscana* 94 (1974): 5–44.

[94] 3, q. 76, a. 3, obj. 2 and 3.

[95] 3, q. 76, a. 3; cf. ad 2. Note that this explanation – the mode of substance – does not explain *how* it occurs that Christ's body and blood is present on the altar according to the mode of substance. The only answer for that would by "by the power of the

The discussion of the dimensive quantity of Christ's living body and blood sets up Aquinas's analysis of the most controverted problem of Eucharistic theology, as borne out by Bulgakov's strong objections (and his radical proposal): how the body and blood can be said to be in the sacrament, when Christ has only one body and it is glorified at the right hand of the Father. Is Christ's body in the sacrament as in a place? The answer seems necessarily to be yes, because one cannot imagine any other way for a body to be somewhere. If Christ's body is not in the sacrament of the Eucharist as in a place, then, it would seem, it is not in the sacrament of the Eucharist in any sense worth speaking about. Any other answer would seem to confirm once and for all that Aquinas is speaking of a ghost-like spiritual presence, not a concrete bodily presence. Furthermore, if the bread and wine are not there in substance, then something must be in the consecrated elements – and that something must be Christ's body and blood.[96]

Yet, Christ's body is *not* in the sacrament of the Eucharist as in a place. It should be clear how close we are here to Bulgakov's iconic understanding of the Eucharist, in which as regards this world the bread and wine are unchanged, whereas as regards the divine realm Christ has made them his body and blood by manifesting himself through them. But it should also be clear that, while Aquinas retains this iconic (significatory) understanding of the bread and wine, Aquinas seeks a solution to Bulgakov's problematic that will give more credence to the Eucharistic conversion as a sacramental bodily change than Bulgakov is willing to do. By his divine power, Christ makes the bread and wine his body and blood; but he does so in a way that cannot be as disembodied as Bulgakov suggests. Christ's body and blood are material realities even in their glorified state (here firmly parting ways from Bulgakov's sophiological anthropology, strongly influenced by Hegel). It follows that if the material realities of the bread and wine are to be changed into the

---

sacrament" or "sacramentally," God's action through the sign. We cannot know the "how" of God's action. As Denys Turner notes with regard to the word "sacramental": "we cannot know what we mean by the word, for it is and must be utter mystery" (Turner, "The Darkness of God and the Light of Christ: Negative Theology and Eucharistic Presence," in *Catholicism and Catholicity*, ed. Sarah Beckwith [Oxford: Blackwell, 1999]: 31–46, at 40). Turner goes to propose "an 'apophatic theology' of the Eucharist, in order to articulate the "absence" (41) that the sign indicates, the absence of the fullness of heavenly communion. Graham Ward makes a similar point about "presence," blaming the late medievals (Ockham) for reifying Christ's eucharistic presence (what Ward calls "a commodification of presence" [186]). See Ward's unfortunately titled "The Church as the Erotic Community," in *Sacramental Presence in a Postmodern Context*, ed. Lieven Boeve and Lambert Leijssen (Leuven: Peeters, 2001): 166–204. Both Turner and Ward nonetheless overemphasize absence. Kevin Hart responds to Ward's article in the same volume (205–11), and rightly urges Ward to avoid a theology that becomes mere gesture.

[96] 3, q. 76, a. 5, obj. 2.

material realities of Christ's body and blood, then this must be a bodily change, not merely a heavenly manifestation that does not truly affect the realm of material bodiliness. It is, after all, at the level of this realm of material bodiliness that our sacrificial communion is won. Bulgakov's complete spiritualization of bodiliness (and corresponding dismissal of any real change in the earthly material realm) does not correspond to the bodiliness of Eucharistic faith. And yet Bulgakov's intuition that the change is not a spatial one, or one involving local motion on the part of Christ's body and blood, is correct, as we will see.

In accord with his principle enunciated with regard to dimensive quantity, Aquinas states, "Christ's body is in this sacrament not after the proper manner of dimensive quantity, but rather after the manner of substance."[97] This means that Christ's body and blood cannot be in the sacrament "as in a place," since place depends upon spatial dimensions and quantity. Indeed, were Christ's body and blood in the sacrament as in a place, we would break his body into bits by "crushing with the teeth."[98] Even so, in their sacramental mode of being, Christ's body and blood *are* in the sacrament. They are in the sacrament according to the mode "in which substance is contained in dimensions."[99]

What kind of mode is this? Regarding the case of bread, it is clear that the substance of the bread is not in the bread according to dimensive quantity. Were it so, if one took a bite out of the bread one would deprive the bread of its "substance" or nature. Similarly, the substance of the body and blood of Christ are not in the sacrament of the Eucharist according to dimensive quantity. On the other hand, in the case of bread, the dimensive quantity of the bread, as an "accident," subsists in the "substance" of the bread. Every accident must exist in a substance. The substance of the bread is the "subject" in which its accidents adhere, and in this sense the substance of the bread is present "locally" in its dimensions.

After the Eucharistic conversion, however, Christ's body and blood do not become the "subject" in which the accidents of the bread and wine subsist. As we have suggested above, Bulgakov's sophiological account of "bodiliness" does away with the material particularity of bodiliness, and therefore cannot adequately describe the eucharistic offering of Christ's one sacrifice. Likewise, it would be ludicrous to imagine that Christ's living body and blood become bready and wine-like.

[97] 3, q. 76, a. 5. Cf. Anscar Vonier, O.S.B., *A Key to the Doctrine of the Eucharist*, 186.
[98] 3, q. 77, a. 7, especially ad 3. Here Aquinas is clarifying the confession of Berengar by which Berengar was formally reconciled to the Church. For further discussion, see J. de Montclos, *Lanfranc and Bérenger: La controverse eucharistique du XIe siècle* (Leuven: 1971) and Henry Chadwick, "Ego Berengarius," *Journal of Theological Studies* 40 (1989): 414–45.
[99] 3, q. 76, a. 5.

Thus Christ's body and blood are not in the sacrament of the Eucharist as in a place, either according to dimensive quantity or as the subject of the bread's dimensive quantity (we will soon return to the latter point in our discussion of question 77). Rather, Christ's body and blood are in the sacrament in the way that a substance or a nature is in bread, in the way that the whole nature of bread is in every part of bread. Clearly, this cannot be conceived through an image, since images require us to think in terms of spatial dimensions. "Substance" can only be conceived through metaphysical *ascesis*, but that does not make it any less real. A human being's status as a human being does not depend upon his or her dimensive quantity: that which underlies changes in accidents such as dimensive quantity is the substance of the human being, his or her deepest reality.

Christ's body and blood, then, are in the sacrament of the Eucharist not according to place – according to the "accident" of place they are in heaven at the right hand of the Father – but sacramentally according to the non-spatial mode of substance. Yet, is this merely another way of saying that their "accidents" stay in heaven, while their "deepest reality" ventures off to foreign territory? No. It is first and foremost a refusal to think of bodiliness solely in terms of "accidental" characteristics. Bodiliness does not consist solely, or even primarily, in the appearances. Rather, there is a profound reality to bodiliness that escapes those who can only think in terms of what appears visibly. Bodiliness, in this sense, is "substantial," "lasting," and "good" in the iconic sense of sharing in the depths of being (in a way that is sometimes mistakenly reserved for spiritual substances). To differentiate the substance of a thing from its accidents is not to postulate a ghost. Instead, this differentiation enables one to escape the imaginative impression that bodily things are sheer flux, lacking any principle of continuity and identity. Second, recall that Christ's "accidents" are not absent from his substance in the Eucharist; on the contrary, they are present, though according to the invisible mode of substance rather than their own mode. By God's power, conditioned to his purposes in the sacrament, the mode of substance here sublates the mode of accidents, rather than the other way around.

Third, Christ's substance does not "venture off" while his accidents stay "at home" in heaven because, as Aquinas affirms with Bulgakov, "Christ's body is at rest in heaven. Therefore it is not movably in this sacrament."[100] The point here is that when one, for instance, carries the consecrated host from one's hand to one's mouth, one is not "moving" or "shaking" Christ. Just as in the case of place, where if Christ were

---

[100] 3, q. 76, a. 6, *sed contra*. See Walter M. Gordon's excellent "Time, Space and the Eucharist," *The Downside Review* 95 (1977): 110–16, which responds to J.A. O'Driscoll, "The Reality of the Real Presence," *The Downside Review* 93 (1975): 201–8.

in the sacrament according to place rather than according to substance he could not be in many hosts at once, so also in the case of local motion. Were Christ moved in the sacrament, then he would (impossibly) move around simultaneously in many different ways every Sunday morning. Neither place nor motion allows for the reality of the glorified, living, one Christ. Since Christ is not in the sacrament as in a place, he does not "move" when the consecrated elements move. Instead, he remains the same in substance, and his substance is present sacramentally according to its non-dimensive mode in many places, just as the substance of bread is present in every part of the bread. In saying this, one must keep in mind also that since his substance is not the "subject" of the dimensive quantity of the bread, Christ's substance is not limited, as the substance of the bread would be, to existing fully under every part of the bread. Rather, Christ's substance can be fully present in numerous consecrated hosts, as well as in his own proper reality in heaven. Since Christ's substance is not the "subject" in which the accidents of bread and wine adhere, Christ's substance is not tied to the accidents in the way that bread's substance is tied to the accidents of the bread. When the accidents of the bread cease to be, the substance of the bread ceases to be. In the case of Christ's substance, in contrast, when the accidents of the bread cease to be, the sacramental relationship by which Christ is present substantially under the accidents of the bread ceases to be; but Christ's substance, living eternally in heaven, does not cease to be.[101]

Bulgakov's concerns thus require a metaphysical *ascesis* that, unlike Bulgakov's own solution, preserves the crucial soteriological reality of sacramental bodiliness. Such metaphysical *ascesis* hardly constitutes a philosophical enslavement of the theological reality of the Eucharist. Rather, it affirms, in terms of the bodily change, that the Church's offering is nothing less than the offering of Jesus Christ, and thus a sharing in his one sacrificial offering on the Cross. This truth is inaccessible intellectually without such metaphysical *ascesis*. As Aquinas points out, the presence of Christ's body and blood in the sacrament, as a substantial (and thus absolutely real and entire) presence, cannot be seen by any bodily eye, even the bodily eye of a glorified human being. Since the accidents of Christ's body and blood are present according to the mode of the substance, rather than according to their own mode, "they do not act on the medium so as to be seen by any corporeal eye"; and "substance, as such, is not visible to the bodily eye, nor does it come under any one of the senses, nor under the imagination, but solely under the intellect, whose object is what a thing is (*De Anima* iii)."[102]

---

[101] 3, q. 76, a. 6.
[102] 3, q. 76, a. 7.

Furthermore, this truth is inaccessible without faith in God's power working in the sacrament. Just as the natural intellect cannot apprehend the divine mystery of the Trinity, but requires faith or the perfection of faith in glory, so likewise the natural intellect cannot apprehend the divine mystery of the Eucharist. Aquinas therefore rules out the notion that Eucharistic apparitions, in which "flesh, or blood, or a child," appears in the sacrament, truly consist in Christ's body in its "proper species," as it appears in heaven.[103] Such apparitions, if true miracles, simply serve to represent more concretely to believers, by a change in the accidents of bread and wine, the truth of Christ's substantial presence in the Eucharist. Bodiliness, in the Eucharist, is always *sacramental* bodiliness.

The "subject" of the accidents

Aquinas's insistence on sacramental bodiliness – the ground of our sacramental sharing (communion) in Christ's embodied sacrifice on the Cross – returns us to a point noted above, but not defended: namely, that the accidents of the bread and wine remain after the consecration without a proper "subject" in which to subsist, since the substance of the bread and wine is no longer present and Christ's body and body, possessing their own accidents, do not become a "subject" for the accidents of the bread and wine. This point introduces Aquinas's discussion in question 77 of the accidents which remain in the sacrament. As Aquinas points out, "it belongs to the definition of an accident for it to be in a subject."[104] It is experientially obvious that without a substance, there will be no appearances. Even so, the living constitution of Christ's glorified body and blood cannot be thought of as changing to become bready and wine-like. We are on the horns of a metaphysical dilemma, but metaphysics, for Aquinas, is not a closed science. "Metaphysics" does not describe "being" in a state *autonomous* from God the Creator and fount of being (as infinite, unfathomable Pure Act). On the contrary, Aquinas's "metaphysics," as a spiritual exercise, instructs believers on

---

[103] 3, q. 76, a. 8. R. Trent Pomplun points out that Scotus sharply disagrees with Aquinas here: "Scotus rebuts this position with an extreme eucharistic realism. 'It is not God's will,' he says, 'to confirm men's faith by imaginary apparitions'" (Pomplun, "Israel and the Eucharist: A Scotist Perspective," *Pro Ecclesia* 11 [2002]: 292). Pomplun explains, "Present upon the altar by means of his resurrection body's eschatological subtlety, Christ's sacramental mode of presence includes his natural mode of presence" (292). With its closeness to Bulgakov's, this position strikes me not as the insertion of the transcendent realm into history but rather as an inability to take the realm of history (materiality/temporality) with sufficient seriousness.

[104] 3, q. 77, a. 1. For further discussion, cf. Édouard-Henri Wéber, "L'incidence du traité de l'eucharistie sur la métaphysique de S. Thomas d'Aquin," *Revue des sciences philosophiques et théologiques* 77 (1993): 204f.

the radically participatory and contingent status of created being, which is a finite created (and continually sustained) sharing in God.[105]

As with a previous metaphysical dilemma in Eucharistic theology – the question of how a whole substance could be converted into a whole substance, rather than simply the matter of one receiving, by transformation (Fagerberg), a new form (which would result in the notion of new bodies of Christ continually being created) – Aquinas appeals to his participatory account of metaphysics in which God the Creator is radically present throughout.[106] He grants that "it belongs to the quiddity or essence of accident *to have existence in a subject.*"[107] In other words, without a subject, accidents would not exist. Yet in the case of the Eucharist, in which God is present in sacramental action, there is no reason why God cannot directly sustain them in existence. God, the giver of being, is not limited as he would be by an "enclosed" or deist metaphysics.[108] The accidents no longer have a "subject" in which they subsist (because God could hardly be such a "subject," as if God could become "bready"), but they nonetheless retain existence because God miraculously – but not impossibly, given the participatory structure of metaphysics – sustains them in the existence that they previously possessed through their adhering in the "subject" of the substance of the

---

[105] This point is made by Catherine Pickstock in "Truth and Language," in *Truth in Aquinas*, 106. The accidents express creatureliness as well by their "signifying and spiritually active purpose," just as every created thing is a trace or an image of God with a teleology ordered to God (107).

[106] As opposed to accounts of metaphysics and ethics that seek (with unfortunate effects, but without explanatory success) to construct an autonomous realm for human action. Without such a metaphysical account of the creature-Creator relationship – which requires the analogy of being, flowing from a recognition of our radical contingency – theology is locked into a self-referentiality that cannot but end up in a nominalist (power rather than participatory wisdom) account of theological claims, resulting in fideism and/or skepticism. For an example of such self-referential theology, see Gianni Vattimo, *After Christianity*, trans. Luca D'Isanto (New York: Columbia University Press, 2002). For a similar rejection of the "analogy of being" as the marker of "onto-theology," see Lieven Boeve, "Postmodern Sacramento-Theology: Retelling the Christian Story," *Ephemerides Theologicae Lovanienses* 74 (1998): 326–43, at 328. For a contrasting reading of Heidegger, see Fergus Kerr, O.P., *After Aquinas: Versions of Thomism* (Oxford: Blackwell, 2002), 89–93. Kerr is intrigued by Hans Urs von Balthasar's reading of Heidegger as unconsciously a defender of the true analogy of being. The best theological study of Heidegger's project that I have found is David Bentley Hart's critical analysis in *The Beauty of the Infinite: The Aesthetics of Christian Truth* (Grand Rapids, MI: Eerdmans, 2003): 129–33, 213ff. Hart makes clear the problems intrinsic to Heideggerian theologies.

[107] 3, q. 77, a. 1, ad 2.

[108] David Power, O.M.I., fearing that the metaphysics of causality has deist implications, proposes an "analogy of being" that lacks an account of causality, although without explaining what then would make intelligible this "analogy": "If the analogy of being is to be kept, it can respond to the issues raised by Aquinas without developing it along the lines in which he wrote of causality" (Power, *The Eucharistic Mystery*: 287).

bread and wine.[109] God sustains them in that condition in order to employ them iconically (Schmemann and Bulgakov), in the sacramental sign by which the whole Christ is made present under the sign of the accidents of bread and wine, for the purposes of our salvific participation in Christ's sacrifice in and through which we attain communion and manifest the New Creation, the *telos* of all created reality, in which Christ will be "all in all." Aquinas adds that in the miracle of the Eucharistic conversion (transubstantiation), God sacramentally sustains them in being in such a way that the cohesion of the accidents now depends upon the accident of dimensive quantity, which thus now *functions* as a "subject" for the other accidents.[110] In other words, so long as there is dimensive quantity, the other accidents will be present; but once dimensive quantity has corrupted, then the other accidents of the bread and wine, too, will cease to be present.

Having accounted for the continuing existence and cohesion of the accidents, which is experientially evident to all, Aquinas turns to another set of experiential issues regarding sacramental bodiliness. These issues have to do with the reality that the bread and wine do not seem to have changed at all (Bulgakov). Just as before the consecration, the consecrated elements can still, as we know from experience, affect external objects, be corrupted and take part in the generation of other material things, nourish us as food and drink when consumed, be broken, and (in the case of the consecrated wine) be mingled with other liquid. As Fagerberg emphasizes, in accord with Dom Anscar Vonier and Catherine Pickstock, the accidents of the bread and wine do not become mere ciphers: they continue to possess effective power by which they signify spiritual realities iconically. Without such power, the accidents of the bread and wine could not serve their iconic sacramental purpose. For example, Aquinas points out, "If they could not change external bodies, they could not be felt."[111] If they could not be felt, how could they signify the sacrificial offering, in which they are lifted up? Likewise, if they could not corrupt, they could not be consumed, and Christ would remain under each (undigested) host forever, thus making our repeated sharing in his sacrifice impossible for our bodies to sustain. If they could not nourish (or if nothing could be generated from them), they would signify quite imperfectly spiritual nourishment. If the consecrated bread could not be broken, they could not be consumed, thereby rendering void their signification of sacrificial communion. If the

---

[109] 3, q. 77, a. 1; cf. ad 3 and 4.

[110] 3, q. 77, a. 2; cf. a. 5 (including ad 3). The miracle is God's directly sustaining them in being; but this miracle does not differ radically from the status of all creatures, since God ultimately sustains *all things* in being. For an opposing view, see Terence Nichols, "Transubstantiation and Eucharistic Presence," 66.

[111] 3, q. 77, a. 3, *sed contra*.

consecrated wine could not be mingled with other liquid, it too could not be truly consumed.

Not only are these things experientially confirmed, therefore, but they are sacramentally necessary. What then is the problem? The problem – and herein lies the greatest reason for the temptation to conceive the Eucharistic conversion as a transformation of the matter – is that the accidents of the bread and wine do not possess the *matter* of the bread and wine. Rather, under the sacramental species, or the accidents of bread and wine, is the whole substance, including matter (though properly understood in light of the fact that dimensive quantity is an "accident"), of *the body and blood of Christ*. However, everything that we associate with our image of "matter" is present as the accidents of the bread and wine. We normally conceive matter in terms of its accidents, not in terms of its deeper reality or substance. Thus, we associate "matter" with things like dimensive quantity, rarity, density, hardness, porousness, breakableness, the capability of sound, and so forth. All these are "accidents" whose changes do not necessarily involve a change in substance: for instance, bread can be soft, big, and fluffy, or hard as a rock and small, while remaining bread.

Nonetheless, the reality that the substance of the (material) bread and wine has been completely changed into the substance of the (material) body and blood of Christ poses an obvious difficulty for Aquinas's theological account of the Eucharistic conversion. Since the issue is a bodily one – namely how can "accidents" continue to act in the same ways after the "substance" is no longer present – Aquinas turns once more to his metaphysics of creation. He notes, "Because everything acts in so far as it is an actual being, the consequence is that everything stands in the same relation to action as it does to being."[112] If it does not change in being, then it does not change in capacity for action. The accidents had previously depended for "being" on the substance; after the consecration, they depend for "being" upon the divine gift of being (which is in fact what they depend upon in depending upon the substance, and therefore not as radical an alteration as would be claimed by a deist metaphysics). Aquinas points out in this regard that "every action of a substantial or accidental form depends upon God as the first agent."[113] Even

---

[112] 3, q. 77, a. 3.

[113] 3, q. 77, a. 3, ad 2. Etienne Gilson argues that the key move here comes from Avicenna, for whom the definition of "accident" does not include being actually in a subject. Describing Aquinas's position with regard to the accidents in the Eucharistic conversion, Gilson writes,

> Now, in the sacrament of the Eucharist, it is not given to the accidents to be not in a subject in virtue of their own essence (which would be contradictory), but to be not in a subject owing to the divine power that sustains them. "And so they do not cease to be accidents, because the definition of accident is not separated from them and the definition of substance does

without the substantial "form" of the bread and wine, upon which the accidental "forms" had depended for existence, the accidental "forms" retain the same power to act because God sustains their existence. It follows that the "sacramental species are indeed accidents, yet they have the act and power of substance."[114] There is no need to posit a transformation of the matter in the Eucharistic conversion. The serious theological problems inherent within a Eucharistic theory of transformation are thus avoided by a richer understanding of creaturely bodiliness in light of the metaphysics of creation, which enables creation to function in the fully iconic fashion that Fagerberg, with the Russian Orthodox theologians, desires.

Sacramental representation

The distinctions that we have made with regard to the accidents recall us to the primary reality: sacraments are signs. In the sacrament of the Eucharist, the Church's offering of Christ's sacrifice – her liturgical sharing in Christ's sacrificial act – occurs through sacramental representation. Aquinas affirms that "the celebration of the sacrament is an image representing Christ's Passion, which is His true sacrifice."[115] As signs, the sacraments are conditioned to everyday human experience. However, they signify the gift of divine friendship in Jesus Christ, which goes infinitely beyond what the resources of the merely human realm could offer. It is not for nothing that Dom Anscar Vonier says that contemplative meditation on this mystery "will make us into true mystics."[116] The sacrament of the Eucharist signifies a past reality – the Passion of Jesus Christ – as well as a present reality (the grace that conforms the believer to Christ's image and thus unites believers in his Body) and a future reality (perfect conformity to Christ in the heavenly consummation of the Mystical Body).[117] Yet, can a sign actually *be* what it signifies? Not in the natural mode of being. In a restaurant billboard, for example, the actual restaurant is present only in idea, not in reality. The billboard unites us only notionally with the actual restaurant, and so if all we experience is the billboard, we go away hungry.

---

not apply to them." So they do not become substances; they subsist without ceasing to be accidents. (Gilson, "Quasi Definitio Substantiae," in *St. Thomas Aquinas, 1274–1974: Commemorative Studies*, ed. Armand Maurer [Toronto: Pontifical Institute of Medieval Studies, 1974]: 111–29, at 124)

114 3, q. 77, a. 5, ad 2.
115 3, q. 83, a. 1.
116 Vonier, *A Key to the Doctrine of the Eucharist*, 40.
117 3, q. 60, a. 3. See Vonier, *A Key to the Doctrine of the Eucharist*, 19–20, 60–3.

God, however, can cause a sign to be what it signifies.[118] In the sacrament of the Eucharist, what is sacramentally represented or signified is Christ on the Cross, that is, the sacrificial pouring out of Christ's blood from his body (cf. Matt. 26:28; John 19:34). Since a sacrament of the New Law causes what it signifies, the sacramental representation causes the change of the bread and wine into Christ's body and blood. [119] In

---

[118] On sacramental representation and causality, see, in addition to Vonier, the valuable treatment by Thierry-Dominique Humbrecht, O.P., "L'eucharistie, 'représentation' du sacrifice du Christ, selon saint Thomas," *Revue Thomiste* 98 (1998): 379–82. Vonier's view is critiqued by Edward Kilmartin, S.J., who argues that the double consecration "has the value of a commemorative sign which elicits the subjective recall of the historical passion" (Kilmartin, *The Eucharist in the West*, ed. Robert Daly, S.J. [Collegeville, MN: Liturgical Press, 1998]: 254). In Kilmartin's view, it is this "subjective recall," not a sacramental mode of being that objectively makes present Christ's sacrifice, that is central to Aquinas's account. Kilmartin explains that for Aquinas "the historical living of Christ is really present in all sacramental celebrations of the Church" (254), because "from the divine perspective, removes of space and time are not relevant to the ultimate intelligibility of the human living of Jesus" (255). It follows that "the presence of the event of the historical living of Jesus signified by the particular sacrament is a presence in the 'recipient' of the sacramental celebration in the sense of instrumental cause modifying the effect of the action of the principal divine cause of sanctification" (255). In other words, for Aquinas, according to Kilmartin, the historical sacrifice is present in the eucharistic sacrifice

> in the willing participant in whose favor the sacramental celebration takes place. It is a presence in the sense of an instrumental cause which modifies the effect of the action of the principal cause, the Holy Spirit, on the subject of the sacrament. This modification of the effect of the divine action consists in the transmission of the historical attitudes of Christ conformed to the situation of the life of faith that is signified by the particular sacrament. (263–4)

Kilmartin, I think, here reads Eucharistic idealism into the texts of Aquinas. For an effort to augment Kilmartin's work metaphysically by means of Bernard Lonergan's understanding of functional specialization, see Raymond Moloney, S.J., "Lonergan on Eucharistic Sacrifice," *Theological Studies* 62 (2001): 53–70.

[119] On the causality of the sacraments in light of Aquinas's development of the thought of his predecessors, see John Yocum, "Sacraments in Aquinas," in *Aquinas on Doctrine*, ed. Thomas Weinandy, Daniel Keating, and John Yocum (New York: T. & T. Clark, 2004): 168–72. Drawing upon an article by H.-F. Dondaine, "A propos d'Avicenne et de saint Thomas: de la causalité dispositive à la causalité instrumentale," *Revue Thomiste* 51 (1951): 441–53, Yocum shows that Aquinas's conception of sacramental instrumental causality develops from his *Commentary on the Sentences* to his *Summa Theologiae*, as Aquinas draws out the sacramental implications of "the idea found in John Damascene and Athanasius, that the flesh of Christ is the organ of his divinity" (170). In his *Commentary on the Sentences*, Aquinas had been influenced by the Avicennian view, adopted also by Bonaventure, that held, in contrast to the Aristotelian-Averroan idea of a series of causes (principal and instrumental), that "there are two distinct lines of causes, the disposing and the principal cause; the disposing cause prepares matter for the formal change, and the principal cause acts upon the form itself" (170). The consequences of the Avicennian view of causality upon sacramental theology are significant: instead of a unified causal movement into which the sacrament is fully integrated, the

so doing, the sacrament retains its sign-character: in sacramental representation Christ becomes present not in his natural or "proper" mode of being (in which he is over five feet tall and so forth), but in his sacramental mode of being (in which he exists under the sacramental sign or species).[120] God makes Christ's body and blood present in the mode in which they are signified, the mode of separation, that is to say in their (salvific) sacrificial mode.[121] For Aquinas, the very "form" of the sacrament of the Eucharist contains this reference to the Passion.[122] As befits the power of Christ's Cross, the signs of bread and wine point to the transformation of the communicants. As Gilles Emery affirms, "Thomas closely links the substantial *conversion* of the bread and wine

---

sacrament becomes simply dispositive rather than causative of grace. The sacramental action is thereby divided in two, with the sacrament itself becoming marginalized. Scotus moves back in the direction of Avicenna on this point (dispositive or moral causality): see David Berger, *Thomas Aquinas and the Liturgy*, trans. Christopher Grosz (Ypsilanti, MI: Sapientia Press, 2004): 74–9.

[120] Aquinas's views on the sacramental mode of being converge with those of the Council of Trent. See, for example, Session 13, ch. 1:

> In the first place, the holy council teaches and openly and without qualification professes that, after the consecration of the bread and the wine, our lord Jesus Christ, true God and true man, is truly, really and substantially contained in the propitious sacrament of the holy eucharist under the appearance of those things which are perceptible to the senses. Nor are the two assertions incompatible, that our Saviour is ever seated in heaven at the right hand of the Father in his natural mode of existing, and that he is nevertheless sacramentally present to us by his substance in many other places in a mode of existing which, though we can hardly express it in words, we can grasp with minds enlightened by faith as possible to God and must most firmly believe. (*Decrees of the Ecumenical Councils*, Vol. 2, p. 694)

[121] Pierre-Marie Gy notes that Aquinas never uses the expression "ex opere operato" in the *Summa Theologiae*, in contrast to 23 times in the *Commentary on the Sentences* and once in the *Commentary on John*, "not because he does not believe the doctrine that Trent would later define, but, I think, because the same thing seemed to him better expressed in the vocabulary of instrumental causality" (Gy, "Avancées du traité de l'eucharistie de S. Thomas dans la *Somme* par rapport aux *Sentences*," *Revue des sciences philosophiques et théologiques* 77 (1993): 222–3); cf. P.-M. Hombert, "La formule *ex opere operato* chez S. Thomas," *Mélanges de Science religieuse* 49 (1992): 127–41. Enrico Mazza interprets Gy to mean that Aquinas is "abandoning the idea of *ex opere operato*" and thereby making "clear that causality is the real root of sacramental efficacy" (Mazza, *The Celebration of the Eucharist*, 209). Mazza argues that Aquinas has in fact abandoned any serious theology of sign, in favor of causality. For Mazza, presence according to the mode of substance "belongs to the order of causality and not to the order of sign" (209). In fact, as the texts show, Aquinas integrates sign and cause in his theology of the Eucharist; the sacrament's causality cannot be separated from the sign. For discussion of the significance of the bread and wine, see Stephen Brock, "St. Thomas and the Eucharistic Conversion"; see also the insights of Catherine Pickstock and David Fagerberg on this topic.

[122] 3, q. 78, a. 3.

into the Body and Blood of Christ (transubstantiation) and our own *conversion* in Christ who is the end [*finis*] of this conversion."[123] At the same time, the sacramental representation means that God need not create anew Christ's body and blood in a sacrificial mode. Christ's body and blood exist in their natural mode in heaven; there are no other body and blood of Christ than the eternally living body and blood.

If the sacramental mode does not cause Christ to suffer anew, but simply represents his past sacrifice, how then God can make Christ's past sacrifice present in the sacrament? The answer consists "in an entirely new mode of being, the sacramental mode."[124] Aquinas distinguishes between Christ's natural and sacramental modes of existence.[125] God causes Christ's body and blood, alive now in heaven, to exist in heaven in its natural mode *and* on the altar in this sacramental mode as participated in and offered sacramentally by the Church. Christ's body and blood once existed in sacrificial separation; by God's power, through the sacramental representation, the Church offers Christ's body and blood in this separated mode. Vonier writes of the mystery of sacramental signification, which both conforms to the level of historical existence (as sign) and exceeds it (as *divine* sign):

> This is the representative role of the Christian sacrament. Such a thing cannot happen anywhere outside the sacramental sphere. Is not the sacrament precisely this mystery of never ceasing repetition or representation of the thing that is immutable in itself? If Christ came to us in his natural state and were offered up in his natural state, this new coming and this new offering would, indeed, be historic events which would form new chapters in the career of the Son of God. The sacramental presence and the sacramental offering are not historic events in the career of Christ; they do not form new chapters in the book of his life, though, of course, the act by which he instituted the Eucharist and offered up himself for the first time are most tremendous deeds in his historic career, but to be offered up in the sacrament does not belong to the historic life of the Son of God. If there is repetition of acts, those repetitions are not on the part of Christ, they are on the part of the Church living here on earth.[126]

---

[123] Gilles Emery, O.P., "The Ecclesial Fruit of the Eucharist in St. Thomas Aquinas," trans. Therese C. Scarpelli, *Nova et Vetera* 2 (2004): 47. Emery goes on to quote from Aquinas's *Commentary on the Sentences*, with reference to *Summa Theologiae* 3, q. 74, a. 2. See also *Lumen Gentium*, no. 26.

[124] Vonier, 218. Laurence Paul Hemming in "After Heidegger: Transubstantiation," *Heythrop Journal* 41 (2000): 170–86 argues that transubstantiation reveals God's power to act in ways "rupture" human reason's understanding of the cosmos.

[125] 3, q. 81, a. 4; see Vonier, *A Key to the Doctrine of the Eucharist*, 116.

[126] Vonier, *A Key to the Doctrine of the Eucharist*, 136.

By causing the sacramental order of being – historically conditioned as an order of *signs* – God makes the substance of Christ's body and blood, living in heaven, to exist sacramentally in a distinct mode, in accordance with the rite's signification. Christ exists naturally in heaven; the same Christ exists sacramentally on the altar and in the tabernacle. God causes the one Christ to exist in two modes. In the second mode, the Church offers up the eternally living body and blood of Christ, but the body and blood are offered up in their sacramental mode, that is, as separated in accord with their separation on Calvary. Vonier affirms:

> The Eucharistic separation of Body and Blood is the memory, the representation of that real separation in historic time . . . As the Eucharistic Body and Blood are such a complete representation of the broken Son of God on Calvary, they are also the most immediate and complete contact of the soul with all the saving power of Golgotha.[127]

In sum, in the "sacrament-sacrifice"[128] of the Eucharist, the Church becomes Christ's Body by offering his sacrifice in him. Recall Ephraim Radner's concern: "Catholics asserted a mode of signification that pointed to something whose reality lies *within* the bounds of the true Church (the transubstantiated elements) but is not itself joined to it in a prior way."[129] As Aquinas, followed by Vonier, shows, the sacrifice signified by the sacrament of the Eucharist does not lie within the bounds of the Church, but rather makes the Church.

3 CONCLUSION

The eighteenth-century philosopher David Hume, while granting that Catholics "are a very learned sect," judged that "there is no tenet in all paganism, which would give so fair a scope to ridicule as this of the *real presence*: For it is so absurd, that it eludes the force of all argument."[130]

---

[127] Ibid., 124, 125; see 3, q. 74, a. 1, where Aquinas proposes that bread and wine are an appropriate "matter" of the sacrament of the Eucharist "in relation to Christ's Passion, in which the blood was separated from the body. And therefore in this sacrament, which is the memorial of our Lord's Passion, the bread is received apart as the sacrament of the body, and the wine as the sacrament of the blood."

[128] Vonier, *A Key to the Doctrine of the Eucharist*, 77ff.; 140–1.

[129] Ephraim Radner, *The End of the Church: A Pneumatology of Christian Division in the West*, 210. Radner is speaking specifically about seventeenth-century Catholic polemicists, but suggests that this mode of addressing the topic continues into the present day.

[130] David Hume, *The Natural History of Religion*, in *Principal Writings on Religion including Dialogues Concerning Natural Religion and The Natural History of Religion*, ed. J.C.A. Gaskin (Oxford: Oxford University Press, 1993): 167. Thomas Hobbes similarly asserts, "That the same body can be in many places at once, neither Aristotle, nor a philosopher,

Hume proceeded to prove the point by means of the fable of the proselyte who, in response to the catechist's question regarding the number of Gods there are, answered "none": "You have told me all along that there is but one God: And yesterday I eat him."[131] Certainly the realities of the Word's Incarnation and Pasch, and their ongoing sacramental presence in the world, must remain "folly to the Gentiles" (1 Cor. 1:23); and yet Christ crucified is "the power of God and the wisdom of God. For the foolishness of God is wiser than men, and the weakness of God is stronger than men" (1 Cor. 1:24–5).

The reality of our full participation in Christ's Pasch is the "foolishness" and "weakness" that the doctrine of transubstantiation affirms. We cannot grasp *how* God accomplishes the miracle (the *how* of sacramental signification), and "substance" remains elusive as describing a bodily but not sensible reality. Nonetheless, in light of the understanding of substance as present "as a whole is in a part," we can apprehend the truth affirmed in faith that Christ does not move from the right hand of the Father and yet is fully present in every consecrated host. We can recognize, likewise, that the same sacramental insight applies to the mystery of the Last Supper, where Christ, present in his living body, nonetheless is able to deliver himself Eucharistically to his disciples under the sacramental species of bread and wine: "This is my body . . . This is my blood" (Matt. 26:26–7). So, too, we can recognize the profound iconic activity of the bread and wine. Other basic problems, such as the fear of cannibalistically crushing Christ while chewing the Eucharistic species and concerns about the unity of the sacrifice, also find resolution. As the *Nizzahon Vetus* requires, we are able to give a reason for our offering of sacrifice and for the content of the sacrifice.

Furthermore, once we apprehend Christ's sacramental mode of being, this insight removes any sense of mechanistic causality (Schmemann, Chauvet, Power) in the sacrament of the Eucharist. The sacramental sign does not disguise an impersonal mechanism by which God conforms us to Christ. Rather, the sacramental sign makes possible our full participation in Christ's sacrificial self-offering to the Father in the Holy Spirit. Precisely in so doing, and thereby constituting Christ's Body the Church, we deepen in the Eucharist our ecclesial supernatural friendship with God by practicing cruciformity in and with Christ. It is the Holy Spirit who enables us to share in the sacrament-sacrifice in this way. Vonier explains our active participation in the sacrament of the Eucharist:

---

nor any sane man can think. But it was useful to them [Catholics] to say this, in order to maintain the real presence of Christ's body in every piece of consecrated bread." See Hobbes, *Leviathan, with Selected Variants from the Latin Edition of 1668*, ed. Edwin Curley (Indianapolis, IN: Hackett, 1994): 475.

[131] Hume, 168.

> The Eucharist is essentially a gift to the Church, not only of Christ, but of the sacrifice of Christ, so that the Church herself has her sacrifice; nay, every Christian has his sacrifice. To participate in Christ's great sacrifice on the cross in a merely utilitarian mode by receiving the benefits of such a sacrifice, is only one-half of the Christian religion. The full Christian religion is this, that the very sacrifice is put into our hands, so that we, too, have a sacrifice, and we act as men have acted at all times when they walked before God in cleanness of faith and simplicity of heart; we offer to God a sacrifice of sweet odour.[132]

For Aquinas, "In the new law the true sacrifice of Christ is communicated to the faithful under the appearance of bread and wine."[133] Certainly Christ is the one who offers the sacrifice of himself, both on Calvary and in the sacrament of the Eucharist. Yet, in the sacrament of the Eucharist (united to the other sacraments as one sacramental organism), the Church, led by her priests, offers up his sacrifice in, with, and through him.[134] Thus Christ's sacrifice becomes the Church's sacrifice, as the Body is conformed to the Head.

We are thereby able to recognize that the instrumental means by which God causes us to share in the redemption won by Christ, is none other than the active means by which we participate in Christ's redemptive work.[135] Aquinas explains that

> one eats his flesh and drinks his blood in a spiritual way if one is united to him through faith and love, so that one is transformed into him and becomes his member: for this food is not changed into the one who eats it, but it turns the one

---

[132] Vonier, *A Key to the Doctrine of the Eucharist*, 223.

[133] 3, q. 22, a. 6. See Vonier, *A Key to the Doctrine of the Eucharist*, 224–7.

[134] Vonier, *A Key to the Doctrine of the Eucharist*, 229ff. See also Gérard Remy, "Sacerdoce et médiation chez saint Thomas," *Revue Thomiste* 99 (1999): 101–18; Jean-Pierre Torrell, O.P., "Le sacerdoce du Christ dans la Somme de théologie," *Revue Thomiste* 99 (1999): 75–100.

[135] For Aquinas's account of divine causality in the sacraments, emphasizing that divine formal and final causality grounds the suitability of the historical sacramental "sign" and thus responding to the widespread criticism (e.g., Chauvet, Power) that Aquinas's account is mechanistic, see Liam G. Walsh, "The Divine and the Human in St. Thomas's Theology of Sacraments," in *Ordo sapientiae et amoris*, ed. C.-J. Pinto de Oliveira, O.P. (Fribourg: Éditions universitaires, 1993): 342f. See also Louis-Marie Chauvet, *Du symbolique au symbole* (Paris: Cerf, 1979); Louis-Marie Chauvet, *Symbole et sacrement. Une relecture sacramentelle de l'existence chrétienne* (Paris: Cerf, 1987), translated by P. Madigan, S.J. and M. Beaumont as *Symbol and Sacrament* (Collegeville, MN: Liturgical Press, 1995).

who takes it into itself . . . And so this is a food capable of making man divine and inebriating him with divinity.[136]

Not mechanism, but supernatural relationship – spiritual inebriation – characterizes this depiction of the sacrament; the eschatological aspect is intrinsic to the sacrifice, as the *Nizzahon Vetus*'s references to the prophets would have led us to expect. The end or goal of the Eucharist is the consummation of our intimate union with a Person, Jesus Christ, in the glory of trinitarian communion.[137] The liturgy of the Eucharist provides us with a foretaste of this communion. In the final chapter, therefore, I will explore the sacramental representation embodied in the liturgy of the Eucharist, a sacramental representation that rules out Eucharistic idealism.

---

[136] Aquinas, *Commentary on the Gospel of St. John*, Part I, trans. Fabian Larcher, O.P. and James Weisheipl, O.P., ch. 6, lect. 7, no. 972 (p. 386).

[137] See Vonier, *A Key to the Doctrine of the Eucharist*, 240. For Vonier, as for Aquinas, the sacrament of the Eucharist flows actively from Jesus in his Paschal mystery, as his great gift: "Sacraments are, then, truly an energy that comes from Christ in person, a radiation from the charity of the Cross, a stream of grace from the pierced side of Christ" (44). Vonier thus emphasizes that "the sacramental grace [the *res* of the sacrament of the Eucharist], is the mystical Body of Christ; Christ's sacramental Body makes Christ's mystical Body. The whole Eucharistic spirit is a spirit of charity, a spirit between the members of Christ" (255). The Church's liturgical sharing in Christ's sacrifice, in the sacrifice of the Eucharist, is "the sacrament of Christ's Mystical Body," a corporate event rather than simply an event of "individual spiritual satisfaction" (257).

5

The Liturgy of the Eucharist

Thus far I have treated the themes of expiatory sacrifice, charity, and Christ's sacramental bodiliness in the Eucharist. All these themes belong to the context of desire for intimacy with God. In this chapter we will examine these themes once again, but now as regards the shape of the liturgy of the Eucharist. As has been the book's pattern, I will begin with the liturgy of Israel – mediated through the work of contemporary Jewish theologians – which expresses the longing of Jacob for an intimacy with God that requires "wrestling" (Gen. 32:24). Jacob's thigh was put out of joint, but he received his blessing and sought the name of God, and even saw God "face to face" (Gen. 32:30). In inquiring into how Christian liturgy likewise involves this kind of "wrestling" and intimate union, I will examine Aquinas's account of the liturgy of the Eucharist as instructive of how Christians learn cruciformity. Vatican II's *Presbyterorum Ordinis* gets to the heart of this liturgical pedagogy in cruciform holiness:

> Through the ministry of priests, the spiritual sacrifice of the faithful is made perfect in union with the sacrifice of Christ. He is the only mediator who in the name of the whole Church is offered sacramentally in the Eucharist and in an unbloodly manner until the Lord himself comes. The ministry of priests is directed to this goal and is perfected in it. Their ministry, which begins with the evangelical proclamation, derives its power and force from the sacrifice of Christ. Its aim is that "the entire commonwealth of the redeemed and the society of the saints be offered to God through the High Priest who offered himself also for us in his passion that we might be the body of so great a Head."[1]

---

[1] Vatican II, *Presbyterorum Ordinis*, no. 2.

1 THE LITURGY OF ISRAEL

In his *Jewish Liturgy: A Comprehensive History*, Ismar Elbogen has described, as best it can be described from the scanty sources, the liturgy of the Second Temple. According to Elbogen, the people had little role in the priestly liturgies of the original Temple. This situation changed with the introduction of *ma'amadot*, in which the people, on a rotating cycle, sent representatives to Jerusalem to witness, in a liturgical role, the Temple sacrifices. In addition, these representatives held four prayer services daily, in which they read aloud key passages from the Torah, along with probably singing psalms and offering petitionary prayers. Elbogen states, "The form of these prayers may be inferred from the prayers in Ezra and Daniel, whose forms are strikingly similar to each other; by analogy we may assume that these petitions began with hymns, and that the statement of the petitions was preceded by the acknowledgment of sin."[2] According to Elbogen, these prayer services were marked by readings from the Torah (creation, the Exodus, the Decalogue), the singing of psalms, the offering of prayers formulated in the context of confession of sin. The prayer services prepared for and assisted the central task of witnessing the Temple sacrifices.

From this description of the ancient liturgy of Israel, it would seem that we have already identified the basic pattern that we will find in the liturgy of the Eucharist. The pedagogy of Israel's liturgy and the pedagogy of the Church's liturgy contain strikingly similar elements. Yet, we cannot too quickly assume that we have reached the heart of Israel's liturgy. Abraham Heschel has voiced doubt that modern human beings can even "conceive of the solemn joy of those whose offering was placed on the altar."[3] For Heschel, the closeness to God, almost a bodily closeness, experienced by those who participated in sacrificial liturgy (in Israel and elsewhere) belongs to a more tangible conception of the sacred than we have today. He writes,

> It is hard for us to imagine what entering a sanctuary or offering a sacrifice meant to ancient man. The sanctuary was holiness in perpetuity, a miracle in continuity; the divine was mirrored in the air, sowing blessing, closing gaps between the here and the beyond. In offering a sacrifice, man mingled with mystery, reached the summit of significance: sin was consumed, self abandoned, satisfaction was bestowed upon divinity.[4]

---

[2] Ismar Elbogen, *Jewish Liturgy: A Comprehensive History*, trans. Raymond P. Scheindlin from the original 1913 German edition and the 1972 Hebrew edition edited by Joseph Heinemann et al. (Philadelphia, PA: The Jewish Publication Society, 1993): 191.
[3] Abraham J. Heschel, *The Prophets* (New York: HarperCollins, 2001 [1962]): 252.
[4] Ibid.

As Heschel points out, the purpose of sacrifice was to enter into communion with God.[5]

Having evoked the spiritual grandeur of sacrifice, however, Heschel also remarks upon its limitations. He notes that while the prophets did not condemn sacrifice, nonetheless they refused to grant sacrifice to be "the essence of piety."[6] Heschel seeks to place us imaginatively in the minds of human beings who, without concern for justice, assumed that proper sacrifices to God (or, in pagan cultures, the gods) would suffice for communion. Such worshippers, he suggests, believed that what God or the gods wanted was acknowledgment, through sacrifice, of the divine power. In contrast, in Amos and later prophets, Heschel finds a critique of sacrifice that asserts that in themselves, without interior justice, sacrificial acts are not pleasing to God, and furthermore that in any event other acts are more pleasing to God. In Amos and later prophets,

> all this grandeur and solemnity are declared to be second rate, of minor importance, if not hateful to God, while deeds of kindness, worrying about the material needs of widows and orphans, commonplace things, platitudinous affairs, are exactly what the Lord of heaven and earth demands![7]

As regards its poetic or imaginative power, Heschel compares this new liturgical focus on righteousness to renouncing a thousand vineyards in favor of "an acre of barren ground."[8]

Heschel tends toward positing the two approaches – sacrificial liturgy versus liturgy as righteousness in daily life – as, in practice at least, opposites. Thus even though he carefully affirms that the prophets did not "condemn" sacrifice *per se*, but only sacrifice without justice, he goes on to say that the prophets "attacked" sacrifice and insisted that "there is something far more precious than sacrifice," namely justice. He contrasts sacrifice, with its "offerings and songs" and its "venerable" schema in which God must be revered for God's "power," with "love, justice, and righteousness" as displayed in the small actions of daily living.[9] The latter, he argues, gets far closer to the truth both about God

---

[5] Ibid., 251.
[6] Ibid., 250.
[7] Ibid., 251.
[8] Ibid.
[9] He differentiates the latter two on p. 256:

> it seems that justice is a mode of action, righteousness a quality of the person . . . Righteousness goes beyond justice. Justice is strict and exact, giving each person his due. Righteousness implies benevolence, kindness, generosity. Justice is form, a state of equilibrium; righteousness has a substantive associated meaning. Justice may be legal; righteousness is associated with a burning compassion for the oppressed.

and about human beings. For Heschel, God, having created human beings and the natural universe, needs human beings to act justly in order to bring his "greater masterpiece," human history, to completion. God's creative action, and indeed God himself, is "at stake" in the molding of history into the pattern of righteousness. Writing with acute awareness of the Holocaust as well as near the height of the achievements of the Civil Rights movement in America, Heschel suggests that acts of injustice, performed so callously, are in fact "fighting God, affronting the divine . . . the oppression of man is a humiliation of God."[10] He compares the offerings of animals and incense with deeds of mercy and righteousness, and concludes that God's "needs cannot be satisfied in the temples, in space, but only in history, in time. It is within the realm of history that man is charged with God's mission."[11]

For Heschel, sacrifice is ultimately a private event between the human being and God that, no matter how solemn and grand, does not involve God in any concern for how we treat our fellows.[12] Clearly, this understanding of sacrificial worship as ultimately unrelated to justice must disparage sacrifice. Yet, Heschel nonetheless continues to see something valuable in sacrifice, which he recognizes as "an essential act of worship" in ancient Israel and as "the experience of giving oneself vicariously to God and of being received by Him."[13] Such an experience, Heschel admits, cannot be but longed for.

Below, in exploring the liturgy of the Eucharist, we will focus upon the conjunction of justice and sacrifice in the liturgy, a conjunction that inaugurates and provides – as Heschel would perhaps have expected had he imagined such a conjunction – a foretaste of deification, in which the grandeur of the heavenly realm converges with the person's daily historical life in the manifestation of justice in Christ. Before turning to this discussion, I will add one further remark upon the Jewish liturgy. The liturgy of Israel cannot be understood outside the variations found within the liturgical year. In this regard, Michael Strassfeld has shown how the cycle of feasts, from Passover to the Feast of Weeks to Rosh ha-Shanah to Yom Kippur to the Feast of Booths to Hanukkah to Purim, reflects an interweaving of the moments of expiation, purification, reparation, absolute self-giving, and covenantal feasting constitutive of Israel's sacrifices.[14] The feasts of Israel's liturgical year locate the participant within the historical and personal pedagogy of God with his people.

---

[10] Ibid., 253.
[11] Ibid.
[12] Ibid., 257–8.
[13] Ibid., 249.
[14] See Michael Strassfeld, *The Jewish Holidays: A Guide and Commentary* (New York: HarperCollins, 2001).

2 AQUINAS ON THE LITURGICAL UNION OF
SACRIFICE AND JUSTICE

Because Aquinas's understanding of the liturgy is firmly rooted in Christ's Cross, he is able both to describe a deifying justice (communion) achieved in the sacramental-sacrificial sharing in Christ's sacrifice, and to suggest that this achievement requires, on the part of communicants, the cruciform practices of true charity which the liturgy, as part of divine pedagogy, teaches us. In order to understand Aquinas's approach, we should begin with his understanding of divine Providence.[15] As Liam Walsh has put it, Aquinas's theology of the liturgy of the Eucharist has its roots in his

> more fundamental analysis of God, his providence, the work of creation and the kind of relationship that exists between God and his creatures. The fact that God is, that he gives himself out of sheer goodness to others, that he directs these others to participate in his goodness by predestinating providence are the ultimate presuppositions for his theological interpretation of the liturgy.[16]

Aquinas's understanding of divine Providence means that history has an "end" that determines it as "history": the right ordering of everything to God, in accord with God's wise plan for history from eternity. This providential ordering of history is God's "eternal law."[17] In this sense,

---

[15] We will thus unavoidably review some of the themes already discussed above.

[16] Liam G. Walsh, O.P., "Liturgy in the Theology of St. Thomas," *The Thomist* 38 (1974): 581. See also Walsh's exposition of the eucharistic sacrifice in his *The Sacraments of Initiation: Baptism, Confirmation, Eucharist* (London: Geoffrey Chapman, 1988): 278–83.

[17] See Carlos-Josaphat Pinto de Oliveira, O.P., "Ordo rationis, ordo amoris. La notion d'ordre au centre de l'univers éthique de S. Thomas," in *Ordo sapientiae et amoris*, ed. C.-J. Pinto de Oliveira, O.P. (Fribourg: Éditions universitaires, 1993): 285–302. This conception of history is so far from the modern viewpoint as to be no longer even contested. In *On "What Is History?": From Carr and Elton to Rorty and White* (New York: Routledge, 1995), Keith Jenkins summarizes current cutting-edge views on historiography and "history":

> History is arguably a verbal artifact, a narrative prose discourse of which, après White, the content is as much invented as found, and which is constructed by present-minded, ideologically positioned workers (historians and those acting as if they were historians) operating at various levels of reflexivity, such a discourse, to appear relatively plausible, looking simultaneously towards the once real events and situations of the past and towards the narrative type "mythoi'" common – albeit it on a dominant-marginal spectrum – in any given social formation . . . [T]he cogency of historical work can be admitted without the past *per se* ever entering into

Louis Bouyer is right in finding "the most primitive meaning of sacrifice" to be "the supreme divine activity."[18] In God, human beings find holiness and renewal. As directed to divine communion in justice, liturgical sacrifice is ultimately God's action, God's gift. Justice, toward which God directs his providential plan, is ultimately accomplished by God in Christ's Cross.

Our sharing in God's enactment of justice involves both God's gifts of creation and of redemption. In the gift of creation, God gives to all human beings a participation in his "eternal law." By the exercise of rationality, human beings may understand what conduces to their right ordering. This rational sharing in God's eternal plan for creatures is called "natural law." The right ordering expressed in God's eternal law is, when put into action, justice.[19] All human beings share in this way in God's eternal law, and it is here that liturgy takes shape.

It belongs to human right ordering to give thanks to the Creator. Put another way, the moral virtue of religion, an expression of the virtue of justice, requires liturgical acts.[20] As rational animals, human beings may know their Creator. This knowledge inspires a gratitude and love that

---

> it – except rhetorically. In this way histories are fabricated without "real" foundations beyond the textual, and in this way one learns to always ask of such discursive and ideological regimes that hold in their orderings suasive intentions – *cui bono* – in whose interests? (178–9)

If, according to Jenkins's nominalist reading, there is no meaning in "history" other than what historians construct in the present, for Aquinas, in contrast, the meaning of history is divinely given and already manifest (though not fully) as the teleological "order" imprinted in creation that is taken up and fulfilled radically by and in Christ Jesus.

[18] Louis Bouyer, *The Christian Mystery: From Pagan Myth to Christian Mysticism*, trans. Illtyd Trethowan (Edinburgh: T. & T. Clark, 1990): 290. Bouyer notes that:

> it can seem that the very notion of sacrifice, as thought of by man without the help of revelation, is turned upside down, since it is no longer for man to offer it to God in order to conciliate him, but it is God who offers it to man, in fact offers himself. Actually we have to say that, instead of being turned upside down, this notion is both brought back to its origin and transfigured, or rather fulfilled in a way that surpasses all men's hopes. (290)

Bouyer's view is correct, so long as the reality that sacrifice is a moral virtue (in gratitude to God) is also recognized and given full weight.

[19] See Russell Hittinger, *The First Grace: Rediscovering the Natural Law in a Post-Christian World* (Wilmington, DE: ISI Books, 2003), as well as my review of this book in *Nova et Vetera* 2 (2004): 223–8.

[20] See 2-2, q. 81, a. 7. Aquinas identifies the virtue of religion as a "potential part" of the cardinal virtue of justice. Romanus Cessario, O.P. explains this categorization in *The Virtues, or the Examined Life* (New York: Continuum, 2002): 115–16. Suffice it to say that the virtue of religion is a potential part rather than an integral part because strict justice between man and God cannot be achieved.

find proper expression in the desire to give a return to the divine Giver. As Aquinas states:

> Natural reason tells man that he is subject to a higher being, on account of the defects which he perceives in himself, and in which he needs help and direction from someone above him: and whatever this superior being may be, it is known to all under the name of God. Now just as in natural things the lower are naturally subject to the higher, so too it is a dictate of natural reason in accordance with man's natural inclination that he should tender submission and honor, according to his mode, to that which is above man. Now the mode befitting to man is that he should employ sensible signs in order to signify anything, because he derives his knowledge from sensibles. Hence it is a dictate of natural reason that man should use certain sensibles, by offering them to God in sign of the subjection and honor due to Him, like those who make certain offerings to their lord in recognition of his authority. Now this is what we mean by sacrifice, and consequently the offering of sacrifice is of the natural law.[21]

Sacrifice as part of the "natural law" indicates why Israel's sacrificial liturgy cannot be separated from justice.

It might seem that liturgical actions could or should be solely interior. As Aquinas recognizes, some have read Jesus' words in John 4:24 as a confirmation of this view of liturgical actions: "God is a spirit, and they that adore Him must adore Him in spirit and in truth."[22] He points out, however, that it is not only in spirit that human beings give due "submission and honor" to God. Rather, since human beings are bodily creatures, the senses and emotions are always involved. He argues that because the human mind learns of the invisible by means of the visible, it follows that "in the Divine worship it is necessary to make use of corporeal things, that man's mind may be aroused thereby, as by signs, to the spiritual acts by means of which he is united to God."[23] Sensible signs

---

[21] 2-2, q. 85, a. 1; compare *Summa contra Gentiles*, III, ch. 120. For further discussion see Cornelius Williams, O.P., "The Sacrifice of the Mass as an Act of the Virtue of Religion," *The Thomist* 27 (1963): 357–84.

[22] 2-2, q. 81, a. 7, obj. 1.

[23] 2-2, q. 81, a. 7. For the influence of Pseudo-Dionysius on this point (see also 3, q. 60, a. 4), see Wayne Hankey's "Reading Augustine through Dionysius: Aquinas's Correction of One Platonism by Another," forthcoming in Michael Dauphinais, Barry David, and Matthew Levering, eds., *Aquinas the Augustinian*. For an illuminating discussion see Charles Morerod, O.P., "Le sens dans la relation de l'homme avec Dieu," *Nova et Vetera* 79 (2004): 7–35.

serve in the liturgy as a pedagogical stimulant, required by humankind's bodily constitution, to desire for union with the invisible God.[24]

Aquinas is well aware, like Heschel, that the goal of the liturgy is the spiritual offering made by the participant. Yet, the union of body and soul is such that the internal expression of the soul, if it is genuine, seeks at the same time an external bodily manifestation. The interior life is sustained by external liturgical acts, even though it is the interior life that fully and accurately evidences the person's relationship to God: "[E]xternal things are offered to God, not as though He stood in need of them, according to Ps. xlix. 13, *Shall I eat the flesh of bullocks? or shall I drink the blood of goats?* but as signs of the internal and spiritual works, which are of themselves acceptable to God."[25] Thus, even though the justice of a human being vis-à-vis God is measured by the person's spiritual condition – and here Aquinas agrees fully with Heschel's point – nonetheless the establishment of this justice between the person and God requires that the person offer visible signs of the inward offering of submission and honor, because it is by outward signs that human beings, as bodily creatures, communicate.[26]

It is here that the moral virtue of justice is associated with the external offering of sacrifice. As bodily creatures, we signify interior sacrifice or self-offering by means of visible signs. Sacrifice of one's own will to the Creator-God, a sacrifice or self-offering that is signified by the visible sacrifice, constitutes the fundamental act of justice – worship of God. After original sin, however, the sacrificial offering, to restore justice, must be the free and loving offering of one's own bodily life, because only such a sacrifice could reflect the returning to God of what human beings, in choosing the creature over the Creator, arrogated to themselves.[27] Only such a sacrifice, in other words, could restore, after the radical disorder introduced by sin, the true teleological meaning of "history" as God, in his gifts of creation and grace, knows and wills it. The Book of Revelation depicts this reality through the image of a "scroll" that only

---

[24] See the discussion in Colman O'Neill, *Meeting Christ in the Sacraments*, 218–21. The Mass, O'Neill points out, ensures that believers "can constantly participate in the supreme act of worship in the bodily fashion that their nature demands" (219). Such participation is transformative: "the praise, thanksgiving and prayer of the faithful, because offered in corporeal union with Christ, are filled out by the perfect worship of Christ; they are united with their source and take their place in the great hymn of love and obedience that goes up from the heart of Christ . . . To offer the eucharistic victim is to adopt a whole program of life" (220).

[25] 2-2, q. 81, a. 7, ad 2.

[26] 3, q. 61, a. 1. See also Robert Sokolowski, *Eucharistic Presence*, 34–5; Robert Sokolowski, *The God of Faith and Reason* (Washington, DC: Catholic University of America Press, 1982): 146–8. Sokolowski rightly points out that such sacramental signs are only thinkable in light of the Christian doctrine of the Creator who is not part of the world.

[27] Cf. 1-2, q. 87, especially a. 1 on the punishment due to sin; as well as 1-2, q. 102, a. 3, ad 5 on sacrificial offerings.

the slain Lamb, by bringing human history to its intended meaning, can "open" (Rev. 5). The sacrifice of animals could, more or less inchoately, signify this expiatory offering, whereas Christ's sacrifice on the Cross perfects it. He freely accepts death, thereby choosing God over his own creaturely life, and he does so out of love for all others. Entering into the heart of the disorder, Christ re-orders death itself to God and re-opens the path of right worship. Christ thereby reveals the full dignity of sacrificial actions in liturgy.[28] It is not for nothing that the book of Revelation depicts the consummation of history in the slain Lamb as a *liturgical* consummation. As the biblical exegete Bruce Metzger puts it:

> In opening the scroll, the Lamb is about to disclose what the scroll contains. In short, Jesus does not change the divine plan; he unfolds its eternal and unchangeable nature by his obedience, even unto death on the cross. No wonder there is praise in heaven, accompanied by incense and harps. The twenty-four elders fall before the Lamb and offer "golden bowls full of incense, which are the prayers of the saints" (5:8). Here is John's first hint of the participation of the church's worship on earth with that of the church in heaven.[29]

History is fulfilled in the eucharistic liturgy, and its *telos* is revealed to be nothing less than sharing in the heavenly liturgy through participation in the life of the Trinity.

This dignity in which human beings become true *givers* and thereby share in the self-giving communion of the Trinity, has been expressed by Catherine Pickstock, who draws significantly on Aquinas in her Eucharistic theology.[30] She focuses on the character of "gift" in the

---

[28] Liam Walsh, O.P. has pointed out here a potential concern, to which he responds well: "There is little doubt that the notion of cult is essential to a theological understanding of liturgy. But whether it is the best starting point for such an understanding may be questioned. Some theologians are slightly suspicious of it insofar as it is a 'rational' notion, derived from philosophico-ethical analysis of the relationship between man and God. This objection has some weight if the idea of worship is being put forward as an a priori concept from which one claims to deduce the reality of Christian liturgy. But when it is simply being used, and used analogically, to provide an understanding of the given reality of Christian liturgy, which is what St. Thomas is doing, one can have little ground for complaint – unless one is prepared to discredit the whole idea of a philosophical theology" (Walsh, "Liturgy in the Theology of St. Thomas," 565–6). See also Thomas Merton, *The Living Bread* (New York: Farrar, Straus & Giroux, 1956): 32–9.

[29] Bruce M. Metzger, *Breaking the Code: Understanding the Book of Revelation* (Nashville, TN: Abingdon Press, 1993): 53; cf. Craig R. Koester, *Revelation and the End of All Things* (Grand Rapids, MI: Eerdmans, 2001): 78–9, as well as Scott Hahn's popularization of this theme in *The Lamb's Supper* (New York: Doubleday, 1999).

[30] See Catherine Pickstock, *After Writing: On the Liturgical Consummation of Philosophy* (Oxford: Blackwell, 1998). For Pickstock's subtitle, see Paul Evdokimov's remark, "Everything is destined for a liturgical fulfillment" (Evdokimov, *The Art of the*

sacrament of the Eucharist.[31] In the liturgy of the mass, she argues, "citizenship" in the community is manifested as depending upon "a genuine flow and exchange of gift."[32] There is no community "outside the offering of gift"; communion depends upon sacrificial gift-offering.[33] God gratuitously offers the gift (Christ's person and work) to humanity, and in Christ humanity offers sacrificially this gift, and all other things ("the overflowing nature of gift"), in return.[34]

For Pickstock, the liturgy demonstrates that our "communion" in Christ's sacrifice is sacrificial at every moment, even in the receiving of

---

Icon: A Theology of Beauty [Redondo Beach, CA: Oakwood Publications, 1990]: 117). I owe this quotation to M. Francis Mannion, "Rejoice, Heavenly Powers! The Renewal of Liturgical Doxology," *Pro Ecclesia* 12 (2003): 45. On the liturgy as a pedagogy in self-giving, see also the superb essay of Peter Kwasniewski, "Aquinas on Eucharistic Ecstasy: From Self-Alienation to Gift of Self," in *The Liturgical Subject: Subject, Subjectivity, and the Human Person in Contemporary Liturgical Discussion and Critique*, ed. James Leachman, O.S.B. (Notre Dame, IN: University of Notre Dame Press, forthcoming).

[31] Pickstock's approach here is influenced by Jean-Luc Marion's Heideggerian attention to "gift." More recently, in "Truth and Language," chapter 4 of John Milbank and Catherine Pickstock, *Truth in Aquinas* (New York: Routledge, 2001): 88–111, Pickstock combines epistemological reflections (evincing a dialectic of scepticism and fideism) with an analysis of Aquinas's Eucharistic theology. As Richard Popkin and Antonio Livi have shown, a dialectic of scepticism and fideism marked the seventeenth century: see Livi, "The Philosophical Category of 'Faith' at the Origins of Modern Scepticism," *Nova et Vetera* 1 (2003): 321–40.

[32] Pickstock, *After Writing*, 238–9; see also 170, as well as her "A Short Essay on the Reform of the Liturgy," *New Blackfriars* (1997): 56–65.

[33] Pickstock, *After Writing*, 234.

[34] Ibid., 240–1. See also Peter Casarella, "Eucharist: Presence of a Gift," in *Rediscovering the Eucharist: Ecumenical Conversations*, ed. Roch Kereszty, O. Cist. (New York: Paulist Press, 2003): 199–225. Drawing upon Robert Sokolowski and Jean-Luc Marion, Casarella speaks of "an analogy of giving whereby what God gives us in the person of the Son is the very condition for our giving thanks back to the Father" (215). David Power, in contrast, attends to the category of "gift" in a way that radically attenuates sacrifice, unless "sacrifice" is understood as a thanksgiving or communion offering. Power writes,

> When the need to atone or propitiate for guilt is given primary importance, the need to offer sacrifice underlines the guilt of those who offer and so promotes alienation from one's sinful body from which one must free the spiritual self in order to receive forgiveness. When sacrifice itself is first and foremost a communion meal, this not only expresses reconciliation through communion with God, but it also affirms the body and integrates body experience into the sacramentality of being the Body of Christ. (Power, "Roman Catholic Theologies of Eucharistic Communion: A Contribution to Ecumenical Conversation," *Theological Studies* 57 [1996]: 587–610, at 601)

Power assumes that the locus of sin is primarily the body rather than the spiritual will. For a comparison of David Power's Eucharistic theology with that of John Paul II (in *Eucharistia de Ecclesia*) and Thomas Aquinas, see my "John Paul II and Aquinas on the Eucharist," *Nova et Vetera* 3 (2005): 637–60.

Christ's body and blood. In such receiving (communion in his body and blood), we receive a *sacrificial* offering, and thus our reception itself belongs to the movement of sacrificial offering. As she remarks, "This confirms that even the receiving of gift is still an offering; that in the liturgy, there is no action outside gift, but only the repetition of the offering which has already been made by God to Himself in the person of Jesus."[35] The result is that no Eucharistic "communion" can be imagined that is not sacrificial. Sharing in Christ's glorified communion occurs in and through sacrifice. She affirms, "It is by thus entering into Christ's action of perfect praise of the Father that we can participate in God's own worship of Himself."[36]

3 THE LITURGY OF THE EUCHARIST AND THE REPRESENTATION OF DIVINE JUSTICE

Yet, if Christ's Cross stands as the liturgical action toward which all others are ordered, the embodiment of communal justice, how exactly do we "enter into Christ's action" in the rite of the liturgy of the Eucharist? Aquinas's account of the rite of the liturgy offers important insights into this question. Obviously some of the liturgical practices discussed by Aquinas are not found in the contemporary Catholic liturgy, and vice versa. What follows, then, is a theological exposition of the contours of eucharistic liturgical action, not an exhaustive treatment of the Church's liturgy. The exposition should make clear that the liturgy of the Eucharist, when understood sacrificially, represents in the world's history the cruciform fulfillment of justice – as Heschel rightly would require – rather than encouraging believers in a flight, however solemn and grand, from history.[37] As the fulfillment of divine justice,

---

[35] Pickstock, *After Writing*, 244.

[36] Ibid.

[37] William T. Cavanaugh points out that Martin Luther, in his *Abomination of the Secret Mass* (1525), "works step by step through the canon of the Mass, showing how nearly every component contributes to the blasphemous view of the Mass as sacrifice (*Luther's Works*, ed. Wentz [vol. 36, Philadelphia, PA: Fortress Press, 1959], 314–27)" (Cavanaugh, "Eucharistic Sacrifice and the Social Imagination in Early Modern Europe," *Journal of Medieval and Early Modern Studies* 31 [2001]: 604, fn. 29). As Luther wrote in 1522, "Once the Mass has been overthrown, I say we'll have overthrown the whole of Popedom" (Luther, *Against King Henry of England*, in *Werke*, Weimar ed., vol. 10b, p. 220; quoted in Cavanaugh, "Eucharistic Sacrifice and the Social Imagination in Early Modern Europe," 586; cf. Francis Clark, S.J., *Eucharistic Sacrifice and the Reformation*, 101). Cavanaugh notes that Luther's "two-part revision of the canon of the Mass – the *Formula missae et communionis* in 1523 and the *Deutsche Messe* in 1526 – effectively expunged all the sacrificial prayers of the old canon" (589–90). In contrast, the fourteenth-century Byzantine theologian Nicholas Cabasilas provides a detailed account of the liturgy which largely parallels Aquinas's, allowing for differences on

the liturgy is thus also a participation in the divine liturgy, in which we share already in the eschatological ordering of humankind to our "end" or goal.[38]

Aquinas identifies in the liturgy a threefold signification:

> in the celebration of this sacrament words are used to signify things pertaining to Christ's Passion, which is represented in this sacrament; or again, pertaining to Christ's mystical body, which is signified therein; and again, things pertaining to the use [reception] of this sacrament, which use ought to be devout and reverent.[39]

Christ's Passion, Christ's Mystical Body, and Christ in the Eucharist are thus drawn together into a significatory pattern that exhibits our radical

---

certain points. See Book V of Cabasilas's *The Life in Christ*, trans. Carmino J. deCatanzaro (Crestwood, NY: St Vladimir's Press, 1998) and his *A Commentary on the Divine Liturgy*, trans. J.M. Hussey and P.A. McNulty (Crestwood, NY: St Vladimir's Seminary Press, 1998); cf. the discussions of Cabasilas in Alfred G. Mortimer's *The Eucharistic Sacrifice: An Historical and Theological Investigation of the Sacrificial Conception of the Holy Eucharist in the Christian Church* (London: Longmans, Green, and Co., 1901): 332–7 and David Bentley Hart's "'Thine Own of Thine Own': Eucharistic Sacrifice in Orthodox Tradition," in *Rediscovering the Eucharist: Ecumenical Conversations*, ed. Roch Kereszty, O. Cist. (New York: Paulist, 2003): 146. Hart identifies Cabasilas as "the greatest Orthodox sacramental theologian . . . whose work constitutes a grand synthesis of the entire Eastern tradition on these matters" (146).

[38] For a depiction of the liturgy of the Eucharist as known and practiced by the Fathers, see Jean Danielou, S.J., *The Bible and the Liturgy* (Notre Dame, IN: University of Notre Dame Press, 1956). Danielou points out:

> If we go through the principal eucharistic catecheses, we find that two chief themes constantly recur in explaining the primary significance of the sacrament: the Mass is a sacramental representation of the sacrifice of the Cross, the Mass is a sacramental participation in the heavenly liturgy. These two essential themes run through the whole Eucharistic liturgy. They are explained mainly in connection with the very heart of that liturgy, the prayer of consecration; but these same themes command the interpretation of the various rites of the liturgy from its beginning. (128)

Danielou, with the Fathers, holds the two themes together. Similarly, he sees how the two themes guide the entire liturgy of the Eucharist. His patristic perspective is mirrored by St Thomas Aquinas, and is quite distant from that of Eucharistic idealism.

[39] 3, q. 83, a. 5. On the aspect of "words" and the Word in the sacrament of the Eucharist, see Thomas D. Stanks, S.S., "The Eucharist: Christ's Self-Communication in a Revelatory Event," *Theological Studies* 28 (1967): 27–50, although Stanks misunderstands transubstantiation. The significance of "word" in the sacrament of the Eucharist is nowhere more clear than in the words of institution. Cf. Joseph H. Crehan, S.J., "The Theology of Eucharistic Consecration: Role of the Priest in Celtic Liturgy," *Theological Studies* 40 (1979): 334–44.

sharing (ecclesial and personal) in Christ's justifying action.[40] This sharing in Christ – in his action as his Body – is deifying: David Bentley
Hart could equally be speaking of Aquinas's theology when he describes "the radically ontological nature of the Eastern Christian understanding of 'atonement' and of the 'drawing nigh' of God in Christ
that Christ's sacrifice achieves for us."[41] Yet, our participation in this
new creation possesses ascetical rhythms. As the Church's mystical
theologians, in whose number Aquinas belongs,[42] have always recognized, we would be unable truly to participate in this liturgical action,
which "represents" and thus sacramentally shares in Christ's sacrificial
action, without undertaking inner preparation. Thus, the liturgy of the
Eucharist begins with spiritual exercises that direct the participant's
attention to the glory and mercy of the holy Trinity.[43] These spiritual
exercises must be seen as a unified whole that shape every aspect of our
sharing in Christ's liturgical self-offering. Lacking an awareness of
this unity, the liturgical theologian Enrico Mazza has rather surprisingly
concluded, "Thomas's understanding of the consecration [the words
of institution] makes the Eucharistic Prayer superfluous, so to speak,
since he assigns it a purely devotional role."[44] Such an understanding of

---

[40] The "manifold presence of Christ in the phenomenon of worship," to use Michael G.
Witczak's phrase, is thus hardly a new insight; what is new is the effort by Catholic sacramental theologians to de-stabilize the objectivity of the Eucharistic conversion and
thereby also to undercut the ordained priesthood's role. For an overview of this effort,
critical of the work of Robert Sokolowski for overemphasizing the role of the priest, see
Witczak, "The Manifold Presence of Christ in the Liturgy," *Theological Studies* 58 (1998):
680–702.

[41] Hart, " 'Thine Own of Thine Own': Eucharistic Sacrifice in Orthodox Tradition," 146.

[42] As John Paul II recognizes in *Crossing the Threshold of Hope*, trans. Jenny and Martha
McPhee (New York: Alfred A. Knopf, 1994): 87.

[43] Catherine Pickstock, focusing on the formation of our desires (ultimately for beatific
union), describes the liturgy as a spiritual exercise. See Pickstock, "Truth and
Language," in John Milbank and Catherine Pickstock, *Truth in Aquinas* (New York:
Routledge, 2001): 100–4. Pickstock's work emphasizes the patterns of participation
inscribed in the liturgy, which thus requires "an ontological coincidence of the mystical
and the real" (93). This coincidence unites the Church and Christ in the Eucharistic
signification. As Pickstock suggests, the liturgical participation in Christ's body and
blood through the sacramental signs, a participation that makes the participants Christ's
Body and thereby (eschatological) participants in the triune life, is aided by a liturgical
pedagogy that enables participants to imitate Christ's cruciform love and to experience
the Eucharist as a foretaste of union. Pickstock's approach has recently been extended
and developed by Peter M. Candler, Jr., "Liturgically Trained Memory: A Reading
of *Summa Theologiae* III.83," *Modern Theology* 20 (2004): 423–45. See also David Bentley
Hart's description of the sacrificial language present throughout the Orthodox liturgy,
in his " 'Thine Own of Thine Own': Eucharistic Sacrifice in Orthodox Tradition," 154f.
As Hart notes, "the 'sacrifice' as such is often rather difficult to locate; it is somehow
shrouded in its own ubiquity" (154).

[44] Enrico Mazza, *The Celebration of the Eucharist: The Origin of the Rite and the
Development of Its Interpretation*, trans. Matthew J. O'Connell (Collegeville, MN:

"purely devotional" superfluity indicates a profound degree of liturgical misunderstanding.[45]

Aquinas begins his account of the rite of the liturgy of the Eucharist with the Introit, where believers offer "divine praise." This praise employs the words of the psalms, since as Aquinas explains, quoting Pseudo-Dionysius, "The Psalms comprise by way of praise whatever is contained in Sacred Scripture."[46] Praise is followed by prayer for mercy. The God who is praised for his greatness is asked to extend his mercy toward sinners. The community prays three times each "Lord, have mercy on us," "Christ, have mercy on us," and "Lord, have mercy on us." Aquinas finds in the pattern of three a threefold mystical reference to the Father, Son, and Holy Spirit; to the circumincession of the three Persons of the Trinity; and "against the threefold misery of ignorance, sin, and punishment."[47] The community raises its eyes toward the Trinity as the source of mercy. The next words of the liturgy, the singing of "Glory be to God on high," combine the prayerful praise of the Introit with the threefold petition's contemplative ascent to the Trinity. Finally, the priest intercedes for the people by praying "that they may be made worthy of such great mysteries."[48]

Liturgical Press, 1999): 210. For a strikingly different perspective, profoundly rooted in the mystical and ascetical understanding of the liturgy, see Jean Danielou, S.J.'s classic study *The Bible and the Liturgy* (Notre Dame: University of Notre Dame Press, 1956 [French edition 1951]).

[45] Mazza argues in *The Celebration of the Eucharist* that the Eucharistic consecration is separated by Aquinas from the whole of the rite, which does not truly participate in the sacramental representation. Mazza writes,

> In Thomas's system the sacramental nature of the Eucharist is reached through a metaphysical analysis of being as applied to the bread and wine, so that knowledge of the Sacrament as a sacrament is obtained through the real distinction between substance and accidents. The rite, however, is not a being but an action. Consequently, the metaphysical analysis of being in terms of substance and accident cannot be applied to the rite, that is, to the eucharistic celebration. From this it follows that the relationship of the eucharistic rite to the passion of Christ must belong to another order than the sacramental. (211)

At almost every point the student of Aquinas would have to stop to correct Mazza's reading of Aquinas here.
[46] 3, q. 83, a. 4. Pseudo-Dionysius's remark is from *Ecclesiastical Hierarchy*, ch. 3.
[47] Ibid. Aquinas recognizes the Trinitarian character of the liturgy of the Eucharist. On the Trinity and the liturgy of the Eucharist – with a valuable comment on the importance of the addition of the epiclesis in the post-Vatican II Roman Catholic liturgy – see Avery Dulles, S.J., "The Eucharist and the Mystery of the Trinity," in *Rediscovering the Eucharist: Ecumenical Conversations*, ed. Roch Kereszty, O. Cist. (New York: Paulist Press, 2003): 226–39. See also Peter Candler's study of liturgical "rhetoric," involving "patterns of 'mimesis'" (Candler, "Liturgically Trained Memory," 427).
[48] 3, q. 83, a. 4.

Having been prepared *actively* by prayer to participate in the trinitarian mystery of Christ's sacrificial offering, the community of believers continues its preparation *receptively* by listening to the instruction of Christ the Teacher. As "a mystery of faith," the sacrament of the Eucharist calls for faith in Christ's words on the part of those who offer, consecrate, and receive it, because it is a true contact with the divine life. First, Christ teaches the community through his prophets (Old Testament) and apostles (New Testament books other than the Gospels). The community indicates its reception of this teaching by appropriate praise: "after this lesson, the choir sing the Gradual, which signifies progress in life; then the Alleluia is intoned, and this denotes spiritual joy; or in mournful Offices the Tract, expressive of spiritual sighing; for all these things ought to result from the aforesaid teaching."[49] Christ's teaching is then directly communicated in the Gospel reading, through which the community receives the perfect teaching of "Divine truth, according to John 8:46, *If I tell you the truth, why do you not believe Me?*"[50] Caught up into the divine mercy, which is the truth that Christ brings, by the petitions and the readings, the community then proclaims its *receptive* (and thus ecclesial) faith in the God of mercy by singing the Creed.[51] Thus, as Peter Candler has remarked, for Aquinas "the liturgy orders our desire."[52] We are transformed into persons truly able to participate in Christ's cruciform love.

---

[49] Ibid.

[50] Ibid. Scripture of course infuses the entire liturgy, as Luke Timothy Johnson has pointed out:

> That Catholics have always been exposed to large amounts of Scripture through the Eucharist needs no demonstration and little reminder. The ordinary of the Mass is built up on the basis of biblical language, from the *kyrie* to the *agnus Dei*. Participation in the Eucharist meant an invitation to the world constructed by Scripture. The proper portions of the Mass included not only readings from Scripture in the Latin Vulgate and preaching on the basis of the readings, but also subtle interpretations of those readings through antiphons, responses, and prayers. Such tropes on Scripture did not fall from heaven. They were the work of skilled interpreters whose mastery of the Bible enabled them to combine fidelity and imagination in astonishing fashion . . . Catholics learned their Scripture through the practices of faith, and those practices also interpreted Scripture. (Luke Timothy Johnson and William S. Kurz, S.J., *The Future of Catholic Biblical Scholarship: A Constructive Conversation* [Grand Rapids, MI: Eerdmans, 2002]: 6)

[51] As Romanus Cessario, O.P. observes, God's merciful goodness is the key to Aquinas's entire theology of the relationship of God and humankind (Cessario, "Aquinas on Christian Salvation," 118).

[52] Candler, "Liturgically Trained Memory," 429. Candler rightly directs attention to the importance of memory for Aquinas.

The participants having been prepared, Christ's merciful justifying action – proclaimed by the Old and New Testaments – is now, in accord with the union of word and sacrament, sacramentally enacted in full.[53] Aquinas writes,

> So then, after the people have been prepared and instructed, the next step is to proceed to the celebration of the mystery, which is both offered as a sacrifice, and consecrated and received as a sacrament: since first we have the oblation; then the consecration of the matter offered; and thirdly, its reception.[54]

The priest prays that the community's offering "be made acceptable to God."[55] The Preface then calls the people once again to praise of Christ. They must "lift up their hearts to the Lord," praise his Godhead by singing with the angels, "Holy, holy, holy," and praise his humanity by saying, "Blessed is he that cometh."[56] Christ's reconciling and deifying action is about to be made fully present liturgically; the people have prepared themselves to share in it as members with their Head. As a final step of preparation, the priest prays that the sacrifice about to be offered will expiate the sins of those for whom the sacrifice is offered, and makes clear that the offering occurs within the context of the communion of saints, the Body of Christ, who offer with, in, and through their Head.[57]

All preparations for the offering of Christ's sacrifice having been made, the priest now consecrates the sacrament by which the Church offers Christ's sacrifice. He first prays that God might effect the consecration of the offering: "Which oblation do Thou, O God . . ."[58] Facing east with the people in a posture of communal sacrificial offering, the priest then speaks the words of consecration *in persona Christi*. These words, by Christ's power in the Holy Spirit,[59] accomplish sacramentally the sacrifice. In describing these words, the "form" of the sacrament, Aquinas quotes Ambrose: "when the time comes for perfecting the

---

[53] The sacrament of the Eucharist enacts what Christ, the incarnate Word, proclaims in the inspired scriptural word of God, namely reconciliation and deification. Any fundamental division between "word" and "sacrament" would be foreign to Aquinas.

[54] 3, q. 83, a. 4.

[55] Ibid.

[56] Ibid. Enrico Mazza claims, "The assembly, too, regarded as so important in the patristic period, has no role to play in the Thomist theological system, because the ordained minister is the complete subject of the celebration" (Mazza, *The Celebration of the Eucharist*, trans. Matthew J. O'Connell [Collegeville, MN: Liturgical Press, 1999]: 208). This statement cannot be squared with Aquinas's actual liturgical theology.

[57] For further discussion, see Colman O'Neill, *Meeting Christ in the Sacraments*, 192ff.

[58] 3, q. 83, a. 4.

[59] Cf. 3, q. 78, a. 4.

sacrament, the priest uses no longer his own words, but the words of Christ."[60] In the perfecting or performing of the sacrament, by which the matter is changed into the body and blood of Christ, the priest pronounces Christ's words "This is my body" and "This is the chalice of my blood" *in persona Christi*, "as if Christ were speaking in person."[61] Aquinas notes that other words are included in the form of the sacrament of the Eucharist so as to show "the power of the blood shed in the Passion, whose power works in this sacrament."[62]

Just as the priest liturgically represents Christ the Head, by virtue of the grace of the sacrament of orders, and acts *in persona Christi* in offering Christ's sacrifice, so also the whole congregation, by virtue of grace of the sacrament of baptism that makes us Christ's members, offers the interior sacrifice (self-giving love) that marks Christ's cruciform dying.[63] The community thus receives Christ's justice by sharing through the liturgical representation in his human liturgical act on the Cross, and by

---

[60] 3, q. 78, a. 1, *sed contra*. Ambrose's statement is from *De Sacram*. iv. For an important discussion of the "form" of the sacrament of the Eucharist, see Benoît-Dominique de La Soujeole, O.P., "La forme de l'eucharistie," *Revue Thomiste* 103 (2003): 93–103. De La Soujeole notes that the traditional Western account of the "form" of the Eucharist as the words of institution rather than the epiclesis focuses attention upon the "acts of the man Jesus" (94), the causality of the Word in his human nature, without taking away from the role of the Holy Spirit who shapes the holy humanity of Jesus. De La Soujeole suggests that

> Consecration by the epiclesis alone, that is to say appropriated to the Spirit, would not recognize the rightful causal place of the humanity assumed. The eucharistic conversion would come about, if one held this interpretation, *at the request* of Christ, by reason of his merits, and not through Christ by reason of his plenitude of grace. This interpretation gives due weight neither to the unique holiness of Christ, nor to to causal importance that it is necessary to grant to his *acta in carne*. These points are at the foundation of the whole of the theology of the sacraments. (101)

As de La Soujeole points out, some Catholic theologians have recently adopted the emphasis on the epiclesis, thereby highlighting pneumatology without fully taking into account the Christological implications. See also Edward J. Kilmartin, S.J., "The Active Role of Christ and the Holy Spirit in the Sanctification of the Eucharistic Elements," *Theological Studies* 45 (1984): 225–53.

[61] 3, q. 78, a. 1; cf. 3, q. 78, a. 4 and q. 83, a. 2, ad 3. For discussion of this point, see Sara Butler, "Priestly Identity: 'Sacrament' of Christ the Head," *Worship* 70 (1996): 290–306; Guy Mansini, O.S.B., "Representation and Agency in the Eucharist," *The Thomist* 62 (1998): 499–517; Lawrence J. Welch, "For the Church and within the Church: Priestly Representation," *The Thomist* 65 (2001): 613–37. These articles respond to a widespread and multifaceted critique of the Church's theology of the priesthood, an ongoing critique that aims ultimately at interpreting the Eucharist as the Church's production.

[62] 3, q. 78, a. 3.

[63] For discussion of the various modes of "spiritual sacrifice," see Gilles Emery, O.P., "Le sacerdoce spirituel des fidèles chez saint Thomas d'Aquin," *Revue Thomiste* 99 (1999): 211–43.

sharing in his offering, his sacrificial body and blood, made present upon the altar.

Christ chose bread and wine for this sacrament, Aquinas suggests, to represent the spiritual nourishment that we receive by sharing in the body and blood of Christ, not merely as a meal but as a sacrifice. The sacrifice is represented by the separation of bread/sacramental body and wine/sacramental blood, just as Christ's body and blood were separated by the spilling of his blood in his Passion.[64] All aspects of the sacramental sign are chosen for their ability to express and manifest Christ's Passion and its effects.[65] Thus water is mixed with wine in performing the sacrament

> because it harmonizes with the representation of our Lord's Passion: hence Pope Alexander says: "In the Lord's chalice neither wine only nor water only ought to be offered, but both mixed, because we read that both flowed from His side in the Passion."[66]

Yet, water is not necessary, Aquinas points out, because the sacramental representation of Christ's sacrifice requires only the representation of the shedding of blood.[67] Even so the water has importance in the sacramental sign because, as Aquinas affirms (following Pope Julius), "by the mixing of the water with the wine, is signified the union of the people with Christ."[68] The liturgical gestures and postures of the priest and congregation, too, belong within this sacramental-sacrificial signification: thus, for example, in Aquinas's day the sign of the Cross possessed a central role, as did the priest's alternation between facing the people and facing East with the people.[69] With regard to the two consecrations, Aquinas similarly states that "the blood consecrated apart expressly represents Christ's Passion, and therefore mention is made of the fruits of the Passion in the consecration of the blood, rather than in that of the body, since the body is the subject of the Passion."[70]

The sacrament of the Eucharist, therefore, makes *Christ's sacrifice* sacramentally present as the Church's (participatory) offering to God. The communion that is the Church is attained in and through Christ's sacrifice as participated in sacramentally. Catherine Pickstock thus describes the Church as embodying an "economy of 'dispossession,'"

---

[64] 3, q. 74, a. 1.
[65] This point is made strongly, from a Heideggerian perspective, by Sokolowski in *Eucharistic Presence.*
[66] 3, q. 74, a. 6; cf. ad 1. Aquinas is quoting Pope Alexander I's *Ep. I. ad omnes Orthod.*
[67] 3, q. 74, a. 7, ad 1.
[68] 3, q. 74, a. 7.
[69] 3, q. 83, a. 5, ad 3, 4, and 6.
[70] 3, q. 78, a. 3, ad 2; cf. ad 5–7.

in which we attain life (communion) by means of death. Comparing the Eucharist to the aqedah, she affirms, "In accordance with Abraham's faith, our sacrifice, by participating in Christ, is obedient to death, does not turn away from death, and so is life-giving."[71] The Church's offering of Christ's sacrifice applies this life-giving effect of Christ's sacrifice to all who in any way share in the Church's offering: this expiatory effect takes place not "only in priests who consecrate this sacrament, and in those others who partake of it; but likewise in those for whom it is offered."[72]

Having consecrated the matter of the sacrament, thereby accomplishing *in persona Christi* the sacramental offering of Christ's sacrifice, the priest, keeping in view that he is a member and not the Head, "makes excuse for his presumption in obeying Christ's command, saying: Wherefore, calling to mind . . ."[73] The priest then asks that God will accept the Church's offering of Christ's sacrifice, and that it will be efficacious for those who share in the offering. Following the order of the liturgy of the Eucharist, Aquinas notes:

> Fourthly, he [the priest] asks that the sacrifice accomplished may find favor with God, when he says: *Look down upon them with a propitious*, etc. Fifthly, he begs for the effect of this sacrifice and sacrament, first for the partakers, saying: *We humbly beseech Thee*; then for the dead, who can no longer receive it, saying: *Be mindful also, O Lord*, etc.; thirdly, for the priests themselves who offer, saying: *And to us sinners*, etc.[74]

In sharing sacramentally in Christ's offering of his sacrifice, the members of Christ's Body receive the effects that their Head's Passion has merited. Christ, acting through the priest (who humbly begs mercy as a sinner), enables his Body to share in his saving action and to manifest its (cruciform) fruits.[75]

In a certain sense, therefore, the sacrament of the Eucharist is "accomplished," as the Church's offering of Christ's sacrifice, by the

---

[71] Pickstock, *After Writing*, 251; cf. 208.

[72] 3, q. 78, a. 3, ad 8.

[73] 3, q. 83, a. 4.

[74] Ibid.

[75] Enrico Mazza holds that "precisely because there is no room in the Thomist system for a theology of the prayer of thanksgiving, the unity of the Eucharistic Prayer is lost from sight, for Thomas succeeds in understanding only the function of the words of consecration, since these alone have a role in a system based on the four causes" (Mazza, *The Celebration of the Eucharist*, 208). It should be clear from the actual texts of Aquinas, however, how profoundly unified around the pedagogy of cruciform love – a charity made possible in and through Christ's saving sacrifice – is the whole of the rite of the Eucharist.

consecration of the matter.[76] Yet, as Aquinas points out, believers benefit unto eternal life from the Eucharist in *two* ways: "this sacrament benefits recipients by way both of sacrament and of sacrifice, because it is offered for all who partake of it."[77] The liturgical sharing in Christ's saving action affects and shapes (cruciform) believers both as a sacrificial sharing in the expiatory justice of Christ's sacrificial action to God, and by the reception of the sacrament of Christ's body and blood. "Receiving," therefore, "is of the very nature of the sacrament."[78] Following the Gospel of John, Aquinas compares the sacramental receiving of Christ by consuming his body and blood, with Christ's incarnational entrance into the world:

> just as by coming into the world, He visibly bestowed the life of grace upon the world, according to John i. 17: *Grace and truth came by Jesus Christ*, so also, by coming sacramentally into man, [Christ] causes the life of grace, according to John vi. 58: *He that eateth Me, the same also shall live by Me.*[79]

---

[76] 3, q. 78, a. 1. Aquinas states,

This sacrament differs from the other sacraments in two respects. First of all, in this, that this sacrament is accomplished by the consecration of the matter, while the rest are perfected in the use of the consecrated matter. Secondly, because in the other sacraments the consecration of the matter consists only in a blessing, from which the matter consecrated derives instrumentally a spiritual power, which through the priest who is an animated instrument, can pass on to inanimate instruments. But in this sacrament the consecration of the matter consists in the miraculous change of the substance, which can only be done by God; hence the minister in performing this sacrament has no other act save the pronouncing of the words. And because the form should suit the thing, therefore the form of this sacrament differs from the forms of the other sacraments in two respects. First, because the form of the other sacraments implies the use of the matter, as for instance, baptizing, or signing; but the form of this sacrament implies merely the consecration of the matter, which consists in transubstantiation, as when it is said, *This is My body*, or *This is the chalice of My blood*. Secondly, because the forms of the other sacraments are pronounced in the person of the minister, whether by way of exercising an act, as when it is said, *I baptize thee*, or *I confirm thee*, etc.; or by way of command, as when it is said in the sacrament of Order, *Take the power*, etc.; or by way of entreaty, as when in the sacrament of Extreme Unction it is said, *By this anointing and our intercession*, etc. But the form of this sacrament is pronounced as if Christ were speaking in person, so that it is given to be understood that the minister does nothing in perfecting this sacrament, except to pronounce the words of Christ.

[77] 3, q. 79, a. 7; cf. q. 79, aa. 1 and 2.
[78] 3, q. 79, a. 7, ad 3.
[79] 3, q. 79, a. 1. As Gilles Emery, O.P. shows, at this level of sign (*sacramentum tantum*) Aquinas repeatedly alerts us to the liturgy's "ecclesial signification" (Emery, "The Ecclesial Fruit of the Eucharist," trans. Therese C. Scarpelli, *Nova et Vetera* 2 [2004]: 45).

By allowing Christ to enter us incarnationally, we receive the merciful and reconciling grace that, by his Incarnation as consummated in his Paschal mystery, he causes in the world. In Christ, the world is re-ordered in righteousness to God even though still seeming to be under the sway of the "principalities and powers"; in the Eucharist, we celebrate the sacrificial feasting of reconciliation. This is the answer to those who, horrified by what appear to be cannibalistic implications, might suggest that if one loves Christ, one would not wish to consume him sacramentally. The sign-character of the sacrament enables us to receive fully the incarnate Christ, and the merciful grace of reconciliation that he brings, without cannibalistically destroying him. The sacrament thus prolongs and extends the Incarnation, in which Christ, and through him grace and truth, is received into the world. We receive grace invisibly by consuming Christ under the visible sacramental species, and this grace, by converting us into Christ's cruciform image not merely as individuals but as his Body, brings us to glory, the unity with God and each other that is eternal life.[80]

Like Augustine, Aquinas, while fully aware of the need to increase the unity of believers, rejoices in the unity in charity caused by the sacrament of the Eucharist, and finds in the very matter of the sacrament a sign of this unity of the Church: "bread and wine are made use of in this sacrament, inasmuch as they denote ecclesiastical unity, *as one bread is made from many grains and wine from many grapes*, as Augustine says in his book on the Creed (*Tract. xxvi, in Ioan.*).[81] As Catherine Pickstock puts it, in the Church's offering of Christ's sacrifice, human time, marked though it is by violence, enters into the divine communion of "peace."[82] It is for this reason that the Eucharist is linked with the sacrament of penance, through which the Christ continues to purify his members and prepare them, no matter their past failings, for full sharing in the eucharistic consummation. Commenting on the York (England) medieval Corpus Christi plays, Sarah Beckwith – influenced by Pickstock's work – has expressed this conjunction of the Body of Christ with penitential members: "If the eucharist is not so much a thing, as a 'performance which makes the body of Christ visible in the present,' if it must therefore be intrinsically related to the sacrament of penance, then there could be no better description of Corpus Christi's relentless focus on the present community, its occlusions and possibilities as a body of Christ."[83]

---

[80] 3, q. 79, aa. 2, 7.

[81] 3, q. 75, a. 2, obj. 3. Colman O'Neill notes that the inspiration for this patristic reflection on the many grains comes from "a faulty translation of 1 Corinthians 10:7," but nonetheless retains its theological value. See *Meeting Christ in the Sacraments*, 168.

[82] Pickstock, *After Writing*, 237.

[83] Sarah Beckwith, *Signifying God: Social Relation and Symbolic Act in the York Corpus Christi Plays* (Chicago: University of Chicago Press, 2001): 117.

Given the importance of the community's receiving well the sacrament of the Eucharist, the liturgy next includes another period of prayer and preparation, just as is found before the offering and consecration. The community in common says "the Lord's Prayer, in which we ask for our daily bread to be given us."[84] Alexander Schmemann points out that "the Lord's prayer . . . is always our ultimate act of preparation for Communion, for being Christ's own prayer, it means that we accept Christ's mind as our mind, His prayer to His Father as our prayer, His will, His desire, His life – as ours."[85] The priest, likewise, offers a prayer on behalf of the congregation. In preparing to receive the sacrament, the community prays especially for Christ's peace, which is the unity in love given by the Holy Spirit. This peace is a special fruit of the sacrament: "the people are prepared by the Pax which is given with the words, *Lamb of God*, etc., because this is the sacrament of unity and peace."[86]

Having prayed for the peace of unity in Christ, the priest and congregation receive the sacrament. Aquinas explains that the priest receives first "because, as Dionysius says (*Eccl. Hier.* iii), he who gives Divine things to others, ought first to partake thereof himself."[87] The priest gives what he has received; all are *receivers* from God. The liturgy ends, Aquinas notes, with a thanksgiving hymn, "the people rejoicing for having received the mystery."[88] Yet this reception, as William Cavanaugh notes, must be a *cruciform* one in order to be true reception: "The fact that the church is literally changed into Christ is not a cause for triumphalism, however, precisely because our assimilation to the body of Christ means that we then become food for the world, to be broken, given away, and consumed."[89] If the Church, as embodied in its members at a particular time and place, does not bear these sacrificial marks, then its "communion" with its Head is a façade.[90]

---

[84] 3, q. 83, a. 4.
[85] Alexander Schmemann, *Great Lent: Journey to Pascha* (New York: St Vladimir's Seminary Press, 1974 [rev. edn]): 61.
[86] 3, q. 83, a. 4. Aquinas refers the reader to his earlier discussion of this point: see q. 73, a. 4 and q. 79, a. 1. See also Godefroi Geenen, O.P., "L'adage 'Eucharistia est sacramentum ecclesiasticae unionis' dans les oeuvres et la doctrine de S. Thomas d'Aquin," in *La Eucaristía y la Paz*, vol. 1 (Barcelona: Planas, 1953): 275–81.
[87] 3, q. 83, a. 4.
[88] Ibid.
[89] William T. Cavanaugh, *Torture and Eucharist: Theology, Politics, and the Body of Christ* (Oxford: Blackwell, 1998): 232. Cavanaugh is not arguing that the Church should become a "counter"-politics, but rather that the eschatological inbreaking of "communion" enables Christians to embody a reality that lies beyond modernity's power-oriented understanding of "politics" (268–9).
[90] Cf. the evocative remarks, drawing upon William Cavanaugh, John Milbank, and Denys Turner, on the Church, the liturgy, and the York (England) medieval Corpus Christi plays in Sarah Beckwith, *Signifying God*, 114–17.

All aspects of the celebration of the liturgy of the Eucharist are thus governed by the mediation of "God's benefits" – conformity to Christ's cruciform and justifying love – that Christ's liturgical action on the Cross has merited for us. In the liturgy of the Eucharist, we are included in Christ's Paschal mystery and thereby attain the communion that, despite our weakness, makes the Church Christ's Body. In discussing the times appropriate for the celebration of the Eucharist, Aquinas states, "Now since, owing to our daily defects, we stand in daily need of the fruits of our Lord's Passion, this sacrament is offered regularly every day in the Church."[91] As regards the liturgical calendar, Good Friday has no liturgy of the Eucharist in order to focus believers on the historical Passion; Christmas Day deserves more than one celebration of the Eucharist, Aquinas suggests, because believers are thereby reminded of the divine benefits of "Christ's threefold nativity": in eternity, in our hearts, and in time at Bethlehem.[92] The time of day in which the celebration of the Eucharist occurs is likewise governed by what aspect of the mystery of salvation is being commemorated.[93]

The same emphasis upon mediation of "God's benefits," won for us by the liturgical action of Christ and in which we sacramentally participate, informs Aquinas's treatment of the place in which the liturgy ought to be celebrated.[94] Aquinas identifies two factors in determining the fittingness of the place (e.g., the building, altar, and vessels) in which the liturgy of the Eucharist is celebrated: "one of these belongs to the representation of the events connected with our Lord's Passion; while the other is connected with the reverence due to the sacrament, in which Christ is contained verily, and not in figure only."[95] Both factors emphasize how the Church's liturgy focuses upon the liturgical action of God incarnate.[96] For example, all the material things in the celebration of the liturgy are

---

[91] 3, q. 83, a. 2.
[92] Ibid.
[93] 3, q. 83, a. 2, ad 3 and 4. See Peter Candler, "Liturgically Trained Memory," 433f. for the significance of time and space in liturgical remembering. Candler observes regarding church architecture, "The entire orientation of the structure is towards the altar, which itself signifies the holiness of Christ, and the cross on which he is sacrificed. Moreover, it points to the disposition of one who enters such space, by signifying 'the holiness required in those who would receive' the Eucharist" (434). As Candler states, "liturgy, as Thomas describes it, takes the activity of remembrance to be coextensive with the journey towards God, not anterior to it" (438).
[94] Aquinas anticipates, and grounds more deeply in Eucharistic theology, the representational sense of "worship space" set forth by numerous contemporary theologians. For insightful discussion see Graham Hughes, *Worship as Meaning: A Liturgical Theology for Late Modernity* (Cambridge: Cambridge University Press, 2003): 154f.
[95] 3, q. 83, a. 3.
[96] The liturgy, as deifying, unites us with the *Trinity*. As Liam Walsh, O.P. cautions, divine action is at the center of the liturgy (Walsh, "Liturgy in the Theology of St. Thomas," 572).

consecrated. Likewise, the liturgy should generally be held in a consecrated "house" or building. Aquinas gives two reasons: to express the fact that the Church is "the house of God," the fulfilled Temple (fulfilled by Christ's liturgical action on the Cross), and to express the fact that this "house of God" extends throughout the world in various buildings.[97] The altar signifies Christ, priest and victim, and is consecrated to express his holiness, "the fount of all the Church's holiness."[98] The altar should be made of stone in order to signify the stone of Christ's sepulchre; the corporal should be made of linen to represent the linen in which Christ was wrapped for burial.[99] Christ's Resurrection is signified by observing for eight days the solemnity of a church's dedication.[100]

4 CONCLUSION

For Aquinas, then, sharing in Christ's liturgical action means, in every way, "representing" Christ by imaging his sacrificial self-offering to God. Insofar as the Church is holy, she is able to be Christ's image and sacrificially enact justice in history, but insofar as she is composed of sinners, she cannot yet fully represent Christ. As sinners we depend upon God's mercy. Thus our liturgical act of sharing in Christ's liturgical sacrifice is an act of God's mercy in two ways: first, as the representation of justice, which itself turns out to be perfect mercy; and second in the very mercy of being able to participate in its ongoing enactment, despite our sinful weakness, in human history. Insofar as people join themselves sincerely to Christ's sacrifice, humankind is on the way to being configured in justice to the image of divine mercy. As Heschel recognized so profoundly, however, we are not yet this image. Indeed, this is why we need the continual nourishment of the Eucharist, recalling us to the representation of what we are called to become. Aidan Nichols, commenting on the eucharistic theology of Augustine, observes, "in the eucharistic liturgy, the Church learns how to integrate her self-offering into Christ's, just as Christ's human self-offering was integrated into the divine self-offering of the Word."[101] As the sacrifice and sacrament of Christ, by which we share in his eschatological fulfillment of human history, the Eucharist builds the Church. Or as Aquinas puts it, "The Eucharist is the sacrament of the unity of the whole Church."[102]

---

[97] 3, q. 83, a. 3, ad 1.
[98] 3, q. 83, a. 3, ad 2.
[99] 3, q. 83, a. 3, ad 7.
[100] 3, q. 83, a. 3, ad 4.
[101] Aidan Nichols, O.P., *The Holy Eucharist: From the New Testament to Pope John Paul II* (Dublin: Veritas, 1991): 53.
[102] 3, q. 83, a. 4, ad 3; cf. ad 6.

When, in the Holy Spirit, this offering to the Father is accomplished in and through Christ's sacrifice, the Church is drawn further into the trinitarian communion of self-giving wisdom and love, and human beings, in history, learn to love God and one another in God. In light of the beauty of the eucharistic liturgy, we can bemoan our failure to participate in Christ's offering with the holiness, the charity, that befits members of his Body. Lambert Beauduin's words in this regard, written in 1914 at the origins of the twentieth-century Liturgical Movement, apply to every age:

> The piety of the Christian people, and hence their actions and life, are not grounded sufficiently in the fundamental truths that constitute the soul of the Liturgy; that is, in the destiny of all things unto the glory of the Father, the Son, and the Holy Spirit; the necessary and universal contemplation of Jesus Christ; the central place of the Eucharistic Sacrifice in the Christian life; the mission of the hierarchy in regard to our union with God; the visible realisation of the Communion of Saints. All these truths, which find expression in every liturgical act, are asleep in men's souls; the faithful have lost consciousness of them. Let us change the routine and monotonous assistance at acts of worship into an active and intelligent participation; let us teach the faithful to pray and confess these truths in a body: and the Liturgy thus practised will insensibly arouse a slumbering faith and give new efficacy, both in prayer and action, to the latent energies of the baptised souls: "the true Christian spirit will flourish again and maintain itself among the faithful."[103]

---

[103] Lambert Beauduin, O.S.B., *Liturgy the Life of the Church*, trans. Virgil Michel, O.S.B., 3rd edn (Farnborough: Saint Michael's Abbey, 2002): 21; cf. 64–5.

6

Conclusion

In numerous recent writings marking the turn of the Millennium, Pope John Paul II exhorted humankind "[t]o contemplate the face of Christ."[1] In his encyclical *Ecclesia de Eucharistia*, he specifies that we should contemplate "the 'Eucharistic face' of Christ."[2] Such contemplation, he argues,

---

[1] *Ecclesia de Eucharistia*, no. 6; cf. *Rosarium Virginis Mariae* (2002); *Novo Millennio Ineunte* (January 6, 2001), especially nos. 16ff.; *Incarnationis Mysterium* (1998), especially nos. 1–4; *Tertio Millennio Adveniente* (1994), especially nos. 1–8, 55. It should be noted that *Ecclesia de Eucharistia* repeats, two decades later, the main points made in Pope John Paul II's apostolic letter *Dominicae Cenae* (On the Mystery and Worship of the Eucharist) which was promulgated on February 24, 1980. On the contemplation fueled by eucharistic participation, Catherine Pickstock has noted (regarding q. 83 of the *tertia pars*) that "Aquinas's instructions for the liturgical promotion of a state of mind able to discern the body" indicate "how, for Aquinas, one is to become capable of, and also fulfill, *theoria* as such" (Pickstock, "Truth and Language," in John Milbank and Catherine Pickstock, *Truth in Aquinas* [New York: Routledge, 2001]: 100). See also the treatment of eucharistic contemplation, focusing on the movement from the sacrament to the *res* of the Mystical Body, in Jean-Luc Marion, *God without Being*, trans. Thomas A. Carlson (Chicago: University of Chicago Press, 1991): 178–82, as well as A. N. Williams, "Argument to Bliss: The Epistemology of the *Summa Theologiae*," *Modern Theology* 20 (2004): 505–26. Williams points out that Aquinas understands knowing in a participatory fashion, so that the contemplation that is the goal of knowing "continues in heaven" (522). Knowing is therefore not a neutral activity, but rather is already teleologically ordered and caught up in God's gracious plan for our participation in his trinitarian life. Williams concludes that Aquinas "relentlessly refuses" all such "distinctions" as that between "the realms of the natural and the supernatural" (522). I would add that Aquinas does not refuse the *distinctions*, which remain crucial for articulating Christian faith, but rather refuses *reified separations*.

[2] *Ecclesia de Eucharistia*, no. 7. For studies of the encyclical, see Don Christoforo Charamsa, "*Ecclesia de Eucharistia vivit*. Introduzione alla Riflessione Tomista sull'enciclica di Giovanni Paolo II," *Doctor Angelicus* 3 (2003): 5–28 and an ecumenical symposium in *Pro Ecclesia* 12 (2003): 394–416 including articles by Susan K. Wood, David Wagschal, George Lindbeck, and William Stacy Johnson. The encyclical should also be read in light of the pastoral instructions given by the Congregation for Divine Worship and the Discipline of the Sacraments in its *Instruction on Certain Matters to Be Observed or to Be Avoided Regarding the Most Holy Eucharist* (*Redemptoris Sacramentum*),

will renew both the Church's life and the theology of the Eucharist. The contemplative believer will recognize Christ's "many forms of presence, but above all in the living sacrament of his body and his blood,"[3] and thereby be united with him more deeply in the faith, hope, and love that unite and build up the Church. As John Paul II states in his apostolic letter *Orientale Lumen*, in which he seeks the reunion of East and West,

> In the Eucharist, the Church's inner nature is revealed, a community of those summoned to the synaxis to celebrate the gift of the One who is offering and offered: participating in the Holy Mysteries, they become "kinsmen" of Christ, anticipating the experience of divinization in the now inseparable bond linking divinity and humanity in Christ.[4]

This participation is necessarily cruciform. As we have seen, all aspects of Eucharistic theology receive their intelligibility in light of the requirement of *cruciform* communion. It is through Christ's sacrifice, participated sacramentally in the Eucharistic sacrifice and sacrificial meal that fully includes us within Christ's action, that God causes the gift of charitable communion in us. By sacramental representation in the liturgy, inspired by the Holy Spirit, we share in Christ's reconciling sacrifice and are included within his relationship to the Father. This inclusion is not metaphorical, but rather consists in the profound intimacy of being changed into Christ's Body by offering, and consuming, his sacrificial body and blood. The intelligibility of the meal comes from its fully inserting us into Christ's cruciform action. Receiving the "communion" that is an abiding in the Spirit in the relationship of the Father and the Son, we share liturgically in the justice that Christ's worship accomplishes. Each of the realities that we have explored – expiatory sacrifice, communion, transubstantiation, and the liturgy of the Eucharist – depends upon the others.

In short, the Eucharist, as thanksgiving, memorial, sacrifice, and meal, is Christ's personal and intimate action of drawing us eschatologically into his cruciform love. Sharing in this love requires, in Christ and by the power of the Holy Spirit, a radical death to self that makes possible communion with God and neighbor. Compare this view with Robert Daly's rejection of the aqedah as a starting point for understanding Eucharistic theology:

---

published March 25, 2004. See also the relevant teachings of the Council of Trent, as well as Leo XIII's now forgotten, but still valuable encyclical *Mirae Caritatis* (1902). On the resonance of *Ecclesia de Eucharistia* with Aquinas's theology, see my "John Paul II and Aquinas on the Eucharist," *Nova et Vetera* 3 (2005): 637–60.

[3] *Ecclesia de Eucharistia*, no. 6.
[4] *Orientale Lumen* (1995), no. 10.

"Have you found out what sacrifice is," asked the pastor when the children had clambered back into their places in the front pews? "Yes!" triumphantly answered the religious education teacher. "Sacrifice means to give up what you love." The pastor nodded approvingly, added a few more words, then moved to the altar to celebrate the Sacrifice of the Mass. The first reading had been from Genesis 22, the sacrifice of Isaac. This happened in a parish church in Germany a few years ago, but it could have happened in any number of churches throughout the world. It strikingly illustrates the theological and pastoral challenges one faces, even from the Church's own pastors and teachers, when one talks about "sacrifice." It is overwhelmed with negative connotations. For if we are correct in seeing the essence of Christian sacrifice as our participation, through the Spirit, in the transcendentally free and self-giving love of the Father and the Son, and if Christian sacrifice is our inchoative, but already real, entering into the fullness of the totally free, self-giving, loving personal life of God, then it is obvious that the common understanding of "sacrifice" does not reveal but rather effectively veils this reality . . . There has been so much incorrect thinking connected with "sacrifice" that a realistic pastoral strategy suggsts that the word should be avoided. For even when, in common usage, sacrifice refers to the most gloriously generous of self-giving human activity, the negative usually remains dominant. Even Jesus' crucifixion can veil, as much as in faith it unveils, his divinity.[5]

The "negative" is not, in light of sin, negative. It is expiatory and salvific, as Israel's mode of sacrificial worship makes clear. Yet, one might still ask: if, *pace* the linear supersessionism that is Eucharistic idealism, the restoration and perfection of the fallen *imago dei* occur in and through our Eucharistic participation in Christ's sacrificial accomplishment of communion, is such transformation worth the cost? Is the Eucharist, understood sacrificially and thus as intrinsically rather than extrinsically "costly," not merely as a celebratory meal that ratifies our acceptance by God, truly *desirable*?[6] Clearly the answer to this question provides

---

[5] Robert J. Daly, S.J., "Sacrifice Unveiled or Sacrifice Revisited: Trinitarian and Liturgical Perspectives," *Theological Studies* 64 (2003): 24–42, at 40–1.

[6] In "Postmodern Sacramento-Theology: Retelling the Christian Story," *Ephemerides Theologicae Louvanienses* 74 (1998): 326–43, drawing upon the work of Jean-François Lyotard, Lieven Boeve undertakes a quest to explore, in light of the "paradigm shift" brought about by postmodernism that has resulted in a "lost authenticity" of the Church's sacramental discourse, "the possibility of being related to the sacred under contemporary conditions" (326–7). Boeve is aware of a radical loss of interest in the

the key to understanding how Christians should expect to live: how the Church, as a sacrificial Body, manifests its *telos* in the distinct and often difficult practices of Christians, and thus evangelizes the world by the divinely given joy of self-giving love.[7]

Given the human aversion to sacrifice and suffering, it may be well to draw at this point upon the insights of a great Russian Orthodox chronicler of human life. In December 1859, Feodor Dostoevsky, at that time a relatively minor novelist who had just completed a ten-year sentence in Siberia for plotting against the Tsarist government, returned to St Petersburg and to the intellectual ferment there heating up. Joseph Frank has written that in this period Dostoevsky "drew the practical conclusions – which would remain essentially unchanged, despite some differences in accentuation, for the rest of his life – from the experiences of his Siberian exile."[8] What were these conclusions? They are touched upon, Frank shows, in Dostoevsky's short novel *The Insulted and the Injured* (1861), particularly in the character of Natasha, who says of her broken relationship with her father, "We shall have to work out our future happiness by suffering, pay for it somehow by fresh miseries. Everything is purified by suffering."[9] Frank explains the kind of suffering that Dostoevsky has in mind:

---

non-sacrificial (as presented in modern catechesis) Eucharist; Catholics in Boeve's country no longer go to mass. Yet Boeve misidentifies the source of the "lost authenticity." For a brief introduction to the new set of postmodern thinkers – Lyotard, Alain Badiou, Slavoj Žižek – see Paul J. Griffiths, "Christ and Critical Theory," *First Things* 145 (August/September 2004): 46–55. See also G. De Schrijver, "Experiencing the Sacramental Character of Existence: Transitions from Premodernity to Modernity, Postmodernity, and the Rediscovery of the Cosmos," in *Current Issues in Sacramental Theology*, ed. J. Lamberts (Leuven: Abdij Keizersberg, 1994): 12–27.

[7] In this book, I can only gesture at the ecclesial-ethical implications of Eucharistic theology. Much depends upon how one understands mediation. On this point hinges the fruitful receptivity and obedience that marks self-sacrificial life in Christ. For explorations of this theme, which I hope to explore in future work, see John Paul II's *Veritatis Splendor* as well as such works in political philosophy/theology as Russell Hittinger, "Social Pluralism and Subsidiarity in Catholic Social Doctrine," *Providence* 7 (2002): 52–69; Reinhard Hütter, *Bound to Be Free: Evangelical Catholic Engagements in Ecclesiology, Ethics, and Ecumenism* (Grand Rapids, MI: Eerdmans, 2004); John Milbank, "The Gift of Ruling: Secularization and Political Authority," *New Blackfriars* 85 (2004): 212–38. Most recent Catholic studies of the Church and ethics are marred by sociological, rather than sacramental, accounts of the Church and of the moral life – and the sociological models themselves are skewed by Enlightenment understandings of the human person. Cf. Bernard Cooke's "*Sacrosanctum Concilium*: Vatican II Time Bomb," *Horizons* 31 (2004): 105–12, in which he argues that *Sacrosanctum Concilium* will ultimately bring an end to priestly mediation, now that "the assembled people are as a community the agents of their worship" (112). The rejection of historically embodied mediation stands at the heart of much ecclesiology and ethics today.

[8] Joseph Frank, *Dostoevsky: The Stir of Liberation, 1860–1865* (Princeton, NJ: Princeton University Press, 1986): xi.

[9] Quoted in Frank, 129.

> Natasha, it is clear, is not referring to material hardship or physical deprivation, but rather to the process by which the ramparts of pride, egoism, and wounded self-esteem are battered down and the way left open for forgiveness and love. It is only in this sense that Dostoevsky will ever maintain "suffering" to be a good.[10]

This process that batters down "the ramparts of pride, egoism, and wounded self-esteem" describes, for Dostoevsky, the life-giving path by which the sinner is transformed so as to be able freely to offer himself or herself in loving self-sacrifice, the opposite of deadly selfishness. Hours after the death of his first wife Marya (Masha), Dostoevsky set out this view of life in a notebook. Frank observes, "The fragment begins with a direct statement and a poignant question: 'Masha is lying on the table. Will I ever see Masha again?' "[11] Dostoevsky's answer is yes; there is a life with God after this life on earth. Christ, Dostoevsky reasons, has embodied for humankind an ideal of perfect self-giving love, but for sinful human beings this ideal is unattainable, in its fullest form, on earth. Aware that the ideal embodied by Christ on the Cross corresponds to the most profound desires of human nature, human beings nonetheless find that the ideal exceeds what human nature in its present condition is able to achieve – thus pointing us to the risen life of Christ. Dostoevsky explains his conclusions about self-sacrifice:

> since the appearance of Christ as *the ideal of man in the flesh*, it has become as clear as day that the highest final development of the personality must arrive at this (at the very end of the development, the final attainment of the goal): that man finds, knows, and is convinced, with the full force of his nature, that the highest use a man can make of his personality, of the full development of his *Ego* – is, as it were, to annihilate that *Ego*, to give it totally and to everyone undividedly and unselfishly. In this way, the law of the Ego fuses with the law of humanism, and in this fusion both the Ego and the all (apparently two extreme opposites) mutually annihilate themselves one for the other, and at the same time each attains separately, and to the highest degree, their own individual development.[12]

What human beings desire is to enter into lasting and radically complete interpersonal *communion* – profound harmony with God and with other rational creatures, not the crabbed self-centered life that all of us,

---

[10] Ibid., 130.
[11] Ibid., 297.
[12] Quoted in Frank, 298–9.

to varying degrees, experience on earth. Dostoevsky describes this perfect harmony as "the merging of the whole *Ego*, that is, of knowledge and synthesis *with all. Love everyone like thyself.*"[13] Such joyous communion would indeed constitute the fulfillment of our created nature; and such communion, in Scripture, is expressed in terms of banqueting with God:

> On this mountain the Lord of hosts will make for all peoples a feast of fat things, a feast of wine on the lees, of fat things full of marrow, of wine on the lees well refined. And he will destroy on this mountain the covering that is cast over all peoples, the veil that is spread over all nations. He will swallow up death for ever, and the Lord God will wipe away tears from all faces, and the reproach of his people he will take away from all the earth, for the Lord has spoken. (Isa. 25:6–8)

As Dostoevsky knew, the Eucharist is the foretaste of this heavenly banquet. Jesus, in the Gospel of John, presents the Eucharist as radical interpersonal communion:

> He who eats my flesh and drinks my blood abides in me, and I in him. As the living Father sent me, and I live because of the Father, so he who eats me will live because of me. This is the bread which came down from heaven, not such as the fathers ate and died; he who eats this bread will live for ever. (John 6:56–8)

Yet, as Jesus reveals by word and deed, such communion is not possible outside of radical *self-sacrifice*: "If any man would come after me, let him deny himself and take up his cross and follow me. For whoever would save his life will lose it, and whoever loses his life for my sake will find it" (Matt. 16:24–5).

Dostoevsky's notes at his wife's deathbed, then, articulate the fundamental Christian truth: our "full development" (communion) comes about only in and through sacrifice, through the radical gift of self, giving ourselves "totally and to everyone undividedly and unselfishly."[14]

---

[13] Quoted in Frank, 305.

[14] Frank suggests that Dostoevsky, in these notes written directly after his wife's death, envisions Christ as a moral exemplar rather than as a redeemer from sin: "Indeed, the sole significance of Christ, as Dostoevsky speaks of him here, is to serve as the divine enunciator of this morality; he fulfills no other purpose, not even the traditional one of redeeming mankind from the wages of sin and death" (299; cf. 305). Dostoevsky's mode of expression is, as with all Russian thinkers of his day, influenced by German idealism. Yet, Dostoevsky understands Christ's saving death, if accepted in faith, as freeing human beings from captivity to sin (i.e. disordered love of self to the contempt of God and neighbor) by enabling us to attain the fulfillment of our nature in self-giving love.

Dostoevsky goes on to point out that even marriage, with its profound self-giving of the couple to each other and to their (potential or actual) children, does not attain to the level of the radical communion of all with all that Christ manifests as the ideal to be attained by human beings in eternal life.[15] The communion of marriage does not suffice, because it is not the radical self-giving of all to all. As Joseph Frank remarks, "The highest aim of Dostoevsky's Christianity . . . is not personal salvation but the fusion of the individual ego with the community in a symbiosis of love; and the only sin that Dostoevsky appears to recognize is the failure to fulfill this law of love."[16] It is no wonder that Dostoevsky repeatedly affirms the crucified and risen Christ, understood as the pattern of free "self-conscious surrender of the will"[17] in pure self-giving love for God and neighbor, to be "something irresistibly beautiful, sweet, inevitable, and even inexplicable."[18] As Dostoevsky writes, "And so, man must unceasingly feel suffering [because of man's sin], which is compensated for by the heavenly joy of fulfilling the law, that is, by sacrifice."[19]

In exploring Eucharistic theology in this book, I have argued that such radical communion is attained most fully on earth in the Eucharist, which as our sacrificial sharing in Christ's sacrifice provides a foretaste of the radical communion that is heaven. In the sacrifice-sacrament of the Eucharist, we learn charity by offering with Christ his own saving sacrifice. The sacrament of the Eucharist is a "school" of charity; it builds the Church by enabling us to enact Christ's sacrifice with him. In the liturgy of the Eucharist, we learn "Jesus Christ and him crucified" (1 Cor. 2:2) and thereby we "[p]ut on the whole armor of God" (Eph. 6:11):

> Put on then, as God's chosen ones, holy and beloved, compassion, kindness, lowliness, meekness, and patience, forbearing one another and, if one has a complaint against another, forgiving each other; as the Lord has forgiven you, so you also must forgive. And above all these put on love, which binds everything together in perfect harmony. And let the peace of Christ rule in your hearts, to which indeed you were called in one body. (Col. 3:12–15)

This is "the heavenly joy of fulfilling the law," the law of self-giving love that the Eucharist, as a sacrament-sacrifice, both enacts and makes

---

[15] Ibid., 302. Frank presents Dostoevsky's view as a condemnation of marriage, but I would suggest that Dostoevsky is simply following the Christian understanding of marriage and the family as a limited end, rather than as the embodiment of full human fulfillment.
[16] Ibid., 307.
[17] Quoted in Frank, 374; cf. 244.
[18] Quoted in Frank, 372; cf. 82, 85.
[19] Quoted in Frank, 306.

present. Christ builds up his Body by enabling us to share sacrificially, through the sacramental representation that the Church enacts, in the offering of his one saving sacrifice. We, body and spirit, are enabled to fulfill, in him, our need (in justice) to offer sacrifice to God and thereby to be in communion with our Creator and Redeemer. Our cruciform communion, in the Eucharist, teaches us the path of the God-centered life by drawing us sacrificially out of ourselves and into the wondrous communion of Christ's Body.[20]

All aspects – theological and liturgical – of the Eucharist should therefore express our Eucharistic sharing in Christ's cruciform Godwardness, which deifies us. Joseph Ratzinger has described the opposite situation, in which the liturgy of the Eucharist, not understood "ecstatically" as a sacrifice, finds its ground in itself rather than in God:

> The turning of the priest toward the people has turned the community into a self-enclosed circle. In its outward form, it no longer opens out on what lies ahead and above, but is closed in on itself. The common turning toward the east was not a "celebration toward the wall"; it did not mean that the priest "had his back to the people": the priest himself was not regarded as so important. For just as the congregation in the synagogue looked together toward Jerusalem, so in the Christian liturgy the congregation looked "toward the Lord". As one of the fathers of Vatican II's Constitution on the Liturgy, J. A. Jungmann, put it, it was much more a question of priest and people facing in the same direction, knowing that together they were in a procession toward the Lord. They did not close themselves into a circle; they did not gaze at one another; but as the pilgrim People of God they set off for the *Oriens*, for the Christ who comes to meet us.[21]

---

[20] Cf. Avery Dulles, S.J., "The Eucharist as Sacrifice," in *Rediscovering the Eucharist: Ecumenical Conversations*, ed. Roch Kereszty, O. Cist. (New York: Paulist Press, 2003): 185. Dulles comments that God's gift of Christ's sacrifice, and our sharing in it, not only draws us away from our self-centeredness but also fulfills "our human longing to offer God a gift truly worthy of himself" (185).

[21] Joseph Cardinal Ratzinger, *The Spirit of the Liturgy*, trans. John Saward (San Francisco: Ignatius Press, 2000): 79–80. See also the fascinating anthropological study, based on fieldwork from the late 1960s and early 1970s that captures the shift in eucharistic understanding from sacrifice to meal, by Suzanne Campbell-Jones, "Ritual in Performance and Interpretation: The Mass in a Convent Setting," in *Sacrifice*, ed. M.F.C. Bourdillon and Meyer Fortes (London: Academic Press, 1980): 89–106. On the depths of meaning contained every aspect of liturgical posture, see, e.g., Graham Hughes, *Worship as Meaning: A Liturgical Theology for Late Modernity* (Cambridge: Cambridge University Press, 2003). Pierre-Marie Gy, O.P., has taken issue with Ratzinger's approach. See Gy, "L'Esprit de la liturgie du Cardinal Ratzinger est-il fidèle au Concile, ou en réaction contre?" *La Maison-Dieu* 229 (2002): 173–5. Ratzinger has defended his approach in "L'Esprit de la liturgie ou la fidelité au Concile: Réponse au Père Gy," *La Maison-Dieu* 230 (2002): 114–20.

I would add that this "procession toward the Lord" advances only insofar as it is cruciform, that is to say insofar as the communion of the pilgrim People of God arises in and through Christ's saving sacrifice and our Eucharistic (sacrificial) participation in it. It is in this way that, in solidarity with our Jewish brothers and sisters, we truly look "toward Jerusalem" in looking "toward the Lord." The Jerusalem in which Jesus went to his passion cannot be displaced by faith in the risen Lord or by a heavenly meal, let alone by an amorphous sense of sacramentality or "the sacred." Rather Christians look "toward Jerusalem" when, with repentance, we participate sacrificially in the saving sacrifice that Jesus accomplished on earth when he turned his face toward Jerusalem (cf. Matt. 16:21), the sacrifice that both takes away sins and reveals the self-giving Love that is the Trinity. As William Cavanaugh depicts the union of sacrifice and communion, "Our offering simply *is* being drawn into the divine life – deification."[22] In and through Christ's sacrifice, we are incorporated into the communion of the new Jerusalem, the fulfillment of the cruciform desire of Israel. In and through Christ's sacrifice, we are enabled sacramentally to turn from self-centered "[gazing] at one another" to contemplating together, in a cruciform communion that accomplishes our deification, the risen life of the Lord.[23]

And they worshiped him, and returned to Jerusalem with great joy, and were continually in the temple blessing God. (Luke 24:52–3)

---

[22] William Cavanaugh, "Eucharistic Sacrifice and the Social Imagination in Early Modern Europe," *Journal of Medieval and Early Modern Studies* 31 (2001): 599. Regarding the Eucharist's Christological revelation of the Trinity, see also David Bentley Hart's "'Thine Own of Thine Own': Eucharistic Sacrifice in Orthodox Theology," in *Rediscovering the Eucharist: Ecumenical Conversations*, 165; Peter Casarella's contribution to the same volume, "Eucharist: Presence of a Gift," 199–225; Matthew Levering, *Scripture and Metaphysics* (Oxford: Blackwell, 2004): 142–3.

[23] See Daniel A. Keating, "Justification, Sanctification and Divinization in Thomas Aquinas," in Thomas Weinandy, Daniel Keating, and John Yocum, eds., *Aquinas on Doctrine* (New York: T. & T. Clark, 2004): 139–58. Keating concludes that "Aquinas' expansive treatment of the virtues in the *Secunda Pars* is much more than an impressive piece of moral theology. It is perhaps the most developed account in the Christian tradition of the possibilities for the divinization of our human nature in the present age" (155). This account of divinization through the virtues and the gifts gives specification to the evocation of a Christological exchange that one finds, for example, in David Bentley Hart's "'Thine Own of Thine Own': Eucharistic Sacrifice in Orthodox Theology," 160f. See also Jean Danielou, S.J.'s chapter on patristic liturgical applications of Psalm 23 in Danielou, *The Bible and the Liturgy* (Notre Dame, IN: University of Notre Dame Press, 1956): 177–90. Danielou notes that the Fathers "show us that the waters of rest in Psalm XXII are the figure of Baptism, the table prepared, that of the Eucharistic feast, the inebriating chalice, that of the Precious Blood" (190). In following (sacramentally and through the life of the virtues) the way of the divine Shepherd, we are already coming to share in eternal life.

There shall no more be anything accursed, but the throne of God and of the Lamb shall be in it [the heavenly Jerusalem], and his servants shall worship him; they shall see his face, and his name shall be on their foreheads. And night shall be no more; they need no light of lamp or the sun, for the Lord God will be their light, and they shall reign for ever and ever. (Rev. 22:3–5)

Name Index

Subject Index